Tarot Skills for the 21st Century

Mundane and Magical Divination

by Josephine McCarthy

TaDehent Books

Exeter

Copyright 2020 © Josephine McCarthy

All rights reserved

Without limiting the rights under copyright reserved above, no part of this publication may be reproduced, stored in, or introduced into a retrieval system, or transmitted, in any form or by any means (electronic, mechanical, photocopying, recording or otherwise) without prior permission of the copyright owner and the publisher of this book.

Published by TaDehent Books 2020
Exeter UK

ISBN 978-1-911134-54-1

Cover image by Stuart Littlejohn
Typeset by Michael Sheppard

Dedicated to my awesome husband Stuart Littlejohn, for being my joy. And to my sister Cecilia Lindley, for being my north star.

Acknowledgements

I would like to thank the following people who, through their love, friendship, advice, support, and feedback, made this book possible: Toni, Tony, Catherine, Christin, Nusye, Jane, and Frater Acher. I would also like to thank Michael Sheppard for being such a wonderful coworker in these writing projects. And thanks to R.A. (Bob) Gilbert for his advice and discussions on Waite.

Contents

	Introduction	1
1	**Whispers on the Wind**	3
2	**Getting started**	13
	Caring for your deck	13
	Making friends with your deck	14
	Doing readings: getting started	14
	Getting good at reading tarot	17
	Reversals?	19
	Tarot's limited vocabulary	20
3	**Major Arcana Card Meanings**	23
	The Major Arcana	23
	How to use this guide	24
	0 Fool	24
	1 Magician	26
	2 High Priestess	29
	3 Empress	32
	4 Emperor	34
	5 Hierophant	38
	6 Lovers	43
	7 Chariot	45
	8 Strength	49

    9 Hermit 52
    10 Wheel of Fortune 55
    11 Justice 59
    12 Hanged Man 62
    13 Death 65
    14 Temperance 69
    15 Devil 72
    16 Tower 76
    17 Star 82
    18 Moon 86
    19 Sun 90
    20 Judgement 94
    21 World 97

4 The Minor Arcana   **101**
    Elements 102
    Numbers 102
    Swords: air, east 104
    Wands: fire, south 107
    Cups: water, west 109
    Coins: earth, north 111

5 Interpretation   **115**
    Vocabulary 115
    Choosing a deck 118
    A snapshot view of a situation 119
    Record and learn 122
    How to construct a useful question 123
    Analysis of question construction 124
    Some points to think about 126
    Timing and time limits 127
    Fate patterns and cycles 130

	Emotions and interpretations	132
	Who is talking to you?	133
	The Self	133
	Esoteric voices	134
	The Inner Library	135
	Parasites and reading hygiene	136
	Responsibilities when reading for others	138
	Reading about death	140

6 Layouts — 143

	What makes a good layout?	143
	Mundane layouts	145
	A simple yes/no layout	147
	Tree of Life layout	148
	Overview layout	150
	Event layout	153
	Directional/location layout	156
	Resources layout	157
	Secondary layouts	159
	Timing layout	160
	Manifestation, causation, and solution layouts	161
	Manifestation/Causation layout	163
	Solution layout	164
	Health layout	166
	Esoteric layouts	172
	Fate pattern layout	173
	Angelic layout	177
	Landscape layout	181
	Map of the Self layout	183

7 Interpretations of Layouts — 187

	Mundane layouts	188

Simple yes/no layout	188
Tree of Life layout	193
Overview layout	200
Event layout	212
Directional layout	221
Resources layout	224
Timing reading	240
Manifestation/Causation layout	244
Solution layout	249
Health layout	255
Esoteric layouts	267
Fate pattern layout	267
Angelic layout	275
Landscape layout	282
Map of the Self layout	290

Bibliography   **295**

Introduction

I began working with a tarot deck in my mid-teens back in the 1970s. It triggered an awakening to many things for me, both mystical and magic. It is now forty-five years later, and tarot, along with the broader concept of using cards for divination and mystical-magical thought, have been constant life companions for me.

At this point in my life and work, I thought it was about time that I wrote a guide to tarot, to cast a light on a path that can be far more profound that it initially appears. I looked around first to see if there was a guide that dug into the esoteric depths while also providing shallow waters for the budding tarot reader to paddle in. I could find no such book—which is not to say that one does not already exist, just that I could not find it.

I decided to write a book that was not too long, and that would be usable by both a beginning tarot reader and an experienced everyday tarot reader—and also by an esoteric seeker of the magical Mysteries. I will not know if I have succeeded in this quest, or failed miserably, until this book is properly put to the test by its readers.

I have laid out basic steps, mundane interpretations, esoteric and magical technical explanations, and layouts both mundane and esoteric; and I have also dipped briefly into the history behind the Rider-Waite tarot, including some of the inspirations that Waite drew on. His Rider-Waite deck has become the *lingua franca* of card divination, the work on which numerous modern card divination decks are based.

Since Waite's day, many card designers have also drawn on the deep well of learning that they have acquired from the Rider-Waite tarot to develop new and exciting decks that move completely away from its system. Some are simply artistically pleasing, and some are astonishing in their reflection of magical evolution.

Hence though this book is designed for a card reader to use with any type or design of deck, the Rider-Waite deck is used both to illustrate the layouts, and as the reference point for the deep meanings of the tarot cards as Waite envisaged them. Once you have learned this universal language, you will have a foundation to launch from in your divination and magical adventures. May you adventure well!

— Josephine McCarthy, May 2020

Alterius non sit, qui suus esse potest
Let he who can belong to himself belong to no other.
— The motto of Paracelsus[1]

---

[1] Hirschvogel 1538.

Chapter One

Whispers on the Wind

The development of cards as a mystical magical tool

But me the scrip and the staff had strengthen'd:
I carried the star: that star led me:
The paths I've taken, of most forsaken,
Do surely lead to the open sea:
As a clamour of voices heard in sleep,
Come shouts through the dark on the shrouded deep.

— A. E. Waite, *Strange Houses of Sleep*.[1]

The tarot trumps in a regular, traditional tarot deck[2] use imagery that originated with magician and mystic A. E. Waite (1857–1942). Waite was a Rosicrucian and founder of the Fellowship of the Rosy Cross (1915), a Freemason, and a member of the Golden Dawn. As such Waite was immersed not only in classical Greek and Latin texts from his education, but also in the mystical and magical imagery of the Western Mysteries. His work was heavily influenced by Eliphas Levi,[3] whose writing Waite discovered in the British museum reading room in 1881.

I have worked with the Rider-Waite deck, among many others, since the mid 1970s, but it was not until I came to write this book that I took the time to really and carefully look at the imagery and

---

[1] Waite 1906, p. 30.
[2] The Rider-Waite deck.
[3] French occultist Eliphas Levi (1810–1875), real name Alphonse Louis Constant.

1. WHISPERS ON THE WIND

symbology within each tarot trump. What I found astonished me: things of great significance that my eyes had simply skipped past, such as ancient magical messages stripped of their usual dressing and clothed in 'ordinary.'

This made me sit up and do a bit of background research on A. E. Waite and Pamela Colman Smith (also known as 'Pixie') and the influences that surrounded them. Where did they get the knowledge for such imagery? Some of it was not commonplace in magical circles of the nineteenth century. I was also careful not to assume that the imagery was all from Waite: I have learned only too well from personal experience that often women involved in such projects were sidelined as 'just the typist' or 'just the artist' when it many cases that was clearly not true.

The imagery hidden in the tarot trumps is pulled from a variety of sources. In addition to hints at Rosicrucian themes, it draws on the mythologies of Rome and Greece, the Kabbalah, Dynastic Egypt, and Mesopotamia. A recurring theme of magical mystical ascent flows through the trump cards, indicating that one or both of the creators of the Rider Waite deck had a solid knowledge of magic and mysticism as well as ancient history and Egyptology. Or at least they collaborated with someone who did.

I quickly found that Waite was a member of the Reading Room club at the British Museum in London, as was S. L. M. Mathers, one of the founders of the Golden Dawn, an esoteric order that Waite would eventually join. Other members of the reading club included his friend the poet William Butler Yeats (also a Golden Dawn member) and most importantly, E. A. Wallis Budge, curator of Egyptian and Assyrian antiquities at the British Museum from 1894 to 1924. Budge had a deep and abiding interest in all things magical, and his knowledge of magic informed his approach to some of his work on, and translations of, Egyptian mortuary texts. Our understanding of the ancient Egyptian language has vastly improved since Budge's time, and his translations have not aged well. However, they can still make for interesting and informed magical reading alongside a modern academic translation.

Budge was also close friend of William Butler Yeats, and as a museum curator he was a frequent attendee of the meetings of the reading club at the museum.

Pamela Colman Smith was also a magician as well as an artist, and she was a member of the Golden Dawn. She mixed with the same crowd who frequented the British Museum reading room, and she did commission work for her friends William Butler Yeats and Bram Stoker, who were both reading room members.

In the late nineteenth and early twentieth centuries, the British Museum reading room club was a powerful focal point for the major writers, thinkers, esotericists, Egyptologists, artists, and occultists of the time. Debates, lectures, and discussions were a frequent feature of the reading room, and many of the major occultists and esoteric thinkers of the age spent huge amounts of time reading and researching in the vast collections of obscure texts that the museum library held.

They also presented their work and ideas to each other, and through his Egyptian translations of funerary and other ancient texts, Budge became a huge influence on the magical thinkers of the day. Budge's translation and presentation of the Papyrus of Ani—a particularly long and beautiful Ramessid Book of the Dead—along with his partial translation of the Book of Gates, opened up whole new vistas of esoteric understanding to the writers and thinkers of the time. Budge's translation of the Papyrus of Ani in 1895, and his work on the Book of Gates in 1905, would without doubt have been studied by Waite and Colman Smith, and the influence of those texts shows up clearly in some of the Major Arcana. The Rider-Waite Tarot was printed in 1909, published by William Rider and Son, London.

The late nineteenth and early twentieth century upsurge of interest in the ancient world and mysticism created a sort of philosophical and magical renaissance that brought forth wonderful, interesting, and at times crazy things. It was a time of rapid change in all areas of society, and it was one of those times in history where all the right people came together to share ideas, argue, and debate. All the necessary resources where there, which allowed for rapid expansion in the worlds of art, literature, dance, music, philosophy, and mysticism. It was an explosion of light before the dark cloud of World War One descended.

In terms of card divination, mysticism, and magic, there was a similar 'magical renaissance' hundreds of years earlier in the sixteenth and early seventeenth centuries that also played part in the development of card divination in the west. And in a poetic sense, the two different times were connected by a similar theme, one dear to the heart of Waite, a mystical thread that wove its way through time to tap him on the shoulder.

Generally, the history of magical interpretations of the tarot and the use of cards for divination is traced back to eighteenth-century writer and mystic Antoine Court de Gebelin (1725–1784) who presented an essay outlining the esoteric meanings behind the tarot trumps in volume eight of his series *Monde primitif: analysé et comparé avec le monde modern*.[1]

However, after an interesting discussion with a dear magical colleague Frater Acher, I started digging into a different area of esoteric history. Frater Acher showed me a collection of the complete

---

[1] Gébelin 1781.

works of Paracelsus in German. Only parts of the work of Paracelsus are currently available in English, so to see a much more extensive collection by this master in German was a major revelation to me. Buried within that extensive work was the seed of a concept that waited hundreds of years to grow.

Paracelsus (1493–1541) was born Phillippus Aureolus Theophrastsus Bombastus von Hohenheim. He was a Swiss alchemist, lay theologian, physician, and philosopher in the German Renaissance. His parents obviously liked long names.

Within the vast collection of works by Paracelsus are thirty illustrations of cards with a commentary. The illustrations are from woodcut prints designed to illustrate the reformist spirit and to prophecize about the downfall the Papacy. Paracelsus argues that the previous commentary on the cards, by the German Meistersinger and poet, Hans Sachs, who was an admirer of Luther, had been done through a subjective and partisan lens.

Paracelsus decided to write his own commentary on the cards, and did an extensive new commentary for each card which remained only in manuscript form in his lifetime. And this is where it gets interesting to us as diviners and magicians. In his introduction to the commentary, Paracelsus explained that there are three ways of divination: one through the agency of the stars, one through the agency of Divinity, and one "through the lens of the magician." He calls the cards 'a Magicum Opus.' He undertook to study the dynamics of pride and evil depicted in the cards, and yet he stated, "nobody should use them to judge, but to remain silent in the Desert like Joannis" (i.e. use them for meditation and mystical thought).

So where did he get these images from?

That question led me to Nuremberg, which in the early to mid-sixteenth century was at the heart of the German Renaissance, and in 1525 took up the Protestant Reformation. Less than a hundred years earlier Nuremberg had suffered from repeated wars and an outbreak of plague, a result of which was the substantial reduction of its population. Out of its recovery sprang a strong and influential literary culture that would endure for centuries.

The images traced back to a publication that appeared in 1527 called *Eyn wunderliche Weyssagung von dem Babstumb* (A Wondrous Prophecy of the Papacy).[1] The publication, edited by Andreas Osiander, included one hundred and fifty verses by Hans Sachs (1494–1576) and thirty illustration woodcuts by Erhard Schön. Sachs, Osiander, and Schön were part of the Nuremberg Reformers of the time.

The images are mainly allegorical images of the Pope, showing for example the Pope in league with the devil as well as depictions of the Papal vices and crimes, and they are littered with political and religious references. Luther makes an appearance dressed as a monk holding a sickle and a rose. Before him is a severed leg: a possible reference to *Isaiah* 40:6:

> Hark! one saith: "Proclaim!"
> And he saith: "What shall I proclaim?"
> "All flesh is grass,
> And all the goodliness thereof is as the flower of the field;

The works were inspired by a thirteenth-century manuscript known as the *Pope Prophecies*, discovered by Osiander in the Carthusian monastery in Nuremberg in March 1525. The text, a medieval prophecy, describes the sins of the Popes, the coming of the Antichrist, and the impending change this would bring. This was taken up by the Reformers of Nuremberg, and in the last paragraph

---

[1] Osiander and Sachs 1527.

of his preface, Osiander says that the work is meant to "admonish the Catholics and show them their fate."

Luther approved of the work, but it was quickly suppressed at Nuremberg, and Sachs was reprimanded by the authorities who subsequently destroyed most of the copies.

Each of the woodcut images in *Eyn wunderliche Weyssagung von dem Babstumb* were accompanied by two rhyming couplets by Sachs, and it ends with a longer poem by Sachs which served as a summary of Osiander's interpretation. The woodcuts designed by Erhard Schön were cut by Hieronymus Andrea, a local formschneider (woodblock cutter) and printer who worked with many of the most prominent Nuremberg artists.

Nuremberg and its surrounding city states in the Reformation were a hotbed of religious, philosophical, magical, and mystical debate. This was the cauldron that eventually gave birth to Rosicrucianism, a mystical path that was important to A. E. Waite.

I find it interesting how these whispers down through time form a delicate and mainly hidden path through magical history, bringing the idea (as well as many other things, including Rosicrucianism) that images can be used magically not only for divination, but also for mystical purposes. Did Waite come up with the concept of the cards as not only divination tools, but mystical and magical tools, on his own? Often wheels are reinvented as curious minds push boundaries. Or did he get that idea from Levi, or from Antoine Court de Gebelin?

At first I thought Waite had probably reinvented the wheel, until I discovered that Waite not only could read German, but was familiar with the works of Paracelsus in German and not just English. In 1894 he wrote a book titled *The Hermetic and Alchemical Writings of Aureolus Phillippus Theophrastus Bombast of Hohenheim, Called*

1. Whispers on the Wind

Paracelsus the Great.[1] I then stumbled across a reference Waite made to the poetry of Hans Sachs.[2] It slowly became obvious that he was familiar with the works of the Nuremberg Reformists, and Paracelsus.

Waite's classical and esoteric knowledge enabled him to embed a wealth of esoteric and mystical symbolism into the imagery of the tarot trumps, thus layering the cards with meanings beyond mundane divination. He was able to draw on a large and deep well of esoteric and ancient writings from the British Museum reading room and from the work of his contemporaries.

Through this wealth of knowledge, he was able to produce a tarot deck that enabled the magical student of the time to draw insight from the more obscure and partially hidden esoteric layers of the images through meditation, visionary work, and study. He brought to fruition the seeds planted by Schön, Sachs, and Paracelsus.

This brought me back to the question of Pamela Colman Smith. When I first started this journey of discovery into the sources for the more obscure occult imagery hidden in the deck, I kept an open mind about who contributed what. However, after discussion with a dear friend of mine, R. A. Gilbert, who is somewhat of an authority on Waite, he passed along to me excerpts from Waite's autobiographical memoir collection *Shadows of Life and Thought.*[3]

In the excerpt I received, from his chapter on tarot, Waite states in reference to Pamela Colman Smith: "under proper guidance (she) could produce a Tarot with an appeal in the world of art and a suggestion of significance behind the symbols which would put on them another construction than had ever been dreamed of by those who (…) had produced and used them for mere divinatory purposes." He adds that part of his task was to make sure that the designs,

---
[1] Waite 1894.
[2] Waite 1933, p. 290.
[3] Waite 1992 [1938].

"especially those of the important Trumps Major—kept that in the hiddenness which belonged to certain Greater Mysteries" and that she "should not be picking up casually any floating images from mine or another mind. She had to be spoon-fed carefully over the Priestess Card, over that which is called the Fool and over the Hanged Man."

These comments clearly outline that for Pamela Colman Smith—while she was a gifted psychic artist and magician—the deeper layers of the Mysteries were more or less unknown to her. Looking at the rest of her artwork, we instead see a deep and abiding theme of nature magic and folklore.

What finally clinched it for me was that at the end of the last chapter of *Key to the Tarot,* Waite writes:

> let anyone who is a mystic consider separately and in combination the Magician, the Fool, the High Priestess, the Hierophant, the Empress, the Emperor, the Hanged Man and the Tower. Let him then consider the card called the Last Judgement. They contain the legend of the soul.[1]

In that last line Waite outlines that those select images have much deeper functions than mere divination: they are the keys to the Mysteries and they are most certainly signposts to various stages of mystical and magical development.

These images have an important role in guiding and catalysing the deeper introspection of the mystic on their path. This is really the same sentiment expressed by Paracelsus hundreds of years earlier: nobody should use them to judge, but to remain silent in the Desert like Joannis.[2]

---

[1] Waite 1971 [1910], p. 316.
[2] John the Baptist who withdrew into the Desert for solitude before emerging as a prophet.

1. Whispers on the Wind

> All poetic inspiration is but dream interpretation
> — Hans Sachs[1]

---

[1] Damrosch, Melas, and Buthelezi 2009, p. 28.

Chapter Two

Getting started

Tarot divination is a fascinating adventure that can take a lifetime to master, and it can be a guiding light in dark and difficult times. Treat divination with respect, curiosity, and common sense, and the world of 'seeing' will slowly open its doors to you.

This brief chapter contains some simple checklists to help you get started with tarot, maintain your deck, and keep yourself energetically clean. Once you have gained a bit of experience and have a good sense of the cards, further chapters in this book will help you explore card divination more deeply.

Caring for your deck

- Get a large, thin, washable cloth that you can wrap your deck in. You can also use the cloth as a surface to lay out your cards. This stops the cards picking up any energetic or physical dirt from surfaces. Silk is the best if you can get it, as it is thin and will easily fit in a box with the deck, but any washable fabric will do. Drop a few drops of some essential oils on the cloth regularly to keep the deck energetically clean. I use frankincense oil, but sage oil, rosemary, or patchouli also work. Wash the cloth with soap and water once it starts to feel grubby.

- Have a box that you can put the deck and cloth into. Drop some essential oils into the box to keep it energetically clean. Keeping

2. Getting started

your deck in a box keeps it safe and discourages others from playing with it. Keep the deck away from children.

- Some readers have the person asking the questions shuffle the cards. This can build up energetic dirt and mess on your deck, and it can also interfere with your tight connection with your deck. How you shuffle is of course a personal choice, but I learned early on from experience to not let people touch my deck.

- When you first get your deck, take out any surplus cards (adverts, etc.) and mix the deck up really well.

Making friends with your deck

- If you are unfamiliar with the deck then lay all the cards out in lines and have a good look at them. Get to know each card: I always say hello to the personalities in the cards when it is a deck I am unfamiliar with.

- Play around with the cards, putting them in groups of personalities and powers—and not necessarily in the official groupings. Let your instinct decide who is related to who: this will help you learn to understand the deeper connections that some cards have.

- Once you have finished getting to know your cards, mix the deck up really well so that it is ready to start work on readings.

Getting started with reading tarot

- First choose your question. Before you even touch the cards, think about your question, how to phrase it, and how much information you need from the layout. Is it a question that just needs a yes/no answer? Or do you need to know details? If you

Getting started with reading tarot

are unsure how to form a focused question that will yield a clear answer, the interpretation chapter contains a section on how to form a question.

- The next step is to choose the layout you will work with. The layouts chapter contains a selection of layouts if you do not already have one you work with. Once you have chosen a layout, if you do not know the layout well, then have the page open that illustrates the layout so that you can look at it while you shuffle. If you keep an awareness of the layout, then the cards can organize themselves to that pattern.

- Now pick up the deck and keep your question in the forefront of your mind. Block everything else out of your mind and focus only on the question and the layout. If someone tries to talk to you while you shuffle, ask them to be quiet while you work. Start to shuffle the cards. Take your time with this, however long you need. Keep the cards moving while you ask the question in your mind and you look at the layout pattern (if you are unfamiliar with it). As you shuffle, think about the question, the layout you will use, and imagine you are searching for something through a mist. Use your imagination to create the sensation of trying to pierce a veil.

- When the reading is ready, you will feel that you no longer wish to shuffle. The more experience you get with cards, the stronger this feeling will get, until you get to a stage where the cards seem to lock in place when the reading is ready. Once you have become accustomed to working with the cards, you may find that the answer you were looking for seeps into your mind even before you lay the cards out. It is as if you get a preview of what is coming. Not all readers have this experience, but for those with

2. Getting started

a strong natural ability, the flavour of the reading often emerges in the reader's mind before the cards are laid out.

- Do not cut the cards. Simply stop shuffling, and holding the pack with the backs of the cards towards you, taking from the top, start laying your cards out. Once the layout is complete, put the rest of the deck to one side.

- First impressions. Before you look up the meanings, just look at the overall reading. How many trumps are there: a lot or a little? More trumps means a stronger fate/picture. Are there a lot of one suite, like a lot of swords or cups? Then sit quietly for a moment and see how the reading makes you feel: what is your first overall impression?

- Now go through each card in the layout sequence and look up the meanings. A lot of cards have multiple meanings so that they can speak to different types of questions. As you go through the sequence, you may find that a story starts to unfold for you, and you start to see connections between the card positions and the cards themselves. The chapter on interpreting layouts contains plenty of advice on how to do this, along with worked examples.

- If it is an important question or reading, photograph it or write it down so that you have a record of it. It is a good idea to get a journal for your readings, and keep a record of them. You can learn a great deal by looking back at readings in retrospect.

- When you have finished, mix all the cards up to break the reading up and disperse it. Wrap the cards up and put them back in their box. Now go wash your hands to remove any energetic dirt that has built up. Liquid soap and a bit of salt in your hands is a good way to do this. Salt strips energetic dirt, and the liquid soap cleans the physical dirt while making it easier to salt wash your hands.

Getting good at reading tarot

The best way to get good at card readings is to not try too hard, but to be curious while using your common sense. In the interpretation chapter you will find a lot of information and tips for developing your skills. But here is a short list to get you going:

- Get to know your deck really well. If you are using a traditional tarot deck, separate out the trumps and group together the people, events, and land powers (sun, star, etc.). Get to know the trumps well, as they are the powers that drive events.

- Don't be afraid to get it wrong. We all get it wrong at some point, no matter how skilled we are. You will make a lot of mistakes but also get great flashes of insight while learning. The key is not to bullshit your way through a reading: if you don't know, be okay with that. I have been reading for more than forty years, and I still get stumped now and again.

- Don't be tempted to 'read' the person who you are doing the reading for. This is a classic mistake in tarot divination. Let the cards speak, and if you have to ask a question of the person you are reading for, don't ask a leading question. Be thoughtful about any question you need to ask them: it should be to discount certain possibilities, not to dig for information.

- Don't be tempted to give the person the reading they want. If they only want good news, they should not ask for a reading. However, if you see a potential disaster on the horizon, tread carefully. Your job is to offer insight and options, not just dump terror on their lap and walk away.

2. Getting started

- Learn to say no. Do not read for everyone just because they ask: you will end up drained energetically. If you feel or have an instinct not to read for someone, then don't. If they do not need a reading, say no. And do not allow people to become emotionally dependant on your readings. Some readers fall into the trap of reading for the same person every week or month, and that is not necessary. It will drain you, and they will unintentionally vampirize your energy. It is not your job to prop people up emotionally.

- Pace yourself. Learn that sometimes it is not a good idea for you to do readings, such as if you are getting sick, or if as a woman you are on your period. Readings, particularly for other people, can take a lot of energy, as it is hard work. Do not burn yourself out for other people's curiosity, and learn to have times when you do not look at anything using divination.

- When you do a reading for yourself that shows something is not good, do not obsess and keep repeating the reading until you get the answer you want. Be sensible. If you see something that worries you, then you need more focused information. Form your next question carefully to extract the maximum amount of information, and choose a good layout. Learn to look at issues from different angles and using different time spans. This is covered in the chapters on interpretation and interpretation of layouts.

- Keep a journal and read back over it often.

- Do not read for every decision in your life, as it will weaken you. Learn to use tarot when you are truly in need of help and advice.

Reversals?

I do not use reversals, as I find them pretty pointless and often inaccurate, and they can easily confuse the vocabulary. Because of the root power nature of the trump cards, any negative aspect is usually conveyed through interpretation in relation to the question, situation, and the position the cards land in. The minor cards, which are how the root powers express in a situation, can be positive or negative depending on their meaning and position. Minor cards also have slightly wider fields of key meanings to explore in relation to the question and their positions. It doesn't help that the actual vocabulary in traditional tarot is not particularly brilliant, but that does give the card reader a chance to really develop their own interpretation skills. The traditional tarot deck really makes you work hard to obtain good divination!

Instead of reversals, I use layouts with negative positions that indicate the negative sides of the question. When a card falls in a negative position it means that the positive qualities of that card are withheld or are problematic. For example, if you were doing a reading to look at a particular job situation and the Empress landed in a negative position, then you would interpret the opposite qualities of the key words for the Empress: lack of harvest, a famine, unloving, uncaring, and so forth. This is saying that the job would be unfulfilling, and that the actual pay would be poor. Layouts with in-depth explanations of negative and positive connotations can be found in the chapter on layouts.

2. GETTING STARTED

Tarot's limited vocabulary

Before you dive into the meanings of the cards, here is something that is seriously worth thinking about. Imagine you had to tell your life story, but you were only allowed to use seventy-eight different words for your vocabulary. Try it, it truly is difficult. This is an issue that many tarot readers do not really think about, as it is something that just does not occur to us. We are used to using a wide vocabulary to describe and relate complex issues.

When you work with a tarot deck, there are two things to always keep at the back of your mind. The first is your seeing range, and the second is your deck's vocabulary. The seeing range is the part of the story that you can see. Looking through a hole in a door only allows you to see what is directly in front of you. To see more details of the room beyond, you have to create more holes. The tarot deck's vocabulary is its seventy-eight cards: these are all the 'words' you can use to gain information.

Because of the tarot's limited vocabulary, each card can have various similar meanings. For any reading, you must decide which meaning you will attribute to each card based on the question you asked and the card's position in the layout. For example, if you wanted to tell your partner that you are going to have a baby, but you cannot use the word 'pregnant' or 'baby'—or you just want to shock them into sitting down, then you could present them with a pair of knitted baby booties.

That same knitted pair of booties could also be a way of conveying the need to tread 'gently and lightly.' The same booties could be used to covey the letter B, or the concept 'feet' or 'woven.' It all depends on the context of the situation and question.

When you are doing a reading and looking at the card meanings, remember there is wriggle room to interpret. Think about how the meaning can be interpreted according to the question and what the cards are trying to convey. Remember the deck's limited vocabulary, and think about creative, sideways approaches to interpretation. Also remember that sometimes a meaning can be literal: if you are asking about a danger, and the Chariot turns up in a position that shows what danger you may be in, this could literally mean "danger with your car."

Another thing to seriously keep in mind is that using tarot for divination is very different from using it in counselling or psychological experimentation. Because the psychologized use of tarot is easier than divination, this has become the most popular way to read the tarot: many books on the market are basically psychology with little or no content about divination. If you really want to learn tarot, then it pays to be clear about what you are using it for and how you want to approach it. If you are clear in your intent, then developing your skills will be much easier.

In divination tarot, the trump or major cards are really powers, fate dynamics, and qualities that *flow through* people, situations, and events. The minor cards represent how those powers, dynamics, and qualities *manifest* in people and events. With this in mind, if you need a lot of information on some subject, it can be worth using layouts that separate the Major and Minor Arcana, then pair them up. More information on that can be found in the layouts chapter.

The more you work with a deck, the more the cards will show you their own meanings in a way that is unique to you. Everyone develops their own vocabulary with divination, and eventually a particular card will have some specific meaning to you that would not work for another reader.

Chapter Three

Major Arcana Card Meanings

Four signs present the Name of every name, four brilliant beams adorn His crown of flame.

— Eliphas Levi[1]

The Major Arcana

The Major Arcana was originally built around the journey of the Seeker of the Mysteries. Its sequence represents the stages, powers, and events that are key markers on the path of those who seek esoteric wisdom and knowledge. The Major Arcana also represents the dynamics and fate powers within the human experience, and as such can be used in divination to convey meaning. Each card has many different layers of meaning, from basic mundane meanings to mystical and magical ones.

The key to interpreting these cards in divination is to interpret them relative to the situation and question. When the question is mundane, then the mundane layers of the cards' meanings must be explored. When the question has a deeper, more magical or mystical significance, then the deeper layers of the cards' meanings are also to be pondered and meditated on.

---

[1] Levi 2011 [1855], p. 78.

3. Major Arcana Card Meanings

How to use this guide

Below for each card is a collection of key words. These are the various meanings that the card has: one or more of those key words will be relevant in the reading.

There is also a longer explanation of the meaning of each card, sometimes with examples. I have also described the esoteric or magical meaning for each card: this should give you a much deeper understanding of the card, while also enabling the interpretation of magical and mystical readings.

0 Fool

Key words

zero, no, empty, foolish behaviour, idiot, innocent, reckless, inexperienced.

Mundane meaning

When the reading is about a person, this card indicates someone who is naïve, inexperienced, someone unaware of their lack of knowledge or inability. It does not mean they are a bad person; they are just not self-aware. Nor are they aware of what they do not know: they are childlike in many ways. Indeed, on some occasions the Fool can represent a child. It can also represent stupid acts, thoughtless behaviour, and self-delusion.

We all have to start somewhere in life, and most of us as teens or young adults stepped out into our adult life full of enthusiasm, yet we had no clue of what the real world was like. Life teaches us lessons, and as we gain experience and start to understand that things are not as simple as they first appear, then we get to a stage where we walk away from being The Fool and towards being The Magician.

The Fool card can represent a young and inexperienced person, but it can also represent the *loss* of experience in such cases as dementia, if the reading is about an old person.

It can come up when something would be a foolish choice, and it can also appear in a reading to say, "no," "not there," or "empty." If you were looking for something and you did a reading for a particular area, and The Fool was the outcome, then the answer is "it is not there."

Esoteric meaning

The Fool represents the person who has no experience to draw on, the person who is driven to move forward, but has no clue about where they are going or why. It can also represent the mundane world, or people wrapped up in the mundane world who do not engage with anything that is mystical, magical, or otherworldly. The dog in the card is the animal companion or spirit that tries to warn The Fool, but the warnings fall on deaf ears. In the distance are the mountains, and the Herculean path up the Mountain of Adversity to the Sun that Initiates climb on their journey of mystical and magical evolution. But the Fool is not treading that path: they are walking into mindless self-destruction. Hence the number of The Fool is 0: they are not on the ladder of the Initiate's ascent into evolution, rather they are trapped in the mindless life of simply existing.

Many tarot guides put The Fool as the beginning of the magical journey, but this is a mistake that has crept into modern magical thinking. The Fool is the Profane, the unclean, the one who is rejected from the outer court door of the temple by the words, *procul, o procul este profane* "begone, oh begone you who are profane." This pronouncement against the unclean and uninitiated appears in book

3. Major Arcana Card Meanings

six of Virgil's *Aeneid* as the seer shrieks out a warning to intruders in a rite. It was taken up and used by freemasons, magicians, and mystics, and was placed over the door of their temples as a warning.

The deepest Mystery of The Fool is that not only is it the first major card in the sequence of powers, but it is also the last, unsaid power. If a tarot deck were to have seventy-nine cards instead of seventy-eight, the last card would also be The Fool. But The Fool XXII would not have a dog yapping at his legs, nor would he have a bundle of his belongings. Instead he would be as The Hermit, alone, with only his lantern of knowledge to guide him. He would step off the cliff in full knowledge of what he was doing: the adept stepping out and crossing the great Abyss, trusting in the Divine, with his worldly belongings discarded and no longer needed.

> Next barks the Dog, and from his Nature flow
> The most afflicting Powers that rule below
>
> — Manilius (first century A.D.) on Sirius[1]

1 Magician

Key words

control, taking measured action, skills, intention, resourceful, organized, clear thinking, intelligence.

Mundane meaning

The Magician is a person who has some power and skills, and who uses them to achieve a set goal. However their deeper wisdom is often rather limited, from a magical perspective.

---

[1] Creech 1700, p. 17.

1 Magician

The Magician has the tools of his magical trade—the four elemental magical implements of cup (water), wand (fire), sword (air) and shield (earth)—on the altar in front of him. He is conducting a ritual to achieve something, and reaches upwards to connect with the infinite power.

When this appears in a mundane reading, it expresses the type of person who uses skilled action to achieve a set goal. It might mean the use of their skills in their job, or their skills out in the world in general, but they are controlling a situation to achieve something. What is *sometimes* lacking in the magician is maturity and wisdom, or emotional intelligence. They are still at the phase of their life where they feel they have to control everything—and sometimes that is necessary, for example in the case of a doctor.

The Magician could easily signify a surgeon or doctor, a stock trader, or a manager: someone with some role to play in the life of the person that the reading is about. Equally it could represent those qualities within the person whom the reading is about.

The Magician can also represent someone who is not above manipulating a person or situation to get what they want. The Magician can represent a woman or a man: it is the qualities of the person, not their gender, that is signified in this card.

Depending on the question posed, this card can also represent these qualities *in general*. It can represent the qualities of The Magician as part of the situational dynamic. For instance, if you are asking about a car you want to buy, and the magician is the outcome, then this indicates that all this car's parts are working properly, or it might represent a highly computerized car. The card can represent the actions of an organisation, or it can be telling you to organize yourself and take action. Say, for example, you did a reading about the best course of action to take in a situation. If The Magician was your answer, then the reading is telling you that you need to take control, and use your knowledge and skills, to organize yourself and get things done.

Esoteric meaning

Esoterically, the mindset of the Magician is one of a person who has learned the foundations of their magical skills, but is not fully aware of the deeper side of magic. They stand with the elemental tools before them and reach for infinity, yet the sacred and mystical has not yet appeared in their orbit.

The Magician is on the first rung of the ladder of magical development: they have learned rituals and foundation skills, but they are not yet magically mature enough to fully grasp the enormity of the magical universe around them. They still use spirits and magic to attain a set goal that is often mundane, and the appearance of this card in a magical reading can signify someone who does magic for hire. It can also simply indicate that *magic is being used*; and when it falls in a difficult position in a layout it can indicate that hostile or manipulative magic is being employed against the subject of the reading. If it is in a good position, then magic is likelier being used to help, or it could indicate that magical action is necessary.

> ...For this is a remnant of Eridanos, that stream of tears, beneath the Gods feet is borne.
>
> — Aratos[1]

---

[1] Brown 1885, p. 42.

2 High Priestess

KEY WORDS

wisdom, truth, honour, deep intuition, maturity, power, spirituality, mystical or spiritual depth, energetic empathy, wise logic.

MUNDANE MEANING

The High Priestess in a mundane reading can either represent a woman of balanced power and/or knowledge, or a woman who has come into her own power. She often has good intuition and empathy, but is not highly emotional: the High Priestess understands that emotion has its place, but should not rule your life. The High Priestess has an ethical code that she will not step outside, but she often has no interest in social norms.

This card can appear when a woman finally comes into her adult power, often through struggle and hard work. It can also represent a female boss, a woman of position, or a highly educated woman. It can also represent a hidden psychic ability, strong ethical code, or mystical depths within a person.

When this card appears in a reading, it can also represent the more intuitive aspects of power for a man or a woman; and it often appears in readings for men when they are coming more into emotional maturity, or if they are developing their deeper intuitive side. In a man's reading, it can also represent a woman coming into their life who will have a powerful effect on them, either in a relationship, or in a job/friendship/teaching way.

When the reading is not about a person it can represent high quality, higher education, ethics, artistic depths, knowledge, medicine, and logic. For example; if you were going on a potentially dangerous journey and did a reading to check if you were going to be safe, and the

3. Major Arcana Card Meanings

outcome of the reading was The High Priestess, then the reading is saying, "you are in good hands and in a high quality mode of transport, you will be safe."

Esoteric meaning

The High Priestess reaches deeper than the magical imagery of the Magician. Whereas the Magician has his tools of magic and is reaching for power, the High Priestess is surrounded by Divine power and holds the knowledge of that Divine power in her hands.

She sits between the two bronze pillars of Boaz and Jachin (Yakin), the two freestanding pillars that once stood at the porch of the Temple of Solomon.[1] The pillar that stands to her right[2] is Boaz, which in Hebrew, in the context of Solomon's temple, is thought to mean "proceed in Strength"[3] and the pillar to her left, Jachin (Yakin) is thought to mean "He will establish."[4] Each word, however, had various applications and language meaning changes over the millennia. Magically, though, it makes perfect sense: if the High Priestess sits within the Tree of Life,[5] then Gevurah (The Strength/Justice of G-D) would be to her right, while Chesed (the Kindness and covenant of G-D)[6] would be to her left.

This dynamic is further strengthened by the word and name Boaz: in Jewish Kabbalah, words and names can convey many layered meanings, and Boaz appears as a person in the Book of Ruth. A small part of the story around Boaz tells that even though he is a prince,

---

[1] Josephus *Antiquitates Judaicae* VIII 3:4
[2] The observer's left side.
[3] In Hebrew Bo (בּוֹא) come or go, Az (עַז) strength.
[4] In Hebrew Yakin (יָכִין) : Masculine; he will establish.
[5] The mundane person looks at the Tree of Life, the priest, priestess, or Hierophant sits within the Tree.
[6] *Psalms* 25:10 "all YHWH's paths are Chesed and truth for those who keep the decrees of his covenant"

he oversees the threshing of the grain.[1] This reflects the dynamic of Strength/Justice of G-D (Gevurah): YHWH threshes his harvest. In magical practice, the right hand is the hand of your own harvest and the left hand is the hand of your path ahead/future action.

So we see the High Priestess sitting at the porch of the temple of Solomon. In parts of the ancient world, the porch of the temple was the place where judges would sit to give judgement in high profile cases,[2] where religious teachers would talk with students, and where philosophers would sit to debate. The High Priestess sits in that powerful position surrounded by sacred and magical imagery. In her hands she holds a Torah scroll, and she sits in the central position[3] between the pillars of Strength and Mercy.

The magical reading of the High Priestess is of a power or person who is seated in balance with the Divine, who reaches into the inner worlds, who holds the sacred knowledge and law in her hands. She mediates between the inner sanctum of the temple and the people beyond the porch. It can represent the inner qualities of the soul of a person, regardless of their outer personality: the deep soul of the person flows through a life fate pattern to achieve what it needs to achieve. Sometimes the Goddess appears as an old bag lady. When the High Priestess appears in a reading, don't take things at face value: deeper, more profound powers of balance are at work.

> The Seven stars to light you,
> Or the Polar ray to right you.
>
> — John Keats[4]

---

[1] Tan., Behar, ed. Buber, viii.; Ruth R. to iii. 7

[2] For example in New Kingdom Egypt where the highest ranking judge was the 'Judge of the Porch.'

[3] The position of Tiphareth on the Tree of Life, the position of balance, the fulcrum of the scales.

[4] J. Keats (1820). "Robin Hood: To a Friend". In: *Lamia, Isabella, The Eve of St. Agnes, and Other Poems*. London: Taylor and Hessey, pp. 133–136.

3. Major Arcana Card Meanings

3 Empress

Key words

female creative power, fertility, harvest, mother, creativity, stability, birth, loving, nature, goddess, understanding, compassion, bounty, intuition, sexuality, beauty, generosity.

The Empress is the female power of regeneration, bounty, love, and the protection of a mother. The Empress is highly emotional and is firmly rooted in the practical world of family, job, and land. This card can sometimes represent the land itself and the power of nature, and in some readings can reflect the female principle of the land or the land as a goddess.

Mundane meaning

When The Empress appears in a reading it can represent a pregnancy or birth, or the fruitfulness of a situation. It is a card of gentle success, where one's needs are taken care of and where home and hearth can nurture you. The success of The Empress is not the aggressive success of business with constant expansion; rather it is the success of survival through having your emotional and physical necessities covered.

It can represent a happy home, a loving female partner, a good harvest, or an older woman who is nurturing, stable, and who will look out for you. The Empress is not weak and is not above lashing out to protect her children, and she can be fierce if her 'children' or harvest is threatened. Her gentleness hides a deep inner strength, fierce courage, and a strong resolve to see things through to the end. The Empress also represents feminine sexuality, and the qualities of femininity regardless of the gender of the person.

This card can also represent too much mothering, depending on the reading and position it falls in: the bounty the Empress brings can also come with an excess of control and/or emotional manipulation. The Empress can overwhelm and smother, and not allow her children to mature to adulthood on their own terms. In an employment situation this card can represent an employer or boss who is kind and easygoing, so long as everything is done their way and no one challenges their authority in any way. They can become overbearing, overcontrolling, and emotionally manipulative, all while smiling sweetly.

Esoteric meaning

The Empress reclines on a throne of soft, expensive cushions. Her body adorned with precious jewels and a voluminous robe decorated with flowers. She holds the wand of authority, and the shield is propped against her throne. Around her are all the signs of nature: trees, water, sunshine, and wheat ready to be harvested.

She is the epitome of the goddess Ceres, the Roman goddess of grain, harvest, civilization, and motherly love. She is the sister of Jupiter and the daughter of Saturn: through hard work (Saturn) comes kingship (Jupiter). This reflects how agriculture brought wealth and power. Ceres was the only one of the Roman gods who was truly invested in the ordinary people: she was their Mother. As such, Ceres was also the goddess of the Plebs, the ordinary people. She was their protector and patron, and oversaw the laws that gave rights to the people. Her Aventine temple in Rome served the Plebs as a cult centre, a place for legal advice, and as a law court. The Roman *Lex Hortensia* (Hortensian law) of 287 B.C. gave Plebian legal protection and rights to all the citizens of the city; and the decrees of the Senate were kept at the Temple of Ceres so that the goddess could oversee and protect them.

3. Major Arcana Card Meanings

So the Empress is not just some whimsical Mother figure: she is a power that feeds a nation, protects the weak and voiceless, ensures a good harvest, and enjoys all the power and wealth of a ruler of the people. When this card shows up in a magical reading it can indicate a female deity is present or is overseeing a magical project, line of work, or magical school. If she is badly placed in a layout it can indicate that a female deity has been angered or that such power has withdrawn from the magician.

> In Pisces, wher Venus is exaltat
> — Chaucer: *The Wife of Bath's Prologue.*

4 Emperor

Key words

stability, order, leadership, responsibility, rank, wealth, authority, war lord, conqueror, the greater good.

The Emperor is the epitome of secure power and all the responsibility that comes with it. The Emperor is a leader or someone of high rank: he represents authority in the world of economics, society, law, military, or any other aspect of everyday society. The Emperor is at ease with his power, but is merciless if his authority is challenged. He is establishment, security, and structure, financial stability and philanthropy. He is connected with the planets Saturn and Jupiter.

Mundane meaning

When the Emperor card turns up in a reading, it can represent a person or quality. The Emperor might represent a boss, a company, a government department, or the government itself; a bank, a judge, a banker, a sponsor, or financial stability. A person who is represented by the Emperor is often older, mature, financially secure, has authority, and is used to being listened to.

The Emperor can also be a father or grandfather, a person who is looked up to, depended on, or who is a father figure. As a root power the Emperor is the archetypal quality of the kingship: he makes sure all his people have what they need, but he also demands obedience to his rule. He restores and keeps order, defends boundaries, limits the strong, and protects the weak; he is fierce in the face of a hostile force and will protect his people and family against invaders and threats. The Emperor educates, casts judgement, oversees, and is the ultimate one who holds responsibility.

Esoteric meaning

The Emperor sits on a stone throne topped with rams' heads. In his hands he holds the tools of kingship—the orb and the staff—and he wears the golden crown of the king. He is older, with white hair and a white beard, and beneath his robes he is dressed in armour, ready for battle. His throne sits on a desert floor. Beyond him are the river and mountains that must be overcome in the journey of ascent to the sun: the trials of the initiate. The Emperor sits with his back to those challenges: in life, the Emperor cannot access the full depths of the Inner Mysteries: instead he has to carry the burden of difficult decisions every day of his life. His is the power of life or death over his subjects. He is the leader in war, the keeper of the nation's wealth, and the ultimate authority over every aspect of the lives of the people in the kingdom.

The decisions of the Emperor affect the fates of nations: his power is purely of the physical world, and while the Emperor may be conversant in the Inner Mysteries, the nature of his kingship excludes him from the deeper understanding gained by direct experience. In

3. Major Arcana Card Meanings

terms of the Mysteries, the job of the Emperor is to facilitate the path of Inner Mysteries for others by providing protection and resources. In return, he has access to wise counsel from Initiates.

The imagery used in the creation of the trump of the Emperor, like most trumps, relies heavily on classical and ancient symbolism. The rams' heads are a reference to Zeus Ammon (or Jupiter Ammon). Ammon refers to the Egyptian deity Amun, one of the key gods of the Egyptian pantheon, a deity who came to major prominence as a guide and kingly ideal at the beginning of the New Kingdom. The main centre of Amun was the temple of Karnak in Thebes, Upper Egypt. Karnak became a major centre of Egyptian theology and learning, and by the Greco-Roman period it was one of the 'go-to' places, along with Alexandria, for philosophers, leaders, and thinkers.

Amun was sometimes depicted as a ram with curled horns, and this imagery became connected with the Greek god Zeus, as Zeus Ammon, and Jupiter, as Jupiter Ammon.[1] Amun and the imagery of the rams' horns became connected, in the classical period, with supreme leaders, kingship, and power. To this end, Alexander the Great, on his return from the Egyptian Oracle of Siwa[2] which had declared Alexander as Pharaoh, had himself depicted with Amun's horns. The Emperor's white hair and beard, as well as his military armour beneath his robes, depicts a leader who is mature and experienced, and is always ready for battle to defend his people and his realm. All the imagery of the Emperor is based around the earthly power of kingship, with little reference to the Inner Mysteries: the power of the Emperor is solely planted in the human world.

When this card appears in a magical reading it can indicate a male deity who fits the description of the Emperor, or it can indicate the planetary spirits, usually Saturn or Jupiter. It can also be a

---

[1] See for example the Roman temple of Jupiter Amun at Siwa Oasis Egypt.
[2] Siwa is an oasis in Egypt close to the border with Libya.

warning to a magician if this card appears in a magical reading: the old kingship deities and planetary spirits will work with you, but they will demand payment. The payment required of the powers indicated by the Emperor card is your first-born son.

This is not a casual remark: it is something I have seen crop up a few times in younger magicians who make deals with such powers. The power returns as a presence to demand their due once the magician has a child. It is a warning to magicians to not dabble with powerful beings if they are not mature enough to understand what is happening, and do not have the depth of magical knowledge required to avoid such 'deals.' Working in collaboration with such powers is often fruitful if the intention and magic is balanced and necessary, and it is not for selfish ends. Making magical deals with such powers always goes badly wrong at some point.

> Though the servant was disposed to do evil,
> The Lord (Amun) is disposed to forgive.
> The Lord of Thebes spends not a whole day in anger,
> His wrath passes in a moment, none remains.
> His breath comes back to us in mercy,
> Amun returns upon his breeze.
> May your *ka* be kind, may you forgive,
> It shall not happen again.
> Says the draftsman in the Place of Truth, Nebre, Justified.
>
> — from the stele of Nebre[1]

---

[1] Eighteenth Dynasty, Deir el-Medina. Berlin Museum 20377. (Lichtheim 1976, pp. 106–7.)

3. Major Arcana Card Meanings

5 Hierophant

Key words

religion, religious organization, religious or spiritual leader or authority, dogma, wisdom, obedience, belief, spiritual discipline, asceticism, structured education, university.

Whereas the High Priestess (originally Papess) is about mystical and spiritual evolution and depth, the Hierophant (originally the Pope) is about structured and dogmatic religion or thought, regardless of religion. It is the power of institutionalized belief that has authority over a population or its followers. It can represent a person of religious authority, or a dogmatic person who casts rationality aside and is fully immersed in a structured and often narrow way of thinking. It can also represent non-religious people who are dogmatic and narrow in their thinking and behaviour: they cannot look beyond their own opinions and cannot absorb and analyse thinking that is different to their own. On the good side it can represent someone who has a high level of integrity, who lives to a specific code of behaviour, and who wields authority.

At its worst extreme the Hierophant can represent a religious fundamentalist or an individual who is obsessive and controlling, who is in the thrall of some particular belief or opinion. At its best, the Hierophant is one who acts as a bridge between Divinity and humanity, and who lives to a highly structured code of behaviour like a priest or monk. The Hierophant does not always have to be part of a particular religion, it is the qualities of belief, discipline, responsibility, ethics, and structure that mark out the person as a Hierophant.

Mundane Meaning

In divination this card can also mean an organization that expresses the qualities of Hierophant. I have occasionally had this card pop up to mean 'university,' but also to mean 'theocracy.' A few years ago I was asked to do a series of readings about a particular nation that was going through a great deal of change and unrest. In the short term, the fate of the country was expressed by the Emperor, but the nation's longer-term picture was the Hierophant. It was clear that the autocratic secular rule was eventually going to change to a religious rule.

When looking at job situations in a reading and the Hierophant appears as an answer, depending on the exact nature of the question, it can indicate either a boss who is dogmatic and moral and who acts with integrity, or a job in an organization with some spiritual, educational, or religious aspect, like a university or an NGO run by a religious charity. It can indicate that a job needs a high level of integrity, honesty, and responsibility.

Esoteric Meaning

Our word 'Hierophant' derives from the ancient Greek word ἱεροφάντης ("hierophantes"), which means "revealer of holy things." It was the title of the High Priest of the Eleusinian cult.[1] This gives us some idea of the root meaning of the word and the card itself. The imagery of the Hierophant card relies heavily on Roman Catholic symbolism, and is based around the Pope. One of the early unofficial titles of the Pope was *Pontifex Maximus*, which means

---

[1] The cult of Demeter and Persephone at Eleusis, Ancient Greece.

"greatest/highest priest." It was a term inherited by the Catholic church from the ancient Roman religion.[1, 2]

The card's imagery shows a high priest—the Pope—seated on a throne between two pillars. In his left hand he holds the Papal triple cross, and he wears the triple crown of the Pontiff. At his feet are the double keys, the symbolic keys to the kingdom of heaven, and beyond the keys kneel two priests in submission for blessing. The triple cross, the triple crown, and the two keys are all part of the traditional papal insignia. The triple crown and triple cross are both symbols of rank and power, but the keys have a deeper esoteric meaning which is directly relevant to the magical understanding of The Hierophant.

> I will give you the keys of the kingdom of heaven; whatever you bind on earth will be bound in heaven, and whatever you loose on earth will be loosed in heaven. [3, 4]

This passage talks about the Hierophant as the power of the bridge between heaven and earth. It says that the acts of the Hierophant or Pontiff are no longer confined to the physical world, but also unfold in the heavens. This is a magical adept dynamic of the highest power, where an outer action has an inner effect and *vice versa*: an action in one realm is mirrored in the other.

This is a magical dynamic that also appears in the text of the *Tabula Smaragdina*, the Emerald Tablet:

> That which is below is like that which is above
> and that which is above is like that which is below
> to do the miracles of one only thing.[5]

---

[1]"Pontifex Maximus" (1997). In: *The Oxford Dictionary of the Christian Church*. Ed. by F. L. Cross and E. A. Livingstone. 3rd ed. Oxford: Oxford University Press, p. 1307.
[2]Tertullian (155-240 A.D.) *On Modesty* Chapter 1.
[3]*Matthew* 16:19.
[4]*cura ei totius Ecclesiae et principatus committitur* (Epist., lib. V, ep. xx, in P.L., LXXVII, 745).
[5]Newton n.d.

5 Hierophant

The Emerald tablet was attributed to Hermes Trismegistus. This is not the name of a person, but more of a title meaning, thrice wise. It came to the west through Latin translations of Arabic texts, which were translations of much earlier Greek texts. The earliest translation to survive appears to be written by Abū Mūsā Jābir ibn Ḥayyān (born c. 721, Ṭūs, Iran, died c. 815, Al-Kūfah, Iraq), a Muslim alchemist known as the father of Arabic chemistry.

The 'as above, so below' dynamic also appears in the writings of the Ikhwān al-safā', the Brethren of Purity, who identified themselves with the "sleepers in the cave,"[1] an anonymous group of eighth-century A.D. early Sufi scholars based in Basra, Iraq, who translated Greek philosophical texts in a series of essays known as the Rasā'il al-Ikhwān al-safā', the *Treatises of the Brethren of Purity*.

The understanding of the Hierophant holding the power to affect both the inner and outer worlds, 'Heaven and Earth,' is an ancient and powerful wisdom that has survived to influence magic, philosophy, and alchemy to this day.

This is the deeper, more mystical reason behind the dogmatic, disciplined, and moral behaviour of the Hierophant. Words and actions can have deeply powerful, long-lasting effects in the inner worlds and the physical world alike. To this end, the Hierophant becomes highly disciplined in their actions and words, as they understand the consequences of thoughtless action. There is also the magical dynamic in which a carefully considered action has powerful effect: the magical adept Hierophant rarely 'does' magic, but when they do, its unfolding can be powerful indeed.

As in all things human, what can start as a discipline instilled from wisdom and necessity becomes a dogmatic adherence to a set of rules without truly understanding why those rules are there. The practical

---
[1] Callataÿ 2005, p. 103.

3. Major Arcana Card Meanings

necessity becomes a dogmatic behaviour based on superstition and belief, not one of understanding. This is the deeper principle behind the mundane understanding of the Hierophant: dogmatic principles or restraint stemming from arcane wisdom.

As you can see, like all the trump cards, each card has various levels of meaning from the deeply mundane to the deeply magical. The reader must interpret at the appropriate level depending on what they are looking at. When this card appears in a magical reading, sit up and pay careful attention. It can may indicate a magical leader or, depending on the question and the position the card falls in, the magical dynamics that slow through this card. It can be a warning to a magician to take care with their power, to hold it carefully and responsibly, and to remember that even a simple magical act by an adept can have unforeseen consequences throughout the different worlds. Such consequences may be actually be necessary and intended: if you are doing a reading for magical advice on a serious issue, this card's appearance can indicate a need for magical action that bridges across the inner and physical world.

> There is no sweeter delight than that the soul should be charged through and through with justice, exercising itself in her eternal principles and doctrines and leaving no vacant place in which injustice can make its way.
>
> — Philo[1]

---

[1] Colson 1939, p. 97.

6 Lovers

Key words

contract, agreement, partnership, union, relationship, love, alchemy, resonance, balance of powers, sustaining.

Mundane meaning

The Lovers is one of the most misunderstood cards in the tarot. Most people assume that it is only about love and relationships, when it has a much wider scope than that. Depending on the subject matter of the reading, it can mean transactions, contract agreements signed, a working partnership, or a balance of powers. It is also the power of two, where two individual people, beings, or things are joined as one or into a collective of one.

As it is a trump card, this card doesn't really depict casual relationships or casual sex; it is more powerful than that. This is the joining of two individuals as one unit: marriage, living together, or a long-term relationship. Depending on the question it can occasionally depict a shorter-term relationship, but one that will change both individuals in a major way.

It can also depict the signing of a contract that brings two parties together, like two companies or two working individuals who will produce something together. I have also had this card come up in a reading to mean a worker's union: an employment collective that bargains for the rights of workers.

Esoteric meaning

The woman and man each stand beside a tree. The woman stands by the Tree of Knowledge and looks upwards to the angel, as she can see the angel: she has knowledge of the angel. (Christian thought considers the Tree of Knowledge as the knowledge of good and evil, which is a greatly diminished understanding of this power.) The man is standing by the Tree of Life, which depicts time. The angel oversees this union, with the Sun behind the angel. In the background is the mountain, which is the struggles of Saturn and/or Hercules: the life path of ascent.

We could spend a long time exploring the deep mystical rabbit hole that is the symbolism of the Tree of Knowledge and the serpent, but the short version goes something like this:

The Tree is the growth of the Mysteries,[1] and the serpent is connected to the harvest goddesses Renenutet[2] or Demeter.[3] The harvest was not just the harvest of grain, but the fruition, harvest, and winnowing of knowledge, wisdom, and the people.

The woman stands by the Tree of Knowledge, looking up at the angel, and is the embodiment of knowledge and wisdom.

The man stands by the Tree of Life, whose twelve flames are the twelve months or fruits of time, and whose leaves provide 'nourishment' for the healing of nations.[4] In ancient Egyptian thought, which highly influenced symbolism and religious thought in the Near East and the Levant, a leaf of the sacred tree bears the name of the new king as well as the length of his reign. The leaves of 'nourishment'

---

[1] The Ished tree, in Dynastic Egypt, bears the name of the king and the length of his or her reign. The Egyptian king was the ultimate bridge between the people and the gods.

[2] One epithet of hers is the Lady of the Granary: *nbt šnwt*.

[3] Hesiod, *Catalogues of Women* Fragment 77: "The snake of Cychreus: Hesiod says that it was brought up by Cychreus, and was driven out by Eurylochus as defiling the island, but that Demeter received it into Eleusis, and that it became her attendant" (Evelyn-White 1950, p. 207).

[4] *Revelation* 22:1–2 "Then the angel showed me the river of the water of life, as clear as crystal, flowing from the throne of God and of the Lamb down the middle of the great street of the city. On each side of the river stood the Tree of Life, bearing twelve crops of fruit, yielding its fruit every month. And the leaves of the tree are for the healing of the nations."

are most likely symbolic of a effective kingship, indicating that everyone is protected and fed.

He is not aware of the Divine or the angel, as he is firmly entrenched in time and the healing power of time/rulership for the nations. Esoterically, this symbolism is an octave of the wisdom in the union between the Empress and the Emperor. The Lovers card is the union of the Emperor and Empress powers that, together with Divine protection, bring wisdom, knowledge, and time: the necessary gifts for a nation to blossom.

When you understand this dynamic as a magician, it brings a whole deeper layer of meaning to the Lovers, and can give you a deeper understanding of the magical interpretation of this card.

[W]ait and be ruled by time, the wisest counsellor of all.
— Attributed to Pericles by Plutarch[1]

7 Chariot

Key words

Forward momentum, movement, the way ahead, ascent, journey, car/vehicle, Divine action, mystical gnosis, action.

Mundane meaning

The Chariot in a mundane reading is about moving forward. and about action that brings movement in your fate path. It can also literally mean a car or vehicle. It is an action card that shows forward momentum that carries you to the next point of your fate. For example, if you are doing a reading about whether you will still be in the same home or job in twelve months' time and the Chariot appears,

---
[1]Clough 1860, p. 315.

3. MAJOR ARCANA CARD MEANINGS

the answer is "no, you will move, but it will be for the better." The Chariot's actions are always positive outcomes, even if at the time they are distressing or difficult. Once you look back at the situation in hindsight, you will see the necessity of the change, and that it helped you to get to a better state/place.

Many years ago while living in a wild and remote place, I started to have warnings in my dreams that I could not make sense of. I knew there was some danger around me, but I could not interpret my dreams well enough to get a concrete idea of what was coming over the horizon. So I did a reading using a layout that identified different aspects of my life at the time. I looked from different angles, using different layouts and questions. The Chariot card kept appearing, surrounded by danger and death cards. I finally got the message that my truck was the issue. I got it checked, and sure enough its brakes were at failing point. Living in a mountainous area with bad brakes is not a good way to stay alive.

This card can also appear when you will travel somewhere important, or when you are about to embark on a serious or long-term project. If you have been waiting for the right time to initiate an action or project and the Chariot appears, then it gives you the go-ahead to get started.

Trumps like the Chariot should always be read carefully and in direct relation to the question. It is too easy to drift into feelgood psychology and make it all about emotions and personality, but when you are asking about events, remember to interpret directly according to the event itself.

ESOTERIC MEANING

The Chariot has a great deal of magical and mystical meaning, and it is heavily wrapped up in the mythos of ascent and the Kabbalistic

Merkabah. It is also heavily entwined with the Ladder of Ascent, Jacob's Ladder, and the Barque of Re.

The Chariot, the Ladder, and the Barque are all ways of describing a Divine structure that helps magician or mystic evolve and to be 'lifted up' to the Divine as a result of their spiritual and/or mystical life and practice. The Chariot itself is an angelic structure that upholds the individual and transitions them from being only in the physical world to being able to flow between the physical world and the Divine inner world.

The Chariot's rider, in the tarot card, is the individual. In Middle and Near Eastern mythology, the rider can be a mystic, a prophet, a deity, or a power. We see deities like Demeter and Apollo as the Chariot's rider, the Prophets as ones who are allowed to step onto the ladder of ascent, and the King, deities, and 'justified ones' as the passengers on the Solar Barque in Egyptian mythology.

In the Rider-Waite Chariot, we see the Chariot rider holding the staff of power. The square on his chest represents the number four, referring to the four directions, which means the physical world. In Kabbalistic Merkabah, the Chariot is made up of the Four Holy Creatures who come together to uplift the rider.

The rider's clothing is covered in symbols, and he wears armour: he has learned the skills of the Magician and the priest, he has been victorious on the battlefield, and he wears the crown of Divinely-inspired kingship: the crown with the star, which is the new beginning. His shoulders hold two crescent moons, waxing and waning, which is the power of Venus, and his canopy is decorated with the stars of the night sky, which is a common ascent motif.

The winged disk on the chariot is the symbol of Divinity, royalty, and solar power. It has its origins in Ancient Egypt and Mesopotamia. The spindle is the spindle of the weaving of destiny, which is connected

3. Major Arcana Card Meanings

to the three fates, known in ancient Greece as the Moirai and in Rome as the Parcae.

The Chariot is drawn by two sphinxes, one black and one white. These are the powers of light and darkness. On one side of the Chariot is a city; on the other, ecclesiastical buildings.

All this imagery and symbolism tells of the Divine angelic vehicle ridden by the human who has achieved knowledge and skill of both temporal and Divine Mysteries, who operates in both the physical and the inner realms, whose actions are balanced and necessary. The Chariot is the gift to the one who has mastered the Mysteries of the Magician, the High Priestess, the Empress, the Emperor, and the Hierophant. One who has mastered all these aspects and wields them in both the physical and spiritual realms is given the gift of *Divine freedom between the worlds*.

When this card shows up in a magical reading it can indicate that the magician is making good magical progress and is moving into more profound areas of learning and practice. It can indicate visionary travel, and if it appears in a layout position for sleep or dreams, it can indicate that the magician is undertaking profound visionary travel in their dream state. If it appears in a magical reading about someone who is dying, it can indicate that their soul, upon their death, will pass into Divine union. In magical readings the Chariot is always profound, and concerns movement of the magician's soul and mind, and their evolution.

> After this speech, [Helios] placed the golden helmet on Phaethon's head and crowned him with his own fire, winding the seven rays like strings upon his hair, and put the white kilt girdlewise round him over his loins; he clothed him in his own fiery robe and laced his foot into the purple boot, and gave his chariot to his son. The Seasons brought the fiery horses of Helios from their eastern

manger; Lucifer came boldly to the yoke, and fastened the horses' necks in the bright yokestraps for their service.

— Nonnus[1]

8 Strength

KEY WORDS

fortitude, endurance, power, strength, stability, protector, triumph over adversity, mastery.

The Strength card is very much about strength acquired through adversity or hard work. It is also the strength that comes from direct experience, which brings wisdom and the powers of endurance. Strength in the tarot is heavily linked to the planet Saturn, where stability, strength, and structure endure. It is not structure that has been allowed to crumble; rather it is structure that is constantly attended to and refined to make sure it survives impacts and the ravishes of time.

The Strength that is the power of this card is not short-term strength gained from going to the gym or quickly boosted though some means; rather it is the strength that comes from long-term application.

When strength appears in a reading, whatever its subject, it indicates that whatever the person is going through, they will have the strength to succeed if they do not give in. Determination builds strength and discipline, and as such brings success. It is those who do not give in when faced with hardship or struggle who triumph, and the strength such struggle gives them will stay with them as a gift for life.

---

[1]Rouse 1942, p. 113.

3. Major Arcana Card Meanings

It is also the strength of wisdom, knowledge, and spiritual communion with the Divine; and the strength to meet every challenge with determination.

Mundane meaning

In a mundane reading, it can indicate the strength of some structure: perhaps a building, an idea, a company, or a venture. It indicates endurance and success. The Strength card speaks of the reserves necessary to weather any coming storm. It also speaks of the strength that comes from honesty and integrity, not brute force.

Esoteric meaning

When you look carefully at the Strength card in the Rider-Waite deck, you will see that the woman is not wrestling with the lion: she is petting him, and the lion is looking up at her and licking her hand.[1] Above the woman's head is the symbol of eternity: she is a goddess. She is clothed in a white robe, which at the time the deck was created symbolized purity, and she is decked with flowers: she is Mother Nature, the goddess of the land and the creatures. In the distance is the ever-present Mountain of Adversity.

The number of the Strength card is eight: a number of Divine completion. The number eight in Kabbalah is the number beyond nature and the limitations of nature,[2] i.e. the Divine miracle or intervention.

The esoteric Mystery of the Strength card hints at a tale from the Book of Daniel in the Old Testament. Daniel was a wise counsellor to the king, and an interpreter of dreams. He was a man devoted to God who lived his devotion in a truthful way, which made him many

---

[1] This imagery comes from the tale of Androcles, and from the tale of St. Jerome.
[2] Seven is the number of creation of the physical world in Kabbalah.

enemies. In the story[1] Daniel is cast into a den of lions to destroy him, but at sunrise when the king comes to check to see if he is still alive, he finds Daniel at peace with the lions who are his friends: it is a Divine miracle.

There are various tales in the Old and New Testament about people of honour, people loyally devoted to God, who through their integrity and compassion are left unharmed by lions. There are also older myths and stories in the Ancient world about companion lions[2] and of course the lion gods and goddesses.

This imagery tells us, in esoteric terms, that true strength comes from not wavering from what you know to be right and true, no matter what adversity should challenge you. If we walk the fate path we know is necessary, no matter how much it scares us, staying true to what we know is right, then the terrifying potentially destructive force of the lion becomes a companion and guardian.

Esoterically this also hints at a similar dynamic that appears towards the completion of adept magical training, where the aspirant adept is cast out to face destruction and survive. If the adept does not waiver in the face of destruction, and has no fear within them, then the destruction will wash through them without harm. "Fear not, for I have called you by your name, and you are mine."[3]

> My soul *is* among lions: *and* I lie *even among* them that are set on fire (...) — *Psalms* 57:4

---

[1] *Daniel* ch. 4–6.
[2] Ramses II is depicted on the walls of his temple at Abu Simbel as having a lion companion named 'Slayer of Foes' who fought with him at the Battle of Kadesh. There is also the Tale of Androcles and the lion (Rolfe 1927, p. 255ff).
[3] *Isaiah* 43:1 (JPS 1917 edition).

3. Major Arcana Card Meanings

9 Hermit

Key words

wisdom in solitude, isolation, trust in oneself, hindsight, introspection, self-examination, careful and bitter experience, the sole path, maturity through adversity

The Hermit stands on the top of the Mountain of Adversity. His lamp lights the way ahead, and his head is bowed from exhaustion. When this card appears in a reading, it tells of a person or situation where adversity has been faced, and bitter lessons have been learned on the path. The Hermit has moved away from society, from religion, and from the norm, and has followed his own star, which has guided him to the peak of learning. At this peak of learning we find ourselves bowed before the sheer vastness of the Divine creation all around us, and we realize how weak we really are and how little we actually know.

In a reading this card tells us to trust our own judgement and to follow truth, to trust in our path where we leave consensus behind and take the hard climb of experience alone. Solitude is something that we can experience even when surrounded by many people: we look around and realize we have nothing in common with others, that we forge a path of discovery that often challenges us to our limits and beyond. But we survive it: we learn hard lessons that bring wisdom, and we learn to trust not in others, but in ourselves and the form of the Divine that we connect to. This is a card of isolation, of wisdom from bitter experience, of survival, and of steadfastness.

Sometimes this card appears when we feel battle fatigued and are almost at the point of giving up or dropping our hard-held ethics. One voice says, "give up, it will be easier" and another voice says, "after you have come so far, don't give up, the star shines a light ahead for you, just put one more foot in front of the other." Those who take one more step and refuse to give up are the ones who are given the gift of change.

The card can also represent great learning that by its nature isolates you. When we know a bit about something, we can converse and interact with others on that subject matter. But the deeper into learning you go, the more complex it becomes, and it becomes harder and harder to find a like mind of similar learning where you can converse as an equal. This brings the isolation that accompanies the gift of great learning. Thus the Hermit can also represent a person or organization who is an as-yet-unrecognized trailblazer.

It can also represent a person or organization that holds strongly to truth and integrity in the face of great corruption. The truthful person shines, and those who are corrupt would seek to tear down the truth. It can be a warning in a reading to guard oneself against such corruption, and not to seek recognition but to continue walking the difficult path in the shadows until the time to shine arrives. The card can warn that you are alone in a nest of vipers, but that you must not give up your light but have faith, wait, bide your time, and stay under the radar.

Mundane meaning

Its meaning in a mundane reading can also be about having patience and thinking carefully before acting. At times it can also mean literal isolation. There are times in our lives when we find ourselves alone, and this card can sometimes herald such a period. If that is the case, the message is not to despair: you are not truly alone. Rather, learn to be at peace with yourself. From that peace comes strength, and with strength the road will open up once again.

3. Major Arcana Card Meanings

Esoteric meaning

The Hermit has overcome the trials of the mountain, but is weary from the challenge and pauses in the darkness to rest. The star in the lantern is held in the right hand, the hand of the initiate's harvest, where their learning and deeds have been threshed and weighed. What remains is the light, the flame of all being, as the star. The star is the ultimate goal of the initiate: to become *as one with the stars*. The Hermit is not at that point yet, but the potential is there, hidden in the lantern, and it is that potential that lights the way ahead for the initiate.

The staff is the magical staff which in magical training eventually replaces the magician's wand. It is held in the left hand, which is the position of the road ahead, the future, and the living fate of the initiate. The staff holds the serpent power of wisdom and knowledge: direct personal knowledge of the Divine, and knowledge of the skills of the initiate. It has the power to heal, to cast out spirits, and to open the way ahead. The staff is not a tool; it is a living companion that travels with the Hermit in service during his most difficult phase of magical development.

Once the Hermit has gathered himself from his ordeals, he will step forward in a single step of faith and trust, a step that will take him from the peak of the Mountain of Adversity towards the path to the sun and stars.

> It is always darkest just before the Day dawneth
>
> — Thomas Fuller (1650).[1]

---

[1] Fuller 1869, p. 208.

10 Wheel of Fortune

Key words

change, change of fate, moving towards true path, change of fortune for good or bad

At a first glance the Wheel of Fortune seems pretty straightforward. It is an indicator of major change, and a coming back on to your true fate path. For the deeper underlying meaning of this card, read the esoteric meaning below.

Mundane meaning

In simple mundane readings, the Wheel of Fortune indicates a change in one's fortune that could be for better or worse. Either way it is a major and often fundamental change. When surrounded by or continued by good cards, it indicates a change for the better. We often think of our fate path as being a single road that takes us from birth to death, when in fact it is a meandering path that sometimes takes us down dead ends or convoluted alleys where we can end up becoming lost.

When the Wheel of Fortune intervenes, something in our fate moves us out of our dead end, or from being stuck in a maze, and puts us back on track towards our fate's destination. Sometimes that intervention is compassionate and helpful: sometimes it is a great gift of a new job, partner, interest, or the birth of a child.

But sometimes, if we have become mired in the mud though our own actions or from stagnation and decay around us, the turning of the wheel can be difficult and at times painful. Pulling us out of the mud can mean that we have to let go of the familiarity that we cling to, and fate does not care if we are tired, or upset, or weary. Fate reaches

3. Major Arcana Card Meanings

out and kicks us up the butt until we move back in the direction we should be heading in.

That is when we remember the lesson of the Hermit, which is to continue to step forward in the face of adversity, as greater things are ahead of us. When you see the Wheel of Fortune appear in a reading, know that change is coming. If you have being paying attention in your life, and making the small changes that present themselves as necessary, then the turn of the Wheel of Fortune will move you along in a strong and productive way. If however, you have resisted all the changes that you could have done for yourself, then the Wheel of Fortune can slam into you hard to push you along the path.

Sometimes the turning of the Wheel of Fortune can bring great good or great bad without any perceivable reason. This is the *seemingly* random nature of fortune. However, usually when you look back, after enough time has passed, you can see how the change was indeed necessary: you just could not see it at the time.

If this card appears in a mundane reading then expect change, usually major change. The cards that come after the Wheel of Fortune in a reading will indicate how that change will play out and whether it will be a good change or a bad one. If the Wheel of Fortune is followed by more trump cards, then the path ahead for you is fateful indeed, and may have a lot of power connected to it.

Esoteric meaning

The Wheel of Fortune has many magical layers, and each layer has lessons for us to learn. Its imagery is an interesting and eclectic mixture of Roman, Kabbalistic, and Egyptian symbolism that when brought together tell us about one of the major angelic powers that operates throughout the physical and inner realms.

10 Wheel of Fortune

In Waite's imagery, the wheel has two words: ROTA and יהוה.[1] ROTA means *wheel* in Latin and the title of the card, Wheel of Fortune, is borrowed from *Rota Fortunae*, the wheel of the Roman Goddess Fortuna, the goddess of fortune who was also known as Atrox Fortuna, the goddess of fate. Fortuna could dispense good or bad fortune, as well as bring death in her role as Atrox Fortuna.[2] She is said to have claimed the lives of the two grandsons of Princeps Augustus. The turning of Fortune's wheel changes the fate or fortune of the individual or a nation.

The use of the Tetragrammaton interspersed with the word Rota, changes the wheel from a wheel of fortune into the *Wheel of God*. This is amplified by the appearance of the Hayyot, the four living creatures: bull, eagle, lion and human. The Hayyot are considered angels of fire who uphold both the chariot of God and the earth. The Hayyot join together to make the body of the chariot, while the Ophanim make up the wheels.[3] The Ophanim are sometimes referred to as the *wheels of Galgallin*. These are the interconnected double wheels of fire and eyes.

On one side of the Wheel of Fortune is a red figure, which is Set. On the other side of the wheel is a serpent. This is Egyptian imagery. Set is the power of necessary destruction and is the one who controls chaos by pinning the serpent of chaos, Apep. The serpent on the other side could be Apep, but it is difficult to know what meaning Waite wanted to convey. There are many different serpents, both good and bad, in Egyptian mythology, and they are usually identified by their shape, species, and name.

It is most likely that Waite was alluding to Apep, as that would make sense with the rest of the imagery: one of the threads of fate is

---

[1] The Tetragrammaton. The four letter name of G-D: YHWH.
[2] Kretschmer 1927.
[3] *Ezekiel* ch. 1, ch. 10.

the constant opposition between necessary creation and destruction, and the unnecessary creation that brings unnecessary destruction. Apep is chaos, brought on by unnecessary creation and unnecessary destruction, while Set is the power that keeps Apep in its place. If Apep gains a foothold in the physical world, then chaos ensues. This is reflected in the rise and fall of nations and empires, as well as the rise and fall of individual fortunes.

The Hayyot, the name of God, and Set/Apep makes for an interesting mixture that points to Maaseh Merkabah. This is the work of the Chariot, otherwise known as the *mysticism of ascent*. It is not traditional mystical Merkabah imagery, which is the territory of religion; rather it is the mysteries of ascent in a magical framework, using images and vocabulary from different traditions to show, not tell, hiding things in plain sight. I have noticed this as a repeated theme in Waite's use of imagery in this deck.

From an esoteric point of view, when this card appears in a magical reading it can simply mean some change, but it can also refer to a deeper *divine movement:* i.e. your work taking you forward on the ladder of magical evolution. If the reading is magical, and there are a lot of trump cards around it or following it, then it likely shows that major developmental changes are coming. How those changes play out will depend on your magical 'harvest' so far. Whether this is good or bad in the short term, in the longer term it is a turn of the wheel that takes you a step closer to what is known in some areas of magic as being the 'Developing One.'

> Then the Ophanim and the Holy Hayot,[1] with a roar of noise, raise themselves toward the Seraphim and, facing them, give praise, saying: Blessed be the Lord's glory from God's place.
>
> — from the *Kedushah* section of the Jewish morning prayer.[2]

---

[1] The Holy Living Creatures.
[2] Zerin n.d.

On rencontre sa destinée
Souvent par des chemins qu'on prend por l'éviter.[1]

One often meets one's destiny
On the path one takes to avoid it.

— Jean de La Fontaine

11 Justice

Key words

balance, justice, conclusion, cause and effect of deeds, scales, sentence, payment of debt, legal matters, policing.

The Justice card represents true justice: justice that is blind to emotional manipulation, excuses, or an offer of compensation to avoid the harshness of justice. The power that is shown in the Justice card is the power of cause and effect. The scales which weigh the deeds are held in one hand, and the sword which delivers justice is held in the other. Justice is about balance and bringing order to disorder, all without emotion or compassion. Sometimes we are swayed in our judgements by emotional stories that are meant to manipulate, and when that happens, often true justice is left undone.

One of the greatest ways for we humans to learn and evolve is by taking responsibility for our actions and learning why our actions were wrong, as opposed to giving punishment out of vengeance. This is the path of true justice, which brings true compassion. Allowing someone to learn a harsh and bitter lesson is a true form of compassion, as it gives a person the opportunity for real learning on a deep level. We can choose to learn, to make good, and to protect others, or we can become bitter and twisted.

---

[1]La Fontaine 1868, p. 515.

3. Major Arcana Card Meanings

Mundane meaning

When this card shows up in a mundane reading, it can indicate literal justice, such as going to court or signing contracts that are legally binding. It can also indicate the police, or gaining justice that has been lacking. In readings that are about health it can indicate a return to health and balance, while in an economic reading it can indicate being in tune with necessity: having what you need and no more.

It can also, depending on the question, indicate that you will get your just desserts: what is due to you. This can be good or bad. If you have been selfless and helpful or have given to those in need, and now you are in need, then what you gave out will return to you. If you have done bad things and so far have gotten away with them without learning or regret, then the appearance of this card can mean that you are about to get what you deserved, be this punishment, arrest, or having something bad happen to you. It is only through our actions coming back to us that we truly learn to not be jerks.

The literal reading of this card can appear in strange and unexpected, but highly obvious ways. Many years ago, my children were under potential threat from a violent paedophile who was on the loose. He had already attacked a woman and two children. I was terrified to let my children out to play. We didn't know where he was, only that he was somewhere in our area. The police had been hunting him for days, but we had not heard anything in the news about his capture. So I did a reading to ask if he was in or near the immediate vicinity of our home: I needed to make a decision on whether it was safe for my children to play outside.

The reading's answer was Justice. I did not understand that outcome at the time, as nothing had been said about any court case. A few hours later we heard on the radio that the paedophile was being held in police cells. He was literally *in* justice, in the police station. So you can see how sometimes these cards can be literal.

Esoteric meaning

The Justice card is intimately connected with the ancient Egyptian dynamic and power of Ma'at, a concept which has to be translated in English as one of various words, such as truth, righteousness, or order. In Egypt Ma'at was both a goddess and concept. The society lived to the rule of Ma'at, from the lowliest peasant to the king himself. In fact, the king was the one who carried the greatest burden of Ma'at, as a king has the power of life and death over his subjects, and has to make difficult decisions for the good of the people. Few kings actually achieved this ideal, but through trying, great societal advances were made.

Justice is about the balance of light and dark, creation and destruction, and the power of the scales that weighs the Initiate's harvest and deeds. Every action has an energetic counterweight, and the more power the magician wields, the more responsibility they bear for the effects of their work.

Justice can appear in magical readings as a warning to weigh the potential consequences of a magical action. It can also indicate that some magical action will rebalance scales that were imbalanced. It can also be a card of completion, where a series of magical actions finally reach their conclusion. It can also indicate a deficit being filled. If as a magician you have *given* much in the way of help, energy, and so forth, and until now you have *received* little in return, then you will be in deficit. The appearance of the Justice card indicates that this deficit is about to be rebalanced. You will receive what is energetically due to you.

3. Major Arcana Card Meanings

> Justice is a certain rectitude of mind in which a man does what he ought to do in the circumstances confronting him.
>
> — Thomas Aquinas[1]

12 Hanged Man

Key words

Self-sacrifice, trials, energetic empathy, service, virtue, self-denial, moral obligation, arrogant martyrdom.

Mundane meaning

The Hanged Man is a complex card and is often difficult to read, even in a mundane sense. At face value, the card is about self-sacrifice for the greater good, but it also immediately throws into question the motives for such sacrifice. Are we truly sacrificing something for the good of others, or are we fantasizing about how we wish to project ourselves to others? The trap of martyrdom is a wide trap indeed, and it can take a person down a dark road. Those who willingly give of themselves or do without for the good of others are rare people. For the most part such sacrifice is a result of personal glamour, where we create a narrative of 'goodness' in a drama of our own making. We then project that drama outwards to feed off the empathy of others.

There is also a deeper aspect to self-sacrifice. Is it truly necessary? Sometimes it is, and sometimes it isn't. If you run in front of a runway truck to push a child out of the way, and in the process put yourself at real risk of getting killed, that is true self-sacrifice. If, however, you decide to go without food so that you can give your teenager money that you know they will spend on entertainment, that is not self-sacrifice, that is stupidity. Such an act is wrapped up in the need to be

---
[1] Zajda, Majhanovich, and Rust 2006, p. 9.

loved. A person who does that wants the teen to love and need them, so really it is not about sacrifice, it is about emotional manipulation.

And that is one of the lessons of the Hanged Man. Is it a real sacrifice that is necessary, or are you fooling yourself in your little drama to get the accolades you crave? The question and situation in a reading will give you the context of this card, and if it appears in a reading, it is well worth spending some time thinking about your motives. Are you being asked to sacrifice something that is truly necessary?

Another lesson of the Hanged Man is guilt. If your self-sacrifice is an attempt to atone for your guilt, then again it is not true sacrifice: you are trying to pay off your deeds. Sometimes such payment is not necessary, and is not about helping the person in need, but about making yourself feel less guilty. In such cases the 'payment' does not really rebalance the scales, and can at times simply make the imbalance worse. Guilt comes when we have done wrong and we know it. You do not truly rid yourself of guilt by being a martyr, but by enduring the pain and suffering that you have caused, and ensuring that you evolve far beyond such actions in the present and future.

You can see how Justice and the Hanged Man are intricately linked. If these two cards come up together, then you must seriously think about your intentions, as they may not be as good as you think. Self-sacrifice to gain merit is an ego trap. Self-sacrifice to become a better person in the eyes of God is also an ego trap. Self-sacrifice because it is necessary is the key to the Hanged Man.

Sometimes the Hanged Man can represent true self-sacrifice, as in working two jobs to make sure your children get a decent education. In such cases the self-sacrifice is recognized by the Divine Universal Power, and fate subsequently brings you Justice when the time is right.

3. MAJOR ARCANA CARD MEANINGS

The Hanged Man's appearance in a personal reading can indicate trials to come; necessary difficulties where you may be pushed out of your comfort zone to benefit someone, or something, other than yourself. It can also mean basic self-sacrifice like donating blood to a hospital, or having to bear an energetic burden for a while—for instance if your child is ill. Sometimes our vital force goes out to uphold our loved ones in time of need.

ESOTERIC MEANING

The imagery of the Hanged Man likely comes from the Apocryphal Acts of Peter.[1] Saint Peter the Apostle was a leader in the early Christian church and is considered to be the first Pope of the Roman Catholic Church. There is a legend that he was crucified, and before his crucifixion he requested to be crucified upside down. There is no reference to this outside the Acts of Peter which is thought to be a late second century text, and the crucifix story does not appear in any other writings of the time. In the story, Peter asked to be crucified upside down as he did not feel worthy of being crucified in the same way as Jesus. He was wracked with guilt for his denial of Jesus, and his death was purported to be on the *dies imperii*[2] of Nero in 64 A.D.: traditionally these celebrations were bloody displays of power. This was the same year as the Great fire of Rome, which had happened only three months previously, and for which the Christians were blamed. It is a story of martyrdom, of feelings of guilt and unworthiness, and of sacrifice to appease the people. It is a warning to all mystics and magicians to be careful of falling into the martyr and saviour traps. But it also has deeper meaning for mystics and magicians about sometimes needing to carry the burdens of others so that those individuals can advance, or even survive.

---

[1] In the *Codex Vercellensis Evangeliorum* — *Actus Petri cum Simone*.
[2] An anniversary of Nero's ascent to power.

The card can describe energetic load-sharing, whether for the magician's loved ones or for wider events that are about to manifest in the world. This happens particularly when the magician has previously taken on magical work in service or long-term projects that would affect a wider group of people, the land, or the nation. As the magic continues to trigger in waves as it brings events into manifestation, so the energy of the magician is pulled on to support that work.

Sometimes the adept must bear a burden for the greater good of others. When this happens, it is without fanfare or drama or emotion. Rather it is a quiet, unseen, and necessary bearing of the burden of another. Most of the time the person being helped is unaware of that help, but the adept knows that such a person must be aided to survive, and that the person will be of great importance to the world in the future. So the act of the adept, their self-sacrifice, goes unseen and unrecognized. That is true self-sacrifice.

> For anything worth having one must pay the price; and the price is always work, patience, love, self-sacrifice—no paper currency, no promises to pay, but the gold of real service.
>
> — John Burroughs[1]

13 Death

Key words

The ending of a cycle, death, change of circumstance, transition.

Mundane meaning

Death is the tarot trump that always terrifies people, as it pokes our deep underlying instinct to survive at all costs. This is a healthy

---
[1]Walker 2001, p. 239.

3. Major Arcana Card Meanings

instinct. And yet we go through little deaths and births throughout our lives: that is the key to this card. It is an ending to a situation or cycle to never be revisited, such as the transition from child to adult, women who have gone through menopause, someone who has been sterilized, leaving high school, and so forth. These are all situations we will not revisit, and that is when the death card emerges. It tells you that a situation will end and it will never be revisited.

If the change is a major one that will totally transform your life, it can often start to appear in your readings many months before the event or transition itself. This can be confusing for a reader, as they may be asking about a job, a relationship, or their spiritual path, and the death card will keep popping up. In such instances, rather than stressing over the appearance of this card, look at the different situations you have read for and think about what they all have in common. Usually the common denominator is where the change or end will occur.

This happened to a friend of mine who repeatedly got the death card appearing in all her readings, and she really started to stress over it. I went to visit her and we looked at the common denominators. One was her, and the other was the town where she lived and worked. So we did two readings. The first reading looked at whether she was going to leave the town within the next 2 years and never return. The answer was yes. We then looked at if she was going to physically die within the next two years.[1] The answer was no. Her stress levels went down immediately, and she started to prepare for an unexpected move, which came a year later.

However, contrary to popular belief the Death card can indeed in some circumstances mean physical death. We are all going to die at some point, so if it appears in a layout and it points to a physical death,

---

[1] Focusing on the *physical* body is important in such a reading.

think about the time span you put on the reading. If you did an open-ended reading about your life and it ended in Death, then panicking is silly: of course you will die at the end of your life. And if you did specify a time span for your reading, then explore the Death theme wider with a more focused reading, to see if it is the death of something to do with your physical body, like a major change, surgery, hormone changes, and so forth.

People often look at their impending death in fear, and that is the worst possible way to approach such a reading. If you are not prepared to face up to an impending death, then do not look. And if you do look at whether you will die within some time span, then it is wise to ask if you would physically survive that 'ending.' A few years ago I had to have major surgery, and the death card appeared as my significator card.[1] I asked *if I would survive that death*, and it said yes. What it was showing was the death of the organ that was being taken out, and how it would change my body permanently.

When you are doing a reading and Death appears, do not assume it is a physical death: mostly this card represents little deaths. Interpret it in direct relation to the question, the layout, and the subject of the reading. Think about the person's age, life circumstances, jobs, and so forth: it should soon become apparent what the little death is.

Esoteric meaning

I think it is wise for any tarot reader or magician to seriously think about their attitude to death in general. Wanting to stay alive to the end of your fate measure is healthy and indeed is spiritually necessary. You have been given a rare gift of life, and it is your job to preserve it to the best of your ability. But it is also important to understand

---

[1] The card that is you.

3. Major Arcana Card Meanings

that death truly is a transition from one state to another, and that the non-physical part of you continues.

As a magician, I have had enough direct and unique experiences of the realm of death, of talking to the dead, and of other related experiences, that I no longer have any doubt in the survival of the self. And I have also learned that the flow of fate is something to trust. These experiences leave me with no fear of death, just a will and determination to do my best in life until my measure is up. And if something threatens that measure, I work hard to shift that threat or to sidestep it.

Divination is an important part of that process: knowing what to look at and where to look, and how to interpret your results, is a powerful tool for getting out of the way of destruction when it is building up in your near future. And it does build up. Destruction and creation are ongoing cycles that visit us throughout our lives in small and major ways. It is the job of the magician to travel through life experiencing these little births and deaths in equal measure, and to draw as much learning and wisdom from them as we can.

Once you get to that more magically mature mindset, it is easier to understand both the physical death and the little deaths we go through in life, which for a tarot reader or magician will help them interpret without fear, but with gnosis. This is discussed in more depth in the chapters on interpretation and approaches.

> The name of the gate of this place is «Which raises the gods».
> The name of this place is «With emerging darkness and appearing births».
> (...)
> The mysterious cavern of the Netherworld[1] at which this great god is born,

---
[1] The Duat, the ancient Egyptian Underworld.

That he goes forth from the Nun[1] and sets at the body of Nut.[2]
This is made like this image which is painted
On the eastern side of the Hidden Chamber in the Netherworld.
It is beneficial for whoever knows it,
On earth, in heaven and in the earth.[3]

— From the Twelfth Hour of the Amduat.

14 Temperance

Key words

Necessity, measure, a middle way, the balance of all things, forward momentum, life and vitality, careful success, protection.

The Temperance card is like a breath of needed fresh air after the trials and tribulations of life's challenges. It is the moment when the storm has passed and the sun comes out: everything comes in measure, every darkness has a light embedded within it, and just when you acknowledge that you cannot take any more pressure from life's challenges, the pressure releases.

Temperance is about getting what you need and no more, ensuring that you have what you need to continue your path without giving you excess, be this resources, love, healing, protection, shelter, or energy. Temperance is the healing spring that nourishes the weary, the tree that gives you shade in the hot sun, and the guardian who protects you but doesn't stop any adversities you bring on yourself.

Mundane meaning

When this card appears in a reading, depending on the question, it can indicate the resolution of hardship, struggle, or sickness, and a

---
[1] The watery Void.
[2] The surface of the sky.
[3] Hornung and Abt 2007.

coming-back into balance and health. It advises you to be moderate with what you do, to tread slowly and meaningfully, to give and receive with equal measure, and to know that you are protected. It warns against all excess, and against narrowmindedness or overzealousness. It also warns against unnecessary lenience or laziness. It is a card that in its positive positions indicates a balance and regeneration, and in negative positions indicates imbalance and loss of inherent protection.

If you are doing a health reading, this card indicates that regardless of what is happening, the body is protected and finding its balance. In economic readings it indicates that your needs—not wants—will be covered. In job readings it can indicate that your position is protected, or that you will find a job that you need, and in a general reading it can show that you will be safe from harm if you use your common sense.

And that brings me to a slightly deeper meaning of the Temperance card and the protection that it brings. Such protection is there to deal with the things that you cannot control, but it will not deal with the things you can do for yourself. If you sit back and expect everything to come to you, then the power of this card will withdraw from you. If you act with stupid abandon, thinking you can do what you like because you have protection, then you will be in for a shock.

Temperance protects and brings balance to those areas of our lives that we have no control over, or that we cannot address for ourselves, whether because of a lack of ability or resources. The power of Temperance kicks in when we make every possible effort to resolve our own problems. We do everything we can, and if Temperance shows up in our lives, it will deal with the rest. If we do nothing, then no help comes.

14 Temperance

Esoteric meaning

The angel of Temperance stands with one foot in the water and one foot on the land. The angel is constantly pouring water back and forth between two chalices, keeping things flowing and keeping balance. Flowers grow by the spring, showing life and vitality, and a road tracks away from the spring towards the Mountain of Adversity in the distance. Over the mountain shines the rising sun. The new day bringing renewal, rebirth, and evolution.

The deeper esoteric meaning of the Temperance card can be found in *Revelation* 10. In this chapter, John the visionary sees an angel that stands with his right foot in the sea and his left foot on the land. The left leg, magically, is the way ahead, the seed of life and the future. The right leg is death, the harvest of life and beyond. This is saying that the gift the angel brings is meant for the future, for the way ahead in life.

The gift the angel brings is a small scroll. The angel gives the scroll to John and tells him to eat it, that it will be sweet on his tongue and bitter in his belly. This is a well-known adept dynamic of the interplay between the digestive system and the inner power of utterance, knowledge, and prophecy. The angel then tells John that he must prophecize again about people, languages, kings, and nations.

One of the esoteric meanings of this is that this power expressed in Temperance is about keeping the cycle of life turning, about passing on profound knowledge into the future until the time when that future will be no more. This means that the angel is one of mercy and compassion to humanity, and that in humanity's darkest days the secret esoteric knowledge necessary for rebuilding and evolving humanity will be passed through human channels and sent into the future as words, prophecies, and wisdom.

3. Major Arcana Card Meanings

This angel tempers destruction with seeds for the future, ensuring that some will find the seeded wisdom, learn from it, and will walk that long path up the Mountain of Adversity to become one with the sun. While ever there are people who answer that call of evolution, humanity will continue.

> And he said unto me, It is done. I am Alpha and Omega, the beginning and the end. I will give unto him that is athirst of the fountain of the water of life freely.
>
> — *Revelation* 21:6

15 Devil

Key words

Temptation, weakness, desire, ignoring self-truth, weakness, self-sabotage, unravelling, dishonesty.

The Devil card is another tarot trump that is often heavily misunderstood because of a Christian cultural mindset that the Devil is an external force that tempts and destroys. This can cause us to project blame onto another—the Devil—instead of recognizing and understanding our own role in our downfall. The power that this card represents is, for the most part, the inability or unwillingness to overcome great temptation that you know will lead to disaster.

Mundane meaning

We have many facets to our personalities, and as we mature from various learning experiences, we find ourselves in a better position to make judgement calls based on past experience. However, sometimes hormones, greed, laziness, or lack of courage causes us to act or behave in ways that we know are wrong. The quiet voice within us tells us that our behaviour is wrong, but we ignore it and carry on regardless, because we *want* something. This is the root of the Devil card in a mundane reading.

The Devil card represents an unravelling power, where a simple but wrong act pulls a 'thread' in your life and its whole stability begins to unravel. When this card appears in a reading it warns of such a situation. You, or the subject you are reading for, is walking in a situation where some desire for love, power, money, position, sex, food, or so forth, will trigger destruction. If the subject of the reading can recognize that their weakness is being tested, and they have the strength and foresight to step back from the precipice, then all will be well. However, if they convince themselves that they can handle the situation—which is part of the power of temptation—then they are at serious risk of destroying everything they hold dear. This is the full manifestation of the power of this card.

It is also important to understand that besides the big, dramatic downfalls that we can subject ourselves to, little downfalls also occur throughout our lives—events that cause us disruption, loss, sickness, and struggle that are really self-inflicted, if we are honest with ourselves. These little downfalls that come and go throughout our lives are teachers and testers, and the more we experience, the more we learn. If we act on what we learn, then we grow stronger and wiser. If we do not, then we gradually descend into weakness and decay.

The Devil can also show up for less dramatic reasons, depending on the subject matter of the reading, though its general meaning is the same. The Devil card can show up in a health reading, or can indicate a health issue in a general reading, depending on its position in the layout. When that happens, the Devil indicates that something about the person's behaviour is damaging their health: they are consuming or doing something that is bad for them.

A good example would be someone eating something they know upsets their system, but they then take medication to dampen its effect. Eventually their body will start to unravel from both the irritant *and* the medication. The same is true for diabetics who insist on eating sugary food and simply take extra medication to keep their blood sugar down. Eventually such behaviour becomes destructive for the body, and their health slowly unravels. This is a perfect practical example of the Devil dynamic: temptation-driven, self-inflicted destruction.

If this card appears in your reading, spend some time thinking about what you are doing in your life. Be brutally honest with yourself. Self-honesty—and acting appropriately as a result—is the key to dissolving the power represented by the Devil. And if you fail to self-assess honestly, and then the Tower hits your life, at least try to learn the lesson of what caused the Tower to fall: it was *you*. The moment you stop blaming others for the situations that you brought on yourself, the quicker you will learn to resist temptation. This is not easy, and we often repeat our mistakes many times until we truly learn. And this is another part of the power of the Devil: it is our greatest teacher. It exposes our weaknesses for us to see, it teaches us about cause and effect and about dishonesty, and it teaches us foresight through bitter experience.

If this card turns up in a reading about a company or organization, it can indicate dishonesty, hidden agendas, theft, and embezzlement. In a reading for a building it can indicate problems with the building, potentially where repairs have been bodged, where dangers (such as bad wiring) have been hidden, or where the structure is unsound due to neglect. The Devil can also indicate actions, such as planned burglaries.

Esoteric Meaning

The imagery of the Devil card is quite modern in magical terms, and basically illustrates trapping through desire. However, the actual power that this card depicts—a power of unravelling—has a much deeper magical meaning. Two dynamics can bring about downfall. One is circumstances or events outside our control, and the second one is self-inflicted suffering. The Devil card represents the second type of downfall. That which we stepped in knowing there was risk, or that it was wrong. In magical thought, two main opposing powers manifest through everything as part of the constant balancing act that is creation and destruction. I call these two opposing powers the Grindstone and the Unraveller. The Grindstone is the power of Saturn. It is the disciplined struggle to achieve, to grow and to overcome difficulties. The Grindstone polishes the rough stone into something beautiful.

The second dynamic I call the Unraveller. This is the power of Pluto. The unravelling power comes along and tests the strength and foundations of what you have built through your engagement with the Grindstone. It will find the flaws, the weak spots, and the cracks. Its power will then lean on those weaknesses until it stresses the foundations of whatever it is acting on. If the foundation is strong then it will buckle a bit, but it will bounce back and bring the weak spot to your attention so that you can work on it. However if your foundation is weak then it will crack the structure wide open until the whole thing falls apart. This is the nature of Pluto, and it is the nature of the Devil card. When it appears in a magical reading, no matter what the situation, it is highlighting a weakness that must be attended to and remedied. If you know your weakness then you are in a perfect position to strengthen. If you make the conscious decision to do so, and practice overcoming that weakness in your life or magical

3. MAJOR ARCANA CARD MEANINGS

work, then you will avoid the catastrophe brought by the next card, The Tower.

The Devil can also represent inner parasites. If an inner parasite is interacting with the magician to feed off their magical actions, then regardless of how that spirit presents itself, the Devil card will represent it in the magical reading. Inner parasites live on our energy, usually emotional energy, and they are quite good at playing with the minds of magicians to tempt or push them into actions that will trigger energetic releases on which they can feed. This is the very root of the Devil card.

> There hath no temptation taken you but such as is common to man: but God *is* faithful, who will not suffer you to be tempted above that ye are able; but will with the temptation also make a way to escape, that ye may be able to bear *it*.
>
> — *1 Corinthians* 10:13

16 Tower

KEY WORDS

Disaster, unexpected calamity, retribution, disgrace, collapse, clearing the ground, downfall.

MUNDANE MEANING

The Tower is the most malignant card in the tarot deck, and unless it appears in a withheld position, it foretells of the downfall the individual or subject of the reading. The Tower is the result of not heeding conscience, warnings, or common sense, and its severity largely depends on the preceding choices, decisions, and actions of the individual. It can at times in divination indicate an unforeseen calamity or accident that is not triggered by the individual, but for the most part, the disasters of the Tower have some connection to an individual's choices or actions.

The Tower tears down what you should have dealt with yourself. If you know your actions are wrong and you still proceed, then the Tower will start to build in your life. It may take you to great heights before it crashes you down. The crash will come at the optimal time for your own learning.

The one glimmer of hope with the Tower is that it removes and destroys what needs removing and destroying. It is not punishment: it is learning or cause and effect. When your tower crashes down you have two choices: learn from your mistakes and start to build afresh, or wallow in self-pity. The Tower always has the dynamics of cause and effect, which is why it is tightly connected to the Justice card. The Tower and Justice can work together as part of a collective rebalancing. When it is this collective in action, the individual who suffers the Tower and its destruction always had a choice, and if the difficult choice was not met as an individual, then that collective Tower will hit them.

The strength of the Tower is always balanced by necessity. The more you have tried to do the right thing, the less of an the impact the Tower will have. The lesson of the Tower is that you can rebuild. You are never given more than you can truly cope with: the Tower can push you to the extreme of your coping ability, but never beyond it. If you can stand amid the rubble of destruction and not give in, but start planning to rebuild step by step, then the Star, the next card in the trump sequence, will appear.

Once the rebuilding process is triggered by your determination, then the learning phase of the Tower begins. Can you look back at your actions and see where your decisions and actions led to the destruction, without offloading responsibility and blame onto others?

3. Major Arcana Card Meanings

Once you do that, you will have truly learned your lesson, and that particular calamity will not revisit you again in your lifetime. You may be revisited by the *circumstances* that led to that calamity as if to test your resolve, and if you spot those circumstances and understand the bad choices you made, and do not repeat them, then the reforming Tower pattern will dissolve.

Each individual has their own deep and unique learning path through fate and life. When you see the Tower hitting others, you cannot sit in judgement of them and say they brought it on themselves: only the individual can do that. And not all calamities are the result of the Tower. It is important to understand that calamities brought by the Tower are often in some way self-inflicted: you played your part in making it happen.

This is not restricted to emotional decisions, but practical ones also. We live in a modern world dominated by psychology, religious thought, and emotions: those are the lenses through which we interpret events around us. In the West and increasingly in the East, the wishes and freedoms of the individual are considered of paramount importance. While this breaks us out of the collective bondage and deep injustice that is so prevalent in the history of the individual, it also brings with it self-responsibility.

However nature is about cause and effect without emotion, without care of extenuating circumstances, and the further removed from nature we become, the less we understand it. A good example of this would be the situation we currently find ourselves in with the Covid-19 pandemic. We can look at the overview of the pandemic and say it is caused by how we interact with wild creatures, the environment, and nature: our collective Tower. But on an individual level there have also been many personal Towers built by poor decision-making or unnecessary risk-taking. In our modern world of excessive comfort and protection, and little apparent danger, our decision-making skills have become weakened.

For example, there are people trapped in far-flung countries, stuck there because of the lockdown to limit infection. They cannot get flights out of the places they were visiting. There are instances of people on holiday with cancer who are on chemotherapy, who are running out of medication and are trapped in unsanitary accommodation with no help from anyone. These are Tower situations indeed, where their lives are in real danger. If they catch the virus or run out of medication, then they will likely not make it home alive.

If we take emotion out of the picture and look at individual situations purely in terms of cause and effect, then you will see—sadly—the self-imposed Towers. It is unwise for a middle-aged or elderly person to visit a distant developing country while they have cancer and depend on lifesaving medication. Doing so while a nearby country is going into lockdown because of an epidemic of a virulent and highly contagious disease is seriously unwise.

People have become complacent in their comfort and freedom. They do not think through the scenarios of what could go wrong, so they do not make wise decisions; nor, if they decide to take the risk, do they make provision for the worst case scenario. Yes, they want to make what could possibly be the last journey of their lifetime, maybe to see something they always wished to see—and that is the emotional justification that can bring about the Tower.

Nature and fate do not care about your emotions, they care about your actions. All this might seem harsh and judgemental, but it is not. It is hard, cold reality—and that is what the Tower gives us: a shot of hard, cold reality. It might be a small warning shot across the bow to teach us not to be stupid, but if we ignore those warnings, then the shots will get bigger and nearer until we listen.

3. Major Arcana Card Meanings

I for one have had my fair share of Towers in my life. They have taught me a lot, not just about cause and effect, but also about my own resilience. Each time I have picked up the pieces and started to rebuild, only to make another, different, bad decision that whacked me across the head. I was a slow learner for many years. But each visitation of the Tower also gave me something: knowledge of fate and its wider actions, knowledge of myself and my own stupidity. It also gave me the knowledge that I can survive whatever life throws at me whether it is self-induced or not. And it is that quality of survival that is the Tower's greatest gift to us.

Esoteric meaning

In the imagery of the Tower, the tower is depicted as having a golden crown that is knocked off by a blot of lightning that subsequently destroys the tower. People fall out of its windows that have flames leaping out of them.

The crown is our own sovereignty. When we forget that we are part of a deep and powerful pattern of creation, we become self-absorbed and think only of ourselves. We think of ourselves as controllers of our own destiny, our own god, and our wishes and desires become the main drivers in our lives. As magicians, regardless of what stream of magic we are involved in, such a thought is a terrible folly that at some point will bring us face to face with the Tower.

A magical-mystical path that places the individual at the centre of the world, the individual as the Divine presence, is one of the deepest and hardest paths to walk without tripping up over an inflated ego that triggers the Tower. And that is the lesson of that path.

For most magicians in various magical systems, the lesson of the Tower is enlightenment the hard way. The deeper you reach into magical learning, the more you learn about the world, about what is behind the veil of the world, and about who you are in your depths. The more you learn from experience, the more you will know the difference between true right and wrong, as opposed to culturally defined morality. When you take an action knowing that it is wrong, you will trigger the fate pattern to bring about a conclusion and learning. This is the sword edge that you walk along as an adept magician—and the more you 'know', the thinner the sword's blade becomes, and the sharper the cut when you fall. The less into the Mysteries you are, the less you know, so the less you have to lose. True innocence is the only protection from the magical aspect of the Tower.

But the magical dynamic is the same as the mundane dynamic. The Tower does not destroy you; it destroys whatever part of your life or magic is built on sand. It destroys the fantasy narrative you have surrounded yourself with, and it holds you in a headlock to make you observe the fruits of your actions and decisions. It then asks, "did you get that?" If you get it—if you drop all self-pretence of victimhood or ignorance, and face up to harsh reality—then fate will dust off your clothing, give you a drink of water, and say "well, don't do it again!"

Willingness to face a disaster, learn your lessons, and accept your part in bringing that disaster about, will give you access, through the gate of magical development, to the next stage of magical power. You cannot handle true power correctly unless you understand it, and truly understand yourself. To understand that power, you need to be fully aware of its full force should it turn on you. That is what the Tower is: the destructive side of power. Self-understanding comes from standing in the ruins of your life and knowing that no one but you can help yourself: you got yourself into the mess, and now you must climb out.

Such a step marks a major shift in your magical self-development: you go from asking "why did God let this happen?" to "well, that was

3. Major Arcana Card Meanings

dumb of me, I shall not be doing that again in a hurry." Without that shift in thinking there is no magical adept, only a magical aspirant.

> I had to learn. All my life. The hard way. And the hard way's pretty hard, but not so hard as the easy way.
>
> — Granny Weatherwax[1]

17 Star

Key words

The dawn after the disaster, hope, self-reliance, seed, Divine guidance, navigation, first step, conception.

The Star is the small but powerful light that shines in the darkness to lead you on your way ahead. When you stand in the rubble of disaster, or have faced a trial so devastating that you feel you are in total darkness, and you have kept as much integrity as is humanly possible in such a situation, this is when the Star begins to shine. When you have seen and acknowledged your failings, weaknesses, and the role you played in your own downfall, when you standalone with no emotion on the edge of the precipice and stare out in to the darkness beyond, then if you do not flinch from it, the Star will appear and show you the safe passage ahead. You must walk that path alone, but the Star will light each step in front of you to stop you falling into the Abyss.

The Star is also the herald of the end of the storm. It tells you that until you are ready—until you have recovered, strengthened, and rebuilt your foundations—you will not be tested again. The Star is a time of rebuilding, reenergizing, reforming, and renewal. The Star

---
[1]Pratchett 1993, p. 356.

will not carry you, nor will it coddle you; rather it will give you safe passage, sanctuary for body and soul, and the space and time to regroup your energy, resources, and necessities. The Star will give you however long you truly need, if you are determined to learn from past experience and forge forward alone to truly become the master of your fate.

It is a card of hope, respite, renewal, and rebirth. It is the gift that comes after the lessons of the Tower are learned. It can appear in a reading to tell you the worst is over, or to indicate the seeds being planted of something to blossom in the future, such as an idea or project. It can indicate conception, or the coming of a different fate path to take you in a different direction. But most of all, the message of the Star is that your suffering has been recognized, your willingness to forge a path ahead has been acknowledged, and the powers of the universe are responding by lighting your path ahead so that you do not get lost.

Mundane meaning

When this card appears in a mundane reading, regardless of its subject matter, it tells you to take a deep breath. No matter how bad a situation is, there is a bright light at the end of the tunnel. It can also say that whatever potential action or decision you are considering will bear strong fruit in the long term. It may be a difficult beginning and a long road to walk, but further down that road you will start to see the life-changing gifts that fate has put in your path. Depending on the question of the reading, and the position in the layout that it lands in, this card can herald the conception of a child, the start of a new cycle of fortune or fate, or the slow climb back to health and balance. It is the card of 1 a.m.: the start of the new day that occurs in the darkness of the night.

3. Major Arcana Card Meanings

Esoteric meaning

The Star is deeply connected with Temperance. It uses similar imagery of the water bearer, but instead of pouring water from one pot to another the Star pours water both into the spring and onto the land, while keeping one foot *on* the water and one foot on the land. This is most likely connected to the *cool water* that appears in Ancient Egyptian funerary texts. Cool water and nourishing bread is given to those who have overcome some of the trials of the Duat.[1]

In the distance of the Star card there is a hill with a tree on it, and sitting on the tree is a long-beaked bird. I have looked at the Star card for decades and never noticed this quiet but powerful message in its background. The bird in the tree is the Benu bird,[2] similar in concept to the Greek Phoenix. The tree it sits in is the Ished tree or the sycamore tree. The cool water is poured for the refreshment of both land and lake by a goddess. These images are all from ancient Egyptian mythology and feature heavily in the Egyptian Book of the Dead[3] and the Book of Gates.[4]

The Benu bird is a bird of new life and renewal, and is the herald of great things to come. It features heavily in funerary texts once the soul has undergone some of its most terrible trials and has survived to begin its walk towards the dawn. The Benu bird appears in the depths of the darkness just before the long journey to light begins. It is also the bird that heralds the birth of the creation of the world from the Benben stone that rises out of the waters. The Benu bird is strongly connected to Osiris and was taken to be the soul of Osiris, who was torn apart, who descended into the Underworld, who was

---
[1] The Duat is the Egyptian Underworld and the realm of the dead.
[2] Benu. Taken from the Egyptian verb *wbn* which means to rise or to shine.
[3] The most recent academic English translation of the Book of the Dead is Quirke 2013.
[4] For a magical translation and commentary of which, see Sheppard and McCarthy 2017.

reconstituted, and who rose again with the dawn as the renewed solar deity called Re.

The sycamore tree also features in the same funerary texts as the tree which is also the goddess Hathor in her connections with the stars.[1] The goddess in the form of a tree offers cool water to the clean soul who has passed some of the trials of the Duat, allowing the soul rest and regeneration before they forge on to the greater trials ahead of them in their quest to rise at the dawn with the sun, and thus into renewal.

The ultimate goal of the soul that rises with the solar barque of Re is to become as *one of the stars*, the Justified Ones. It is perfect imagery for the Star, together with the goddess who pours water onto the spring and the land, and the new bright star that shines among the others on the trump card. It is clever way of quietly using Egyptian imagery to convey hidden meaning to *those who have eyes to see*.

The collective imagery for the Star tells of the deeper, layered, esoteric meaning of this card. The Hermit and his lamp, lit by a star, forges forward alone in the darkness to face the trials ahead of him. On the other side of those trials, the star is no longer the wisdom and harvest of the adept; the adept themselves is *becoming the star*.

When this card appears in a magical reading it tells of new seeds that are starting to grow. Those seeds will blossom into fate paths or events that will take the magician to the next step in their magical development. It is a sign in the darkness that the best days are still to come. By not giving in, the magician will develop into a better, more evolved version of themselves.

---

[1] Book of the Dead ch. 59 (see Quirke 2013, p. 145).

3. Major Arcana Card Meanings

To me belongs yesterday, I know tomorrow.

What does it mean?

As for yesterday, that is Osiris. As for tomorrow, that is Re on that day in which the foes of the Lord of All were destroyed and his son Horus was made to rule. *Otherwise said:* That is the day of the 'We-remain' festival, when the burial of Osiris was ordered by his father Re.

— Book of the Dead ch. 17.[1]

And so they become clothed in Gold;
Their faces in the stars,
Their feet in the waters,
And their minds cast to the road ahead.

— Josephine McCarthy.[2]

18 Moon

Key words

fantasy, hidden, creative, tides, delusions, madness, hormones, stealth.

The Moon is a card of many faces. Just as the moon can present as a full, new, or crescent moon, so its meanings can ebb and flow in their strength and meaning. The Moon card appears when someone is not truly seeing what is there. They see in 'moonlight': in shadows and without clarity. This can mean anything from self-delusion and self-ignorance, to something literally being 'hard to see.' For example if you are hiding from danger for some reason, and you ask the cards if you are hidden enough and the Moon card appears, then it is saying "yes, you are unseen, you are in the shadows, in the mists."

---

[1] Faulkner 1985 [1972], p. 44.
[2] Sheppard and McCarthy 2017, p. 296.

Mundane meaning

The appearance of this card in a mundane reading can also mean loss of clarity of thought or vision: you are not seeing everything in the situation that you are reading about. Sometimes that lack of clarity is the result of your not being objective; sometimes it is because there are unseen, still-forming elements in the situation, making it difficult to get a clear reading.

The Moon can also show up in a health reading if something is going on that is unseen or not yet fully formed. It can also indicate hormone cycles in women.

When it is surrounded by negative cards it can indicate a hidden enemy, someone who seems nice and positive, but is forever working behind the scenes to destroy you.

The Moon can also indicate mental instability or mental illness that can affect the subject matter of the reading. For instance if you are doing a reading to look at the suitability of someone for a particular role or job, and the Moon card is prominent in their reading, then it is likely that no matter how 'together' they appear, the person has a high chance of suffering from a mental illness. If the cards and result of the reading are positive, then such an illness should not badly affect their work—but you need to be aware of it so that you can adapt your working method to take their disability into account. If the reading is surrounded by disaster cards then it is more likely that they would not be suitable for the role, and that the pressure of such a role could aggravate their illness.

A prominent meaning for the Moon card is illusions and self-delusion. We have all been there at some point in our lives: we are convinced that something is 'right' when it is not, and often when we look back we can see that we *wanted* it to be right and so did not see—or chose not to see—the harsh reality. We have all fallen in love with

3. Major Arcana Card Meanings

the wrong person and refused to listen to the small internal warning voice. That is the power of the Moon.

Sometimes we are trapped in illusions for good reason. When we are really ready and capable of handling the truth then the sun will come out and drown out the shadows of the Moon, so we at last see clearly and learn from that.

The Moon can also herald a creative phase, where the illusions of the Moon are put to good use in creating art, literature, music, etc. The Moon is the patron of artists and her power flows through us to create something beautiful and otherworldly. Depending on the question and subject matter of a reading, the Moon can indicate a creative phase or job that is lining up.

Esoteric meaning

The esoteric meaning of the Moon, just like its mundane meaning, has many faces. The Moon on the Kabbalistic Tree of Life belongs in Yesod, the ninth Sefirot, which itself has many layers, and their meanings are roughly the same.

The Moon holds power over tides: the tides of the sea, the rhythm of breeding and procreation, the hormones, and the mind/imagination. Because of this the Moon can represent bloodlines and tribes in magical readings. The meaning that the Moon throws up in esoteric readings is its 'Hidden' aspect.

The Moon hides things in plain sight. Whatever it is, it is there, but the light is so poor that you can only see shadows. The power of the Moon can be used magically to veil and shield things from sight, and to deflect attention into the shadows. Similarly, if you are trying to get a clear view of something in a magical reading, and the Moon turns up in the reading, then whatever it is you are looking for is there, but it is either naturally veiled because it has not yet taken a full and complete form, or it has been magically hidden.

When something is forming, be it a magical fate pattern or something being built magically, it is first *envisioned*. The inner structure is built first, and when that is finished it can express itself in the physical world. If the inner structure is not complete, it is hard to get a fix on it, either in vision or in readings, as it is still in the formation stage. When that is the case, the Moon will often come up in a reading to say, "there is too much fluidity in what you are trying to look at, so you will not be able to see it."

Personally, I find that if there is something I am not meant to see for some reason in a reading, then the Moon card will turn up as the outcome. Often this is a protective mechanism where a response or reaction/action from me would be detrimental either to the situation or to myself. So I am blocked from seeing something so that I do not respond to it.

There is also the magical dynamic of "if you don't look, they cannot see you." Sometimes it is best simply to trust in the process you are working on and stay off the radar. When that is the case, the Moon will appear in the reading.

If as a magician you are looking at the potential effects of a specific magical working or project, and the Moon plays a prominent part in the answer, then depending on the question, and the position of the Moon in the layout and the subject matter, the Moon could either be blocking your ability to see the answer, or it could be a direct warning that the work would affect your mental stability. The Moon connects strongly to mental health and self-delusion. So if it appears, tread carefully. It might be an idea to focus your reading on a specific question, such as "how will this work affect my mental and physical health over X number of months or years?"

Occasionally in my experience the Moon has literally meant "the full moon" when the reading is about the timing of a proposed action. The full moon has a lot of tidal pull, and as such it can be used magically and homoeopathically as a perfect time to initiate particular actions. The moon when full is at the peak of its power, and that can used to energize whatever you are doing.

For the most part, in both mundane and esoteric readings, the appearance of the Moon should make the reader pause for thought, and they should carefully reconsider the wisdom of whatever proposed actions the reading is looking at.

> Modern science says: 'The sun is the past, the earth is the present, the moon is the future.' From an incandescent mass we have originated, and into a frozen mass we shall turn. Merciless is the law of nature, and rapidly and irresistibly we are drawn to our doom.
>
> — Nikola Tesla[1]

19 Sun

Key words

Success, achievement, favour, expansion, earned status, successful completion.

The Sun is the epitome of success earned through constant application, determination, and hard work. The Path of Hercules up the Mountain of Adversity will push you to your limit, but when the Sun appears all your struggles, mistakes, missteps—and most importantly persistence—pays off. You reach the Sun and bask in its glory.

---

[1] Tesla 2001.

The Sun card appears in our readings when we are about to harvest the fruits of our labours, when all that effort and persistence is about to pay off with the success we need. Note that I say *need*, not want. Sometimes we set our sights too high or too low on what we want as an outcome, but the Sun gives the success that you need to progress forward, to evolve, to be nourished, and to be recognized.

Mundane meaning

When the Sun appears in a mundane reading, it tells of success and achievement. It is a big "yes" if you have posed a yes/no question. For example if you are asking about a job interview or test and the Sun is the conclusion card, then it is telling you that you will be successful in your endeavour.

Depending on context it can also represent things like heat, fever and drought. In a health reading it can represent inflammation or fever. Too much heat in a body is not good!

One caution with the Sun card, however, is that if you spot it in readings about your future, and you then decide to slack off because you think your success is guaranteed, then the Sun will turn into the Moon: self-delusion. Success comes from effort that is sustained right up to the conclusion of the project, event, or situation. Anything less and the Sun will become obscured by clouds.

In fact, this is a general danger with divination. The cards answer questions on the understanding that the path you are currently walking is how you will continue. If you drastically change your path by suddenly taking the pressure off your sustained effort, then you are changing the potential outcome of your actions. See the appearance of the Sun in your reading as a cheerleader as you run the last lap of your race.

3. Major Arcana Card Meanings

Esoteric Meaning

The child of the Sun is crowned with flowers, rides a white horse, and holds a banner. In the background the Sun is watching, and below the Sun is the garden and garden wall. There is a lot of interesting esoteric meaning wrapped up in that simple image, and once again, as in some of the other Trump cards, it draws on Persian, Egyptian, and Kabbalistic understanding.

The child of the Sun is modelled on the idea of the young sun that has successfully risen out of the darkness. We see this sort of solar deity in various forms around the known ancient world, for example the Egyptian *Heru-pa-khered* or Horus the Younger, Mithras the child emerging out of the rock, and the deities Helios and Apollo.

Similarly, white horses in the ancient world were considered particularly special, and were the steeds of gods, kings, and prophets. A couple of examples would be the white spirit horse al-Buraq which carried the prophet Muhammed to heaven and back in one night,[1] and the pure white Nisean horses of the Persian Empire which were kept for kings and gods.[2] White horses pulled the solar chariot of the deity Mithras, and white horses were also considered powerful spirit animals to the Celts of the British Isles. They are often worked with in magic today as visionary guides and companions for magicians seeking to explore the realms beyond the physical.

The theme of the successful sun and the white horse is deeply embedded within mythic symbology around the world. The garden wall with flowers in the tarot image of the Sun is likely connected to the mystical idea of the walled garden of Eden: Paradise. This collective symbolism taps into the reoccurring theme, in the deck's major cards, of the evolution of the magician through walking the

---

[1] *Hadith* vol 5, book 58: *Merits of the Helpers of Medinah*, no. 227.
[2] Olmstead 1948, p. 25.

Path of Adversity up the Mountain to the sun: mystical ascent. The same theme is often hidden in many fifteenth— and sixteenth-century grimoires in which planetary rituals seem to be the main theme of the magic, but when you dig below the surface this hidden aspect of the work of ascent emerges.

The message of this card, in an esoteric reading, is similar to the mundane reading: it depicts success and the completion of something. However, whereas in mundane readings it points to worldly and physical success, when it appears in a magical reading it is most often pointing to deep mystical and magical success. The path of the Initiate is turning into the path of the Adept.

In esoteric readings there is another theme signified by the Sun, which is the anger and destruction of a solar deity. If the card is surrounded by destructive cards and there is a destructive outcome, then it can point to the little known and little understood solar aspect of Divine Anger. This destructive solar theme has a long and deep history in our collective Neolithic heritage, and was likely the cause of human sacrifice to the sun that was fairly widespread until around 3000 B.C.. Fragments of this destructive side to the sun can be found in the ancient Egyptian story of the Eye of Re and the destruction of mankind known as the Book of the Heavenly Cow.[1]

> O thou Sun, send me as far over the earth as is my pleasure and thine, and may I make the acquaintance of good men, but never hear anything of bad ones, nor they of me.
>
> — Apollonius of Tyana[2]

---

[1] Hornung 1999, p. 148.
[2] Phillimore 1912.

20 Judgement

Key words

Decision, culmination, resolution, knowing yourself, self-responsibility, literal judgement, rebalance.

The Judgement card often terrifies people, particularly if they have been raised in a culture containing the idea of final judgement, as is found in Christian mythology. They associate this card with death and the judgement of God. However, the Judgement card has deep layers, both mundane and esoteric.

The Judgement card represents the culmination of a cycle of fate, where decisions, actions, and events all come together to a conclusion. Once that conclusion has passed then life will change, whether for good, bad, or a mixture of the two. One of the most prominent dynamics of the Judgement card is *knowing yourself*. How you judge yourself in the culmination of events is far more important than how others judge you. Once you have survived the trauma of the Tower and have picked yourself up under the light of the Star, then it is time to examine your subsequent steps and actions, and to pick through the rubble of the Tower to understand what happened and why.

Not all judgements are bad ones; sometimes the conclusion of events that is heralded by the Judgement card is good. We reap what we have sown, and we can look back without excessive ego and see where we played our part in something that was good and successful. The conclusion brings the fruits of those labours and weighs our efforts against our needs. What we need is then put in our path so that we are resourced for the next new cycle of fate that we will be walking into.

20 Judgement

MUNDANE MEANING

In mundane readings, this card can appear when a major decision has been or is about to be made. The Judgement card is not about changes brought by fate, but about our own decisions, such as marriage, divorce, moving home, and changing career. It can also appear when we are being judged, as in a court case or dispute. If the cards around Judgement are good ones and it is followed by good cards, then the judgement will lean in our favour.

The Judgement card can also herald the end of a cycle triggered by the Wheel of Fortune. The harvest of that cycle, both its good and bad parts, are weighed by the universe/powers of fate. Things are either taken from you or given to you to balance your scales, so that you can start a new cycle of fate. The trick of the Judgement card is to accept that judgement and its results, learn its lessons both good and bad, then move on. It is also important to learn not to judge yourself too leniently or harshly, but to look at your past actions without emotions and learn from them, accept their harvests, then move forward with a sense of renewal.

If the judgement or change that comes is harsh, then there is always a gift hidden in the struggle: a helping hand, a guide, shelter, or compassion. There is no real punishment, only learning, and whatever you need to move forward in that learning will come to you if you pay attention. Conversely, if the judgement or change was spectacularly good, then there will always be a little dark corner to remind you of human frailty. Don't get too complacent. Enjoy the fruits of your labour, but always realize that it will not always be this good, and that if you slide into poor decision-making then the results will eventually bite you in the ass.

3. Major Arcana Card Meanings

Esoteric meaning

The Judgement card is deeply connected to the Justice card, and as such is closely connected to the Egyptian concept of Ma'at, of balance. Where the Justice card looks at the harvest and weighs it, Judgement decides what fate action will be necessary to balance out that harvest. The harvest is our actions in life, and this theme of harvest, scales, and balance has played a major role in most types of magic for millennia.

The harvest of the deeds is winnowed, which is to say the major deeds, both good and bad, that hold precious learning and development are sifted from deeds that have no learning value. The harvested and winnowed deeds are then weighed against pure balance, and in all humans the scales in life will never be truly balanced. It is a lesser version of the scales and weighing in the Underworld.

Where there is deficit in the weighing of the deeds, the Wheels of fate start to turn to trigger events in life to give you opportunities to strengthen your harvest. Where there is excess in the weighing of the deeds, again the Wheels of fate turn to give you an opportunity to distribute that excess. This process, from an esoteric perspective, is what is reflected in the Judgement card.

We can bring that process right into our lives by doing the weighing and winnowing ourselves, by looking back at the series of events and our response to them, and seeing what was valuable that was learned, and what was truly a waste of time and energy for all concerned. By doing this ourselves the inner processes need not trigger. The more you engage these deep magical inner processes and brings them into your own sphere of influence, the more you will learn about power, evolution, and yourself.

It is also wise to note that this is not about good and bad actions, but about necessary and unnecessary ones. It is about order and not chaos. Sometimes destructive actions are necessary and are part of order, and if done with the full knowledge of necessity without emotion, self-interest, or self-delusion, those actions are creative deeds for the harvest. This can be a hard concept for some to wrap their heads around if they have been raised in a culture where only the good deeds count, where only happiness and youth is important. I call it the Disney realm of magic, where love and light is all that matters. Constant light kills things just as effectively as constant darkness. The whole deeper esoteric power behind Justice and Judgement is true balance, and acting in a way where we strive towards true balance in our path up the Mountain of Adversity. This action brings magical maturity and evolution for ourselves and for everything we connect to. And it bears the healthy fruits of deeds to be harvested on the scales of Ma'at.

> Many that live deserve death. And some that die deserve life. Can you give it to them? Then do not be too eager to deal out death in judgement. For even the wise cannot see all ends.
>
> — J. R. R. Tolkien[1]

21 World

Key words

Completion, self, fulfilment, opportunity, security, stability, acclaim.

"The world is your oyster." This would be a perfect saying for the World trump card. The World card tells of the successful struggle against your own ignorance and weaknesses, your survival of what the Devil and the Tower bring to your door, and your introspection and determination to rebuild, to succeed against all odds. All these

---

[1]Tolkien 2005, ch. 2.

3. Major Arcana Card Meanings

struggles were weighed and harvested by Judgement, and in return you are given the World.

Mundane meaning

When this card appears in a mundane reading, it signifies the world of the subject of the reading. It can signify yourself in a personal reading, and it can also signify your world, home, job, interests...everything that makes up who you are and what you do.

It can also indicate success, and the security and fulfilment that comes from it. This card, when it turns up in a reading, says that everything in your world is good; that no matter what you are worried about, it will be okay, as your foundation, your world, is solid.

In a yes/no reading, the World is a big and successful yes that is not fleeting. If it appears in a health reading with a health layout then it can indicate that all is well and healthy in the part of the body it represents. If it is the concluding card then it indicates strong robust health.

The card can also, depending on the question, indicate that the person or subject is protected to some extent. In the imagery of The World, the four holy creatures[1] surround the central figure as guardians. If you are where you should be, and doing what you are supposed to be doing on your fate path, then inherent protection can often draw close to you. It is one of the gifts of fate.

The card can sometimes be literal. I have found The World card turn up numerous times to indicate the land around me or my garden. This is useful to know if you are doing a reading to find something or someone who is missing: the World can indicate that they are home or close to home. They are in their world.

---

[1] *Revelation* 4:6-8.

Esoteric meaning

Beyond the obvious and mundane meanings that can also apply in esoteric readings, the world can have a much deeper connotation. It can literally be the gift of the world. Through the various stages of magical development, we are ground, sandpapered, and polished. There comes a time in the life and development of the adept where you are presented with a choice, with Judgement. You can check out from the hamster wheel of life and continue your journey in the Underworld, or you can choose to take a rest, where you withdraw from the depths of magical patterns and live a simple, normal life for a while. Such a life is depicted by The World: you choose life, and as part of that choice, you have to be able to gather all your magical skills and patterns into yourself. It is a bit like a hibernation, but it is also a cauldron of regeneration.

It is a major stage in individual magical evolution. Can you gather everything together and allow it to flow through the mundane? Can you *become* magic? This is the point where the magician ceases to conduct specific magical acts but allows their magic, and the magic of the universe, to flow through them unheeded as part of their everyday life. The magician is in the centre of the World card: they are enclosed by an elongated shen,[1] which is the same concept as a cartouche. It denotes protection, eternity, the sun's cycle, and the limits of the world. In the four corners are the four holy creatures, the angelic guardians, and in the centre the mystical magician, or Developing One, holds two wands: power in life and death.

The deepest meaning of the World is that the world, as an active consciousness, accepts you as the magician or mystic and guards you.

---

[1] The ancient Egyptian *shen* ring, which when elongated becomes a cartouche, provides encircled protection to guard the name of a king and associate him with the sun.

3. Major Arcana Card Meanings

You are in the garden[1] while in life, walking among the mundane, doing mundane things, while all the time the power of the universe flows through you to effect necessary change. This is the point where you become *as one with the world*. You do not live in the world; you *are* the world. There are many magical rabbit holes you can explore in that concept!

In an esoteric reading it can have all the same meanings as in a mundane reading, but it also tells you that whatever action or situation you are reading is part of the order of your world. It is good, it is balanced, and it is as it should be.

> We must close our eyes and invoke a new manner of seeing, a wakefulness that is the birthright of us all, though few put it to use.
>
> — Plotinus[2]

---

[1] The metaphorical Paradise.
[2] O'Brien 1964, p. 42.

Chapter Four

The Minor Arcana

While the Major Arcana tells us about the core powers and principles of humanity, fate, and progression, the Minor Arcana tells us about the everyday ups and downs of how those fates and powers express.

The meanings of the Minor Arcana are simple and to the point, yet they can develop nuances particular to the individual tarot reader. Over time you will begin to realize that some cards have particular meanings for you that seem to contradict the official meanings. This is normal for readers, as they develop their own internal vocabulary. This happens not by 'wishing' a card would mean something else, or from ignoring its more dire warnings, but from a card repeatedly showing up in certain circumstances. If you record your readings so you can revisit them, you will start to see patterns of behaviour emerging from various card meanings.

The Minor Arcana cards, besides their individual meanings, also have overarching characteristics, which are elements and numbers. If you get stuck on the meaning of a particular minor card, then refer back to the elemental and numerical meanings to understand what it is trying to tell you. Here is a breakdown of those characteristics:

4. THE MINOR ARCANA

Elements

AIR

cold, breath, words, sword, east, beginning, storms, intellect, learning, tactical war, focus, enemies, knowledge, ritual magic.

FIRE

heat, magical wand or staff, creativity, future, south, intelligence, fate, development, wisdom, righteous conflict, inspiration, medicine, rage, shamanic magic.

WATER

immaterial, vessel, west, changeable, emotions, dreams and visions, fading, arguments, spirit, intuitions, psychic.

EARTH

solidity, shield, north, storage, substance, practical skills, anchor, past, buried, ancestors, growth, entanglement, nature magic.

Numbers

Each number has a divinatory meaning or quality. Your understanding of a number can be used to expand your understanding of a card's meaning.

ACES

are intermediary powers between the Major and Minor Arcana. They are more important than the rest of the Minor Arcana, but not so important as the Major Arcana. An ace brings more power to the cards that surround it, and they emphasize the strength of the element they represent. For instance an Ace of Wands brings a lot of fire to a situation: this could be good or bad.

Two

is a number of polarity, conflict, and equally matched powers which balance each other. It is a power of duality, of conversation, and polarized action.

Three

is a number of action, where the polarity of two produces a third. Whether this action is good or bad, it creates something and is therefore a number of producing something.

Four

is a number of stability, where all four elements and directions come together to be equally balanced. It doesn't create or destroy, it simply *is*. Thus four is a number of stasis and at times stagnation.

Five

is the number of humanity and struggle. It is the number of the everyday challenges that we overcome to survive and thrive.

Six

is the number of the past, memories, inheritance, and how the past affects the present and the future.

4. The Minor Arcana

Seven

is the power of evolution of the mind and soul; a number of personal self-development and the maturation process.

Eight

is the number of Divine awakening, of events that awaken us out of everyday slumber and trigger us to search for deeper meaning.

Nine

is the number of cause and effect, where our past actions, for good or bad, trigger events for our present and future, so that we may learn. "By their fruits shall ye know them."

Ten

is the number of the completion of the circle, where whatever fate cycle we are currently on is coming to a close. The saying of number ten is "this too will pass."

Swords: air, east

Ace of Swords

Law, enemy, conflict, difficult change, heavy responsibility, loss.

Two of swords

Peace offering, friendship that develops with former enemy, contentious but productive debate, intellectual discussion, writing.

Three of Swords

Divorce, separation, the breaking up of something, enemy, disillusion, conflict, loss.

Four of Swords

Illness, exhaustion, withdrawal, seclusion, need for silence and rest, waiting.

Five of Swords

Setback, temporary failure, gathering oneself after battle, arguments, loss of face, test of determination, not giving in when faced with defeat.

Six of Swords

Journey, an unexpected traveller, moving away from difficulty, leaving the past behind, travel over water, putting knowledge in a safe place for the future.

Seven of Swords

Evading disaster, Divine intervention, spirit help, successful strategy, legal help, a need to enhance home security.

Eight of Swords

Trapped, enemy, the fear to act, indecision making a situation worse, imprisonment, lung illness, injustice, bullying, slander, struggle against adversary, taking action that relieves the situation.

Nine of Swords

Hatred, attack, enemy, suspicions, grief, suffering, pain.

Ten of Swords

Defeat, collapse, the darkness before the dawn, rock bottom, complete loss, intense suffering.

Page of Swords

New Moon, difficult child, secret enemy, underhand communications, hidden hostility.

Knight of Swords

A young person who cannot be trusted. Emotionless but projects normality, has harmful intent, untruthful and manipulative, can be violent and ruthless.

Queen of Swords

Strong minded woman, territorial and combative, sharp legal mind, unemotional and highly intelligent, selfish, focused, and can be a devastating enemy when crossed.

King of Swords

Male lawyer or figure of authority in law, military, higher education or digital technology. Can be either a helper or enemy depending on the situation. As a helper this person will consider it their duty to protect or help you. As an enemy, they will not stop until they have destroyed you or have been destroyed themselves.

Wands: fire, south

ACE OF WANDS

Creative beginning, inspiration, success, immune response, guidance, warmth, overcoming difficulties, the single flame, a doorway.

TWO OF WANDS

Creative or business difficulties, discussions and collaboration, emotional arguing that is ultimately productive, equal balance of power.

THREE OF WANDS

Good luck, moving a project from concept to practical building, a good foundation, creative resources.

FOUR OF WANDS

Social interactions, happiness, friendship, all that is creatively needed comes together.

FIVE OF WANDS

Overcoming creative or business differences, obstacles that can easily be overcome with thought and creative thinking.

SIX OF WANDS

Victory, success after struggle, reaching a happy compromise. Be careful of complacency.

4. The Minor Arcana

Seven of Wands

Holding your ground, not giving in when faced with uneven odds, determination brings victory eventually, minor sickness.

Eight of Wands

Communication, speed, inspiration, rapid learning, burst of energy, mild fever.

Nine of Wands

Battle weary, struggle, adversity, a warning of dishonesty, injury, treachery.

Ten of Wands

Burden, withdrawal, retreat, leaving conflict, struggle, difficult fever, energetic burden that must be carried, load-sharing.

Page of Wands

Financial or creative good news or communications, favourable communication, a creative student with potential, beginning of a writing project, first quarter moon, faery being, the rising sun.

Knight of Wands

Young person, creative personality, open and honest, can be unstable at times, a good solid friend, youth and inexperience, a fickle lover, fiery temper when pushed, competitive personality.

Queen of Wands

Female. Teacher, influential thinker, creative female artist, maturity and wisdom from experience, truthful, volatile temper, dangerous if crossed.

King of Wands

Family man, business man, reliable and helpful but can be dangerous when angry, a person within their own power who can be learned from, a person of experience who will advise, teacher.

Cups: water, west

Ace of Cups

Happiness, love, healing, a good outcome.

Two of Cups

Friendship, love affair, happiness, best friend, joyful communication, connection with nature.

Three of Cups

Fulfilment, happiness from completion of something, creative success and recognition.

Four of Cups

Emotional stability in living situation, can indicate emotional complacency, can be a warning to not take loved ones for granted.

4. The Minor Arcana

Five of Cups

Emotional insecurity or immaturity, emotional weakness, unfounded pessimism, emotional disappointments, not seeing with clarity. Love is there, but unseen.

Six of Cups

Gentleness, innocence, idealism, happy memories, past events, naïveté.

Seven of Cups

Glamour, not seeing the true treasure before you, physic ability, the beginning of a quest, magical awakening.

Eight of Cups

Emotional overload, walking away from comfort, the beginning of the Lone Quest, dissatisfaction of life or relationships, seeking the unknown.

Nine of Cups

Emotional security, good omens, a time of contentment, peace.

Ten of Cups

Happiness, fulfilment, success after adversity, peace, abiding love, celebration.

Page of Cups

Full Moon, love or support letter, gentle child, new project that needs protecting, creative ideas.

Knight of Cups

A young person of high emotions, can get easily depressed, creates much drama, romantic but unrealistic, artistic and musical, tendency to gaslight, emotionally clingy.

Queen of Cups

A soft and gentle woman, easily moved to tears, loving and passive, loves beautiful things, can be narrow minded, unthinking, and spiteful when crossed.

King of Cups

A kind-hearted man, often single, artistic, can be religious or a religious figure like a priest, can be overemotional at times, but is a generous and kind-hearted soul.

Coins: earth, north

Ace of Coins

Material success, a financial gain, solidity, foundation, a block in the path that protects you, substance, ancestors, shield, physical strength.

Two of Coins

Balance of money in and money out, monetary necessity but no excess, keeping balance, help when needed, passing things forward, simple satisfaction, action/reaction, balance of powers, maintaining physical integrity, giving and receiving.

4. The Minor Arcana

Three of Coins

Work, a job, productivity that brings monetary gain, creating something physical (such as sculpture, art, furniture, or books), physical work that produces something, a work or business proposal.

Four of Coins

Financial security, can indicate overcautiousness or hoarding, a family dinner or party, stability.

Five of Coins

Loss, financial difficulty but not disaster, loss of physical energy, hardship that can be over come, struggle.

Six of Coins

Getting your due, payment for work done, paying your debts, the balancing of scales, a loan that must be paid, financial disputes.

Seven of Coins

Satisfaction, completion of a job or project, the fruits of hard work, improvement in financial matters, a gift or unexpected windfall.

Eight of Coins

Craftsmanship, artistry, mastery of craft brings prosperity, a well-paid job, fruits of one's labour, practical self-development.

Nine of Coins

Happiness, fulfilment, resources, fruitfulness, pregnancy, a good harvest, material gain from past effort, security, a gift.

Ten of Coins

Overgrowth, wealth, a large gift, coagulation, property, long-term resources, burden of resources.

Page of Coins

Last quarter moon, financial letter, strong child, new growth, a garden, a token gift.

Knight of Coins

A hardworking young person, slow to anger, not creative, enjoys physical pleasures, can be passive-aggressive and abusive when crossed.

Queen of Coins

Earth mother, woman of substance, prefers family and gardening over socialising and career, can be possessive and domineering, likes to control everyone, protects her family strongly, is not easily pushed around, is highly practical and solid in her quiet confidence.

King of Coins

Man of substance or wealth, a man who works with finance or agriculture, dependable and hardworking, mature and not without wisdom, does not expect to be disobeyed but protects his own.

Chapter Five

Interpretation

> Happy the person who has learned the cause of things and has put under his or her feet all fear, inexorable fate, and the noisy strife of the hell of greed.
>
> — Virgil[1]

Interpreting a tarot divination reading is not quite as easy as it first appears, and often people can spend years practising tarot and trying to make sense of what they are looking at, which can be frustrating. I hope that this chapter can help people bypass a lot of that frustration. If you understand the process and how to approach the process properly, it should enable you to develop good solid divination skills that you can apply not only to tarot, but to other forms of divination too. Just remember, interpreting tarot is truly an art form, and like all art forms, it takes time, patience, and lots of practice.

Vocabulary

The first thing to think about when approaching tarot is understanding that it has a vocabulary of seventy-eight 'words' or meanings. Imagine you had to convey an important and at times complex message to someone and you could only use seventy-eight different words. It would be a tough job, and the more complex the subject

---

[1] Durant 1928, p. 138.

5. Interpretation

matter, the tougher it would be. Each word will have to have more than one meaning—and to decode your message, your reader will have to work out the intended meaning of each single word by placing it in context of the subject matter, the question asked, and the other words.

Approaching tarot like a code and puzzle switches your thought processes away from conversation and towards pattern recognition, which allows you to think sideways and creatively. The key is to be neutral in your interpretations, and not let your emotions fill in the gaps, which is something we will look at a little later.

Here is an example. Let us think of an image that would convey the following concepts: pregnancy, feet, small, fragility, comfort, and new beginnings. I would use an image of a pair of baby booties. Let us look at questions where that one image would give a defined answer:

- "Am I pregnant?" "Baby booties!" Yes, you are.

- "Where is the root of my sickness in my body?" "Baby booties!" Look at your feet: sometimes a small cut can trigger an infection and this often goes unnoticed.

- "Am I strong enough to do this job?" "Baby booties!" No, your energy is frail, like a baby.

- "Would staying in this situation be good, or would moving to a new situation be better for me?" "Baby booties!" New paths would be better. (Baby/new/feet/path).

- "Will I find my cat in a big building or a small one?" "Baby booties!" A small one.

- "Should I stay with the big company I work for, or take up the offer from the small startup company?" "Baby booties!" Take the startup company offer (baby/new/small).

Vocabulary

You can see how one image can be deployed for meaning across a variety of subjects while remaining specific enough to be useful. That is basically how card divination works. Some decks are designed to be particularly vague, so that they only act as a catalyst for the reader's own thoughts, and some decks are specific enough in their meaning to be useful for divination.

The traditional tarot deck, the Rider-Waite deck, is a halfway point between those two points. One of the reasons for that is that the Rider-Waite deck was designed for two purposes: card divination and esoteric exploration. Sometimes the two different vocabularies overlap, which can be helpful when doing a difficult reading; other times it can leave the reader blinking in confusion. It is most important that you understand the dynamics that operate through divination, as that will also shift your approach to interpretation and understanding.

The best way to learn a vocabulary is to get to know the cards. Lay them out, group the families together, look at their images and numbers, and get to know their personalities. Look through whatever book comes with a deck, and look at the pictures. Choose a keyword or two for each card based on the information you have, and write that keyword on the card (or on a bit of tape stuck to it). Just as a child learns to read by recognizing single words at a time and may not get the whole sentence in one go, so a new tarot reader needs to learn their keywords for each card. Don't dive into a card's mystical-magical aspects: just get to know its surface presentation to start with.

Treat tarot, and divination in general, like everything else in life: it can be terrifying and daunting at first, but once you begin to grasp the skill you start to learn from your experiences, and you learn that not all bad things are really bad. Treat learning divination as being like a child learning to play out on their own for the first time. It can be stressful, and at first everything can be perceived as a threat. But as you learn to interpret, you will become more comfortable with your readings, and you can look, decipher, and act as though they were everyday things.

Choosing a deck

When choosing a deck to use for tarot reading, don't be lured by clever pictures. Cards covered in weird-looking symbols, letters, and numbers may look mysterious, but they can be really useless for divination.

I make my magical students start with the Rider-Waite tarot deck simply because it has enough esoteric symbolism (some is cleverly hidden) *and* enough mundane images to make it useful without being too easy. Apprentices have to work hard to draw meaning from those cards, which helps them to develop their interpretation skills and teaches them to spot coherent patterns. Once they have the basics, they go on to work with other decks.

If you feel drawn to nontraditional decks, again, do not be lured by the artwork. Some decks are beautiful but magically illiterate and therefore useless. Some are wrapped up in psychology to the point that they, too, are useless. Think about the limited vocabulary: does the deck you are interested in have a coherent and potentially wide-ranging vocabulary?

Before I gained enough skill to properly design my own decks with useful imagery, I used to make my own decks out of index cards and key words. Each card would have a colour and a key word, and occasionally a scribbled image. Working with a deck like that taught me a great deal about how to focus right in on meaning without getting lost in glamour. It is an interesting exercise to try!

A snapshot view of a situation

Once you understand the limitations of trying to communicate and decipher a message using only seventy-eight 'words,' the next hurdle to understand is how divination works practically. The human brain can process information at an impressive speed, and we are so used to this that we do not think about how much information streams into us every second or every day, and where that information comes from. Understanding this process will help you understand how to approach divination.

Let's say you see an old lady fall down in the street: suddenly your attention is focused. Your eyes look at her and around her: was she pushed, or did she fall? Are people going to help her? Are *you* going to help her? You decide to go help, and you have to cross a busy road to get to her. Your eyes and ears weigh up what cars are coming towards you and what speed they are going, and your brain calculates the safest moment to cross.

When you get to the old lady you can hear that she is rambling, and you wonder whether she has dementia or has had a stroke. But when you get close up beside her, you can smell alcohol, sweat, dirt, and urine. Your brain decides she is an alcoholic with fallen over and cannot get up. Someone has called an ambulance so there is nothing more you can do, so you leave.

In that whole scenario, you have used your eyes, ears, and nose to glean information, and your brain has been busy sorting, cross-referencing, analysing, and triggering decision-making, all while navigating a busy street of cars and people. Pretty impressive! Your brain made an emotional and social decision about empathy, social responsibility, cause and effect, and weighed them against necessity and social behaviour. A huge amount of data was drawn from various

119

5. Interpretation

'sensors' in your body, and was processed and interpreted to come to a conclusion that made sense.

Later, you read in the paper that an old lady in the last stages of untreated cancer, who had fallen through the social safety net, had died on the street. It was that lady. You read an emotional report about how she could not afford treatment and had turned to alcohol to treat the pain. But her ageing heart could not deal with the strain of the cancer and the alcohol. She died alone, in pain, and in a puddle of her own urine on a busy street. Your brain processes again and reconsiders its initial conclusions. You ponder of what you would have done if you had known, and you question what you actually did. That is all normal for everyday occurrences.

This might all seem a bit long-winded and irrelevant to tarot reading, but it has everything to do with it. Here is why.

Tarot is about people's stories, and how we approach those stories. However, when you use a tarot deck, while you can 'see' present, past and future, unlike the scenario with the old lady on the street, you do not have eyes, ears, a nose, or a complex processing brain to sift through all the incoming data. Your brain only has seventy-eight images that convey a limited meaning.

And that is how all 'inner sight' works: when you have a vision of the future you are seeing only snapshots of a situation. Look at it this way. Imagine a wall between you and the event with the old lady. That wall has a few holes in it, and you can look through those small holes, but they only show you sections of the event unfolding. You cannot touch, smell, feel, or hear; you can only see. That is how psychic ability works, and is also how tarot divination works.

But you *can* open more holes in that wall using tarot. That is what makes card divination—a skill you can train—so much more useful than simply relying on your natural psychic inner sight. Inner sight gives you a snapshot of an event, but tarot can then open up exploratory avenues to glean more information. Once you have a blurry snapshot, say, the lady in the street event, then you can focus that picture by asking key questions and using specific layouts to give you more information.

You can ask: "will the lady will be okay if I do not help?" *No*. You can ask: "is the lady ill?" *Yes*. You can then ask, "is she dying?" *Yes*. Then you can ask, "would it benefit her if you went and sat with her as she died?" *Yes*. Obviously you cannot do a set of tarot readings in the street in the middle of a situation, but hopefully you get the point I am trying to make: properly approached, tarot can give you quite detailed information.

As you become more experienced in doing readings, or having flash insights or visions, you will learn how to interpret what you are seeing by using your past divination experiences as well as logic, assessment, and the rule of thumb that probably the simplest explanation is the right one. It is much easier to do this for others' stories, as you are not so emotionally invested in the outcome of their readings; but when you look at your story, common sense often goes out of the window. For example, where the cards say, "slow down, you will get sick—maybe a light infection" your emotional brain sees "Plague! OMG we are all going to die!!" You get my point.

When people first turn to tarot it is new, uncharted territory, and generally they do not engage their hard-won assessment skills: emotion takes over. Understanding the process of tarot interpretation will disengage this emotive approach that serves no purpose, and will trigger the process of hooking the new skill into your already-developed assessment skills. In the chapter on interpreting layouts, we will look practically at sample readings and at different approaches

121

5. Interpretation

to interpretation, as well as at 'panic' interpretations and what can go wrong.

Record and learn

I dabbled with tarot reading when I was young in the 1970s, but there came a critical point where I really needed to learn properly. I asked out loud for help, and sure enough a few months later someone made a passing comment at me. They said, "cards are more complicated than you realize. If you really want to learn, then write down each important reading you do, and keep it. When the event happens that you were reading about, go back to your records and you will see what meaning the cards were trying to convey."

That was the best advice I could ever have been given, and I started to record my readings religiously. And sure enough, when the events I had spotted in readings happened, often they did not play out as I had expected: the cards were showing me meanings that were not in the little book of interpretations I had for reference; but they were parallel meanings. The cards were *always* spot on. What was deficient was my ability to interpret them.

I kept reading and recording, pondering, and taking notes for years. Slowly I built up a wider vocabulary as each card revealed its various meanings. Some cards seemed to have meanings that were specific to me as a reader. Gradually the cards and I found a good way to communicate. Still, over forty years later, it is an ongoing process, particularly as I now design my own decks that do not follow the traditional tarot format. It is like meeting new friends and slowly getting to know them as deeper layers of their personalities gradually reveal themselves.

I advise you to get a notebook and write down and/or photograph each important reading. Take a note of the date you did the reading, and most importantly record the *exact* question you asked, not just a summary of it. Also record your interpretation. Once the events kick off, go back and look carefully. Take time to ponder each card, and compare the reading with how events actually unfolded. This will teach you far more than any online course on tarot ever could.

How to construct a useful question

The first stumbling block for successful interpretations of tarot is poorly constructed questions. If a question is open-ended and vague then the reading will be similarly open-ended and vague.

When someone asks us a question, lots of extra processing happens that allows us to understand what they really mean, which makes it easier for us to give a meaningful answer. Just as in the scenario we looked at above, the brain is an astonishing tool and will fill in gaps for us. It can tease meaning out of a jumble of input, and use experience and logic to come to a final conclusion.

When you use card divination, all that goes out the window. We are back to a limited vocabulary and the limitations of the question. For anyone who has asked questions of an AI, you will immediately understand what I mean.

Here is an analogy. Imagine that a precious ring has been dropped into a small pond, and you need help to retrieve it. If you say to someone, "something precious is in the pond, please get it for me," and you give them no further details, then the person goes off to the pond, rolls up their sleeve, and starts rummaging around. The pond is muddy so they cannot see, and they have to go by a sense of touch. They do not know what you have lost, whether it is big or small, hard or soft, and before long they are thinking "what do I consider precious?" The helper decides it must be something like a wallet. They plunge their hand into the dark water and start feeling about, stirring up the sediment as they search for something that feels like a wallet. They can feel rocks, pebbles, leaves, clumps of mud, little things, and big things, but nothing wallet-sized. After a while they give up.

If you had instead said to them, "I have dropped a ring in the pond, can you get it for me?" then immediately they would have focused on feeling out a small ring shape. As they reached their hand into the muddy pool, they would carefully sift through the bottom of the pond, feeling their way for small round things. The helper understands that they need to be delicate and careful. They gently scoop up handfuls of the mud from the bottom of the pond, put them on the ground, and look through them. Eventually they find your ring.

It is just the same with tarot. What or who you are working with to get answers needs clear, focused questions. We will get to the what/who issue later: for now, we will look at how questions are structured. We will look at the common mistakes made when asking questions, solve the mistake by discerning what the questioner actually wants to know, and then work out what the question should actually be.

Analysis of question construction

Wrong question: "Show me my life in general."

What do they actually want to know? Their whole life? Their relationships? Work? Self-development? Events? Let's say that the person wants to know the major events in their life over the next year.

Correct question: "Show me the major events that will potentially happen to me in the next twelve months."

The original question was too open-ended and would prompt a reading showing the rest of the questioner's life. The correct question gives a time limitation and a subject focus. It asks for major events—often the things that rattle us most, which we need to be prepared for, are the unexpected events. Getting an overview first, with a good layout, will indicate not only the events, but whereabouts in our life that event will play out: work, relationship, health...Once you have identified what area of your life it will affect, then you can do further focused readings to get more information. The question also uses the word 'potentially.' That sweeps in not only events that are fixed in fate and are about to play out, but events that *potentially* will happen *if we continue our daily life as we currently intend.* If we get enough warning in time, we can change those potential events. We will compare potential and fixed fate later in this chapter.

Wrong question: "Am I sick?"

What they actually want to know is whether they have cancer (or some other disease that is worrying them).

Correct question: "Will I have an active cancer illness in my body in the next twelve months?"

Again the question was too open-ended, and additionally it specified a timing of here and now. The person is stressed because they suspect they may have cancer, and they need a clear answer so that can decide how to act. But they could also be incubating a cold or minor infection, and the answer would still come back as "yes, you are sick." Because they asked the question about the immediate present, the answer will only account for the immediate present, not two months ahead, for example. Sometimes we get instincts that something is going wrong, but we could be picking up on something months away. The correct question asks about the specific illness the person is worried about, and defines "active illness": cancer is a weird set of different diseases, all which have cell proliferation as

125

their basis. There are probably many times in our bodies that such cell proliferation starts, and it is almost immediately squished by our body's defence system. The term "active illness" in the reader's mind defines what we consider to the be the illness of cancer: active cancer cell proliferation that will make us ill.

Wrong question: "Does he/she love me?"

What the person really wants to know is whether their partner will stay with them.

Correct question: "Will my partner still be in a relationship with me—or living with me—in twelve months' time?"

Now even this is a loaded question, as love is not always the reason why a relationship works, or why people stay together. And it also leaves the door open as to what kind of love is intended. As the questioner really wants to know whether their partner will stay with them, love should not really be part of the question: you can love someone but not want to be in a relationship with them. The correct question is time limited, as relationships rarely last a lifetime: the original question was too open-ended time-wise.

Some points to think about

To construct a good question to give you the information you need, think about these points:

1. Include a sensible timeframe that is not overly long or open-ended so that the really pertinent information can be focused on.

2. Think about the *core* of the situation and ask about that: don't get trapped asking about peripheral details.

3. Think about what, within the proposed situation, you really need to know.

4. Use a layout that will give you the information you need. If you need a yes or no answer, choose a simple layout that will provide that. If you need an overview, or need to find the root of a situation, use a layout with positions that show different aspects of your life: home, work, health, and so one.

5. If a reading throws up more questions than it answers, go through a filter process again to decide your next question. Again, focus on what you need to know.

Timing and time limits

We have already looked at the folly of asking open-ended questions without time limits. Indeed, as far as the tarot is concerned, 'now' is a fleeting second: so if you ask about something happening 'now,' you will likely not get an accurate answer. Instead, specify the timeframe you need information about: today, the next three hours, the next week, etc.

When you do a lot of short-term readings, sometimes small but difficult events can present as disaster cards, and this can terrify an inexperienced reader. The more readings you do on a subject, the narrower your focus will become, and the more likely you will find powerful cards representing small but uncomfortable events. If this happens to you, it pays well to widen the timeframe out by a few months. Most of the time, the 'disaster' will reduce to minor difficult cards or vanish completely.

There is another interesting dynamic with divination and timing that I have noticed over the years: divination will often throw up the next big event no matter what timeframe you specify. For example,

5. Interpretation

say you do a general life reading for the next twelve months, and a powerful card turns up. If nothing of any real note is fated to happen in your life over the next twelve months, but in two years there is going to be a major change for you, then that powerful card may relate to it, even though it falls outside the reading's scope.

This can understandably be confusing, but eventually I figured out that you can pin down what is happening with careful follow-up readings. Here is an example:

A twelve month general overview reading has The Tower in a position that means 'future path'. This could mean that the Tower is active within the next twelve months *or beyond*. The next step would be to do a reading using a layout that sections out different aspects of life: relationships, work, health, resources, home, and so forth. The Ten of Swords falls in the 'home' position. The Ten of Swords has a similar meaning to the Tower, and the rest of the reading looks fine. So the home is the area where the trouble will strike.

The next step is to do a yes/no reading with a suitable layout. The question is asked: "will this Tower strike in the home in the next twelve months?" The answer is the Four of Coins. That means 'no': in this context, a disaster card would be a yes. Now you need to pinpoint which year, then what month, this disaster is likely to strike. You use a 'year timing' layout to look at the next four years. You deal the four cards. The Devil card falls in year two. The rest are benign cards. So the problem comes in year two. The next step is to do a twelve month reading, using twelve cards, for that year to see which month it appears in. If the fate pattern is already set in place (fate patterns are discussed below) then you can pinpoint the exact month. If the pattern has not set in place, you may turn up two or three potential troublesome months. Then you can note those troublesome months down. This is the tarot equivalent of making more holes in a wall so you can see more.

Now you can push further, to see the nature of the trouble. Again, if the fate pattern is locked in place, it will be easier to figure out what the exact problem will be. If it hasn't locked in place then it will be more difficult to get a fix on the exact nature of the problem. This is done by a layout that looks at causation, with one position each for various potential disasters: theft, home intrusion, fire, natural calamity, etc. It also includes benign positions to create a balance in the reading. (All these layout approaches can be found in the layout chapter.)

A quick example of this was with a family member who got a strong instinct something bad was going to happen in their house. She did readings and it pinpointed a home invasion. So she got extra locks and bolts for the doors, checked the windows, and so forth. All seemed good, but the warning kept appearing in readings. A week later she got locked out of her house without a key, so she went around the back. She always kept a high kitchen window open, as she assumed it would be too high and too small for anyone to get in. But she had forgotten that she had a ladder propped against the back of the house. She was in the house within five minutes. The reading was right: the house was not as secure as she thought. So that was immediately remedied, and the warning vanished from the readings.

Sometimes the weak spot that allows something bad to happen can be as simple as that, and it is often a simple fix to remedy it. And that takes me to the next subject in this chapter: fate cycles. Understanding fate cycles and how they work can go a long way to helping a reader really use tarot properly. Although this tends to be a subject that only esotericists and magicians make use of, I think it is valuable information for any tarot reader.

5. Interpretation

Fate patterns and cycles

Fate is a complex subject, and even the best magician among us can never really get a full grasp of its complexity and reach. However, magicians have worked with fate patterns for millennia, and as such are a well placed to understand their basic dynamics.

A fate pattern forms in response to an action. Its reach can be long, complicated, and vast, or it can be short and simple. A fate pattern can form, reform, branch out, and connect with other fate patterns. Within that fate pattern there are often junctions of time and event that create what I call a hotspot: a convergence of energy and potential than can 'out' itself in a major event or change.

Fate patterns mostly appear to be organic and changeable as opposed to fixed runways, until a fate pattern has locked itself in place. Once that happens, the pattern of event behaviour is pretty much unchangeable. This can happen years before an event, or an hour before. Even so, there is always personal choice, even with a totally fixed fate path: how you act and react decides *how* you get to a certain point in fate, the easy way or the hard way.

I have also found, after years of working as a magician and a card reader, that people often appear to have one overarching fate path through life, but within that are many fate patterns that constantly shift and change according to the actions and choices of the person. So fate gives the runway of life from A to B, but how they get to B is more changeable.

When we do tarot readings for divination, we are basically looking at these fate patterns and their potential hotspots. It can show us the small roads that are short cuts, the dead ends, the potential potholes and bumps in the road, and the different choices of route we might take. Then we can make informed choices: within our fate pattern we decide what is triggered and what isn't. Such decisions often change a fate pattern dramatically.

One thing I have learned through direct experience with divination and fate patterns is that it is unwise to try and avoid every single bump in the road. Knocks, disappointments, and little disasters often serve a purpose not only for our fate, but also to strengthen and mature us, just as an immature immune system evolves from having to deal with minor bugs. Some big bumps on the road are worth the hassle, and some are best avoided.

As a tarot reader you can get a sense of which ones to avoid and which ones to grit your teeth and get through. This is done by stretching the timing of a reading. If you see a potential disaster in the short-term future, you can do a second reading to ask, "if I do not avoid this, what will be the long-term consequences for me over a five (or ten) year period?" If the longer-term outcome is good, then it is possibly best to go through the disaster—and now you are forewarned, you can plan to survive it in the best possible way. You can also look, for comparison, at the same long-term outcome if you do everything within your power to avoid the situation. If that outcome is better, then it may be worth dodging it. But always make sure in the question that you state everything *within your power* and that you are willing to do that. Then you will have to use readings to look at what you can do to ameliorate the effects of the event.

Some bullets you cannot dodge, no matter what you try, and when that becomes clear in a reading, at least you have been forewarned and can cushion the blow and be as proactive as possible. That way you will survive it intact and will draw the best possible fate path out of it. Currently (2020) we are going through the Covid-19 pandemic. I started to get a 'heads up' in 2019 that something big and bad was coming that I had to prepare for. No matter how many ways I looked at it, and no matter what aversion actions I read for, it was still there. What became clear from readings was that I had to make sure I had a three-month supply of food and necessities, a good stock of medicinal herbs, and lots of bleach.

I presumed it was the UK Brexit disaster looming on the horizon, as we would lose not only access to some foods, but to also medicines. There was also discussion in the news about potential issues with clean water etc. if we crashed out of Europe without a deal. But it was the pandemic. So always keep in mind that you may not pin down exactly what disaster is coming, but you can pin down what you need to do to prepare and survive it intact. The key to any disaster reading is to approach it calmly and with minimum emotion, which brings me to the next subject that is so important in tarot reading: emotions.

Emotions and interpretations

Emotions are a vital part of our make-up and are what help us survive as a species. But there are times when they can get in the way of things, such as if you were in a dangerous job or were a surgeon. Emotions can also interfere with your magic. Divination is one of those areas of magic where emotion is counterproductive. If you react emotionally to a reading, you are far less likely to get a balanced, truthful interpretation. A tarot reader is also far more likely to attract parasitical beings that feed off emotional energy. These beings can cloud your judgement and at times push you to interpret badly, making you terrify yourself to give them more energetic food.

When we plunge ourselves in the unknown, we react emotionally. Tarot is ground zero for such reactions. We see the Tower and think it must always mean death and total destruction, whereas it could also mean the loss of a job that keeps you financed but is killing you slowly. By going through the Tower you are freed from a bad situation that you felt you could not escape; and after the dust has settled, a much better and healthier life option emerges.

Who is talking to you?

In the previous section on emotions I mentioned parasitical beings. These beings are well known to magicians, and it is best to avoid them as much as possible. And this throws up a question that I am often asked about tarot: what is speaking to you through the vocabulary of tarot?

There is no easy answer to that question, as there are many different answers, all which are valid. Tarot is a window, and what speaks to you through that window can vary a lot depending on who you are, what you are doing, how you are doing it, and why.

The Self

One of the core lines of communication in tarot comes from your subconscious,. speaking to you through the medium of tarot. This is usually the first voice that emerges in a beginner tarot reader. The subconscious mind takes in a lot of information that our conscious mind is not aware of, and that information can be sifted through and organized to become a well of information that guides us. The tarot simply provides a vocabulary and external interface so that such communication can happen.

Then there is the deeper self, beyond the subconscious, the timeless soul, the real you. One of the stages in magical training is to learn to connect, and communicate, with that deeper self. This is the 'you' that decided to come into this life, and the you that will survive your death in this life.

5. INTERPRETATION

It is not a part of you that you can hold a conversation with, as it is too remote, unlike your subconscious mind, which is more than happy to step in and chat with you through an externalized form. But that deeper self tends not to emerge for everyday readings; rather it emerges when you engage a powerful magical or mystical life path, when you are in mortal danger, or when you have to make critical choices that will affect the rest of your life.

Now let us look briefly at the more esoteric side of what can speak to you through a reading. This section is more for magicians, but it will give other tarot readers something to think about.

Esoteric voices

When you are a magician, often the reach of your consciousness goes far beyond everyday life. This makes you pretty visible to lots of other types of consciousnesses who may have their own agendas. This is something, as a magician, to be aware of and to keep an eye out for.

This book is not the place to go into detail on this issue, and we cannot discuss esoteric meanings, reasons, and details in a few short paragraphs. So for magicians reading this, I have just outlined as briefly as possible some of the more frequent 'reading invasion' types that happen. You can look further into the possibilities for yourself.

Sometimes beings will manipulate not only the reading itself—what cards come out—but also how you interpret those cards: literally, they can mess with your head. After that had happened a few times to me with important magical readings, and I did not trust what had come out of the reading, I thought sideways, and decided to do a yes/no reading, focusing on asking the question "is this reading true?" to my deepest self. The answer that came back was "no." As I suspected, something was manipulating my readings to push me to act in a certain way.

I had not heard or read anywhere else in magical texts about such a situation, and I was pretty young at the time, so I asked a much older magician whom I trusted. She nodded and said, "yeah, that can happen: you have to really be careful with some readings, and focus intently on whom you are asking." At that point in time, I had not even thought about focusing on whom I was asking; I just focused on the question.

As a result of that experience and conversation, I decided that when I had to do important magical readings, I would ask the one collective I knew I could trust: the Inner Library.

The Inner Library

The Inner Library is a term that magicians use for a collective consciousness of knowledge and experience within humanity that spans millennia. Often worked with in vision, it is the sum total of the knowledge of many individuals whose knowledge was jettisoned upon their deaths. Over time, humanity has collectively envisioned this collection of knowledge as a Library. I have also found that future knowledge often first appears in this pattern before it appears in the physical world.

Magicians tap into the Library intentionally to learn—and also deposit—knowledge. In some cultures the Library appears as a forest, to others as a single book, to some as a library, and to other cultures as a collective of 'people' who advise. It has become clear to me, over many years of working with this interface, that how it presents is based heavily on how we imagine knowledge is stored. There is a big, deep rabbit hole that magicians can explore with this pattern, not only to work with it, but also to investigate what it 'actually' is, why it is, and what its potentials are.

5. INTERPRETATION

Many people do not interact intentionally with this non-physical structure, but tap into it naturally. When you have worked with the Library for a few years, you will start to see the classic signs of its interactions with those who naturally connect with it, as it informs their work. Nikola Tesla is one famous scientist that I feel strongly was connecting with the Inner Library without realising. He would dream and wake up with a fully-formed concept or idea, and not need to go through the usual processes in order to glean the information he needed. Stravinsky, as a composer, did exactly the same thing. To a magician, this is a classic sign of someone tapping into the Inner Library in their dreams.

Sometimes when doing readings, particularly if the reading is about a critical event or critical learning, the reader can connect unknowingly with the Inner Library, and that communion of information is interfaced through the card vocabulary. Such readings certainly have a distinctive feel to them, and are for the most part highly accurate and to the point.

Parasites and reading hygiene

Parasites are the biggest problem of all in readings. Parasites are non-physical beings who exist by living off the energetic vital force of living physical creatures. They are not weird and wonderful, or some strange alien force; they are an ordinary part of normal life, and are everywhere, like fleas or ticks. If you know the basics about them, then like avoiding ticks, you can navigate your way through readings without too much interference from them. Just be warned that readings can be like feeding stations for them: when you do a reading, you become energetically visible. It is like walking through long grass or a forest with bare legs: you will pick up a tick or insect bite if you don't use your common sense.

Parasites are drawn in by emotion—one of the many reasons that emotions should be kept in check when doing divination readings. If you do a reading and it shows something bad, most readers will have an immediate emotional reaction. If they do not immediately reel that reaction in, but start doing emotionally driven, obsessive readings to get more information, then they will be at high risk of a parasite feeding frenzy. The reader will be manipulated emotionally to interpret the worst of the reading in the worst possible light. This drives their emotions deeper and deeper, which causes more feeding. The same is true of any sort of reading that elicits an emotional response: relationships, jobs, security, health...If the infestation gets bad enough, the readings themselves will be 'untruthful,' because what cards come out will be manipulated by the parasites to get you to panic.

This is a common hazard with readings, and one that magicians and readers in general need to get to grips with early on in their reading practice. The way to do this is fairly simple, but takes discipline. Here are some simple methods for limiting or eliminating such infestations from your readings:

- If a situation that you are reading for is too close to home or too much of an emotional subject matter for you to be clear about, get someone else to do the reading for you.

- Keep emotions in check. Your questions, shuffling, and interpretations need to be done from a place of calm and logic, not emotion and panic.

- Do not over-read on a subject that you are heavily emotionally invested in. Work out carefully what you really need to know, and what can be left to fate. Don't keep repeating the same questions to get a better answer!

- When you have done a reading, particularly a potentially emotional one, get a bag of dry salt—ordinary fine-grain cooking salt. Put your cards in, and give them a good shake. Then wash your hands with liquid soap, salt, and water. Salt breaks energetic connections and the energetic dirt that builds up on hands from doing readings. I wash my hands after each reading session, and always salt clean my deck after a difficult reading.

- If you are a commercial reader, wash your hands and smudge your deck after each client. Salt shaking is best; frankincense smoke is second best.

- Do not fall into the trap, as a commercial reader, of doing too many readings for a client. Often such clients are obsessive and overemotional and they will likely be heavily parasited. Their infestations can transfer to you, if you are not careful.

Common sense is the key to a lot of reading problems. In terms of energetic hygiene, apply the principles of everyday hygiene to your reading work. If you shake hands with a lot of people, you are going to need to wash them. If you have a job cleaning drains, then you need to wash well after each job. Doing readings for other people is like cleaning drains: really you are plunging your hands, mind, and energy into the murky water of people's energetic and emotional lives.

Responsibilities when reading for others

When you read for others, commercially or otherwise, there are some simple principles of responsibility that you need to think about, not only for the person you are reading for, but also for your energetic health and wellbeing, to keep you safe from getting stuck in other people's fate patterns. Many commercial readers have their own set of principles and develop a good awareness of personal responsibility.

But for those who do not have that, or have not thought about it, here are some pointers:

- Truthfulness. If you don't understand a reading then say so. Don't make shit up. No one is 100% on the ball with readings all the time, and sometimes a situation being read about can turn out to be far more complicated than you realize. This can cause incomprehensible readings, not only because the subject is too complex to cover in one reading, but also because often the client is asking the wrong question. With care and insight, once you admit you have no idea what the reading is about, you can then explore further to get a better fix on what is happening. This process cannot happen if you just make shit up.

- Do not make decisions for others based on the outcome of a reading. Your job as a reader is to present what you have seen, not what they should do. You can make decisions for yourself based on your readings, but not for others. Allowing someone to put that responsibility onto you can entangle you in their fate mess: your energy can get sucked into working on their fate pattern. This is one of the many reasons why commercial readers get chronic fatigue: another is being parasited.

- If people do not want to know the future or cannot face it, then do not read for them. Some people in the past have come to me for a reading, then promptly said, "I don't know if I want to know." In those cases I always used to put down the deck and refuse to continue the reading. If people want to know something, then they have to take responsibility for it.

- Don't do readings about other people you know unless there is a seriously good reason for it. Respecting people's privacy is important with tarot. Tarot readings can easily tip into spying or invading someone's privacy, so they should not be used to look at an individual without a really good cause. When it comes to your family, use common sense: if there is a potential emergency, then use it. When there is not, then do not spy on your family. And the same goes for readings about other people: divination can have all sorts of consequences both energetically and in life dynamics, so tread ethically and sensibly.

- Don't read for couples with both parties present: uncomfortable truths can come out, such as hidden affairs, that can seriously damage a relationship.

- When you need to practise you can use public figures. They, by nature of their job, have chosen to put their life out in the public eye. You can do readings about them, and in hindsight you will discover whether you were right about what the cards were telling you.

Reading about death

Many times a reader will be asked whether a person will die. Of course they will die at some point; it is just a matter of how and when. Ninety-nine percent of the time, such questions are unnecessary and should not be indulged, for your psychic health as well as theirs.

Looking at a potential death with tarot is not as simple and straightforward as many people think, as there are so many variables not only with fate, but also with the vocabulary. The death card most certainly does not always mean death; conversely, in most actual death readings the death card does not appear. So this is not something for a casual reader or a beginner to take on; rather it is something for readers with a lot of experience in working with their card vocabulary and/or who are highly psychic. Even then, a massive irreversible change in someone's life can look at first glance like a death reading, so it pays to be cautious and thorough in how you approach it.

If someone is clear that they think an impending death is a real risk due to sickness, and they want to see if there are ways to avoid it, then that is fine. Just be aware that such readings can be complex, and you will need to tread carefully when exploring the various possible avenues. Sometimes you will see potential paths that may steer the person away from such a threat, or where the threat will draw near as a potential but will not manifest as an outcome, in which case you advise accordingly.

If it seems that death is a clear and active potential, then you can, without emotion, look at timelines. I did that for my mother, who was dying of cancer. I managed to track which month her death was most likely to happen—and bear in mind that such timelines can change, so you need to keep an eye on them. Giving her a timeline gave her enough information to know when to get things in order, and to plan her time appropriately. She died on the last week of the month that looked to have the most potential for her death.

In my late thirties I did quite a lot of magical work with people who were very sick, and I would track their progress with readings. One thing became apparent over and over again: not all death readings present with the death card, or even a death pattern.

A few times, when I was working with coma patients—trying to reach them in vision, which often worked quite well—their death reading would describe them suddenly becoming healthy, happy, balanced, and regenerated. At first I thought I had just done a poor reading and would redo it, but the same description persisted. By the time this happened a few times, I realized something different was going on. The reading was showing me how they were going to be *after* their death. This was a common occurrence when I was reading for

5. Interpretation

people who were in comas, or in late stages of cancer. Such readings only happened when there was absolutely no chance that they would survive, which is what confused me so much at the beginning. By coming to terms with their own mortality, the transition from physical life to non-physical life was smoother and far more regenerative. This was reflected in the readings as birth and regeneration.

To conclude, no matter how skilled you are, or how much of a beginner you are, tarot is a skill that truly takes a lifetime. You never really master it, because as soon as you think you have, another layer of learning starts. The real key to mastering tarot is to approach it as a work in progress, and to keep reading: practice makes the road towards perfection!

> The Lord whose is the oracle of Delphi neither utters nor hides his meaning, but shows it by a sign.
> And the Sibyl, with raving lips uttering things mirthless, unbedizened and unperfumed, reaches over a thousand years with her voice, thanks to the god in her.
>
> — Heraclitus[1]

---

[1] Russell 2004 [1946], p. 70.

Chapter Six

Layouts

Fifty percent of the success of a strong, accurate reading comes down to a good functional layout whose positions are specific to aspects of the question you are wishing to pose. Most good, experienced readers end up developing their own layouts that work well with the types of questions that reader needs to ask.

In this chapter we will look at various different layouts. Deeper explanations of each layout, and examples of how they work and how they are interpreted, can be found in the interpretation of layouts chapter.

What makes a good layout?

The key to an accurate, stable layout is its underlying pattern. What do I mean by this? Card divination is an aspect of magic, and magic works by connecting with energetic patterns that energy, potential, and information can flow through in a stable and generally predictable way.

When you ask a question of the cards and begin shuffling them, and you keep in mind what layout you are using, the energetic patterns start to form like highways that information can flow along. The positions of a layout really have two layers: two patterns. One is the energetic pattern, and the other comprises the 'home' positions—

6. Layouts

layout positions—for specific aspects of life: family, work, health, evolution of self, past, present, future, and so forth.

A reading layout, whether mundane or magical should have positions which interrelate, which slowly teach the reader cause and effect, and which teach how some fate patterns unfold. Remember, tarot—and indeed any card divination—looks at fate probabilities. The more complex the layout, the more all of its positions should harmoniously interconnect.

For example, in the Overview layout in the mundane section below, the first position is family. This is where we come from, and is what affects us deeply, whether we realize it or not. The seventh position, which is placed beneath the first, is conflicts. Now, how we relate to each other is often the source of conflicts, so the two positions can often be read together to gain more understanding not only of the nature of the conflict, but also about *our programmed response to that conflict*. By adulthood we have a programmed set of responses that we learned from the adults around us when we are children. It can take many years to become aware of the nature and sources of our responses, and then to adapt in order to change them.

A simple reading pattern can be used for mundane, simple questions, but when the reader wishes to delve into the more serious questions involving magic, fate, and how fate can play out over time, then the more complex patterns are needed to facilitate the flow of information. It is a bit like electric circuitry.

The energetic and positional pattern enables a coherent flow of information, and enables the magical 'opening' of the highways for information to pass along—you need to build a road for the vehicle to drive along.

Though in the last few decades tarot has passed into popular culture, much of the knowledge required to work with it successfully has fallen by the wayside. People toss out a card a day, or three cards, without any real focused intent—sometimes this works, a lot of the time it doesn't. The success of such 'readings' lies purely with the individual, and mostly they are pointless anyway, as they do not give enough information. It becomes a habit, like brushing your teeth, and is more about the person's needs than actual divination. There is nothing wrong with such a way of working with tarot cards, and a lot of people do it, but if you really want or need to use divination for an actual reason, or get information, then a smarter approach is necessary.

In this chapter we will look at a wide variety of layouts. Some are for mundane questions, some are for more esoteric, magical questions, and some are secondary layouts to pinpoint an event or to extract more information. In the interpretation of layouts chapter, we will look at these layouts in action and interpretation methods for them.

Mundane layouts

Mundane layouts are useful for ordinary, everyday life events. You can use them to get an overview of your next twelve months, for a yes/no answer, to find a missing object, to pinpoint the timing of an event, to check your available resources, and so forth. Magicians can also use them to look at the specifics of an event.

6. LAYOUTS

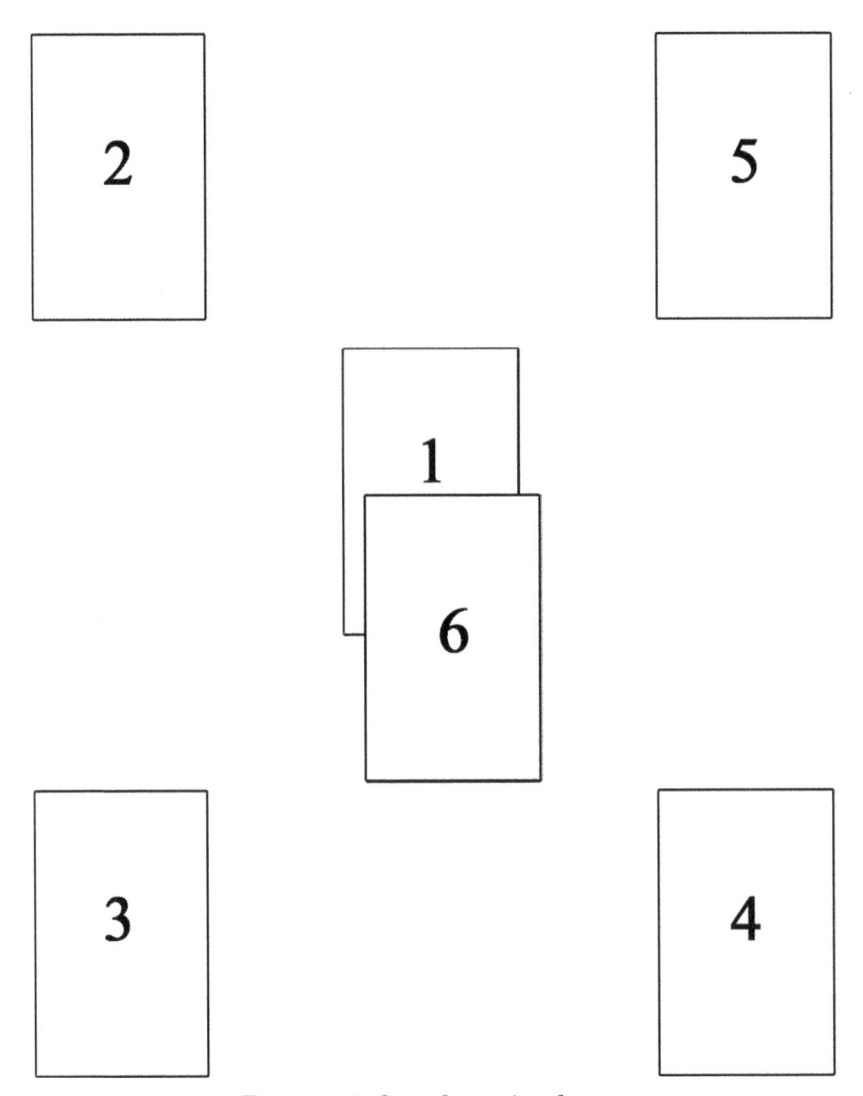

Figure 6.1: Simple yes/no layout

A simple yes/no layout

This layout is good if you need a simple, straightforward answer. However, because it is a focused layout, your question needs to be equally focused, and not vague in any way. For help forming a focused question, see the interpretation chapter.

1. What the question is about.

2. The relevant past: what is in the past that led up to the event in question.

3. Difficulties to be overcome.

4. Help you are given.

5. The future outcome: what the answer will lead to.

6. The answer.

6. Layouts

Tree of Life layout

The Tree of Life layout is based on the dynamics of a Kabbalistic map of creation. It can be used esoterically, but it can also be used for mundane readings. It is a stable magical pattern with many layers, and for some who are learning magic, working with this map in a particularly mundane fashion can be useful. Because it is a map of creation, it can also be worked with for yes/no answers while giving details of how that answer comes about.

The following is a list of the meanings of its positions for a mundane reading. If you are using the layout for a yes/no reading, your answer falls in position number ten, and the rest of the reading tells you how that answer comes about.

1. What the story is about.

2. What positive or giving aspect helps form the story.

3. What is hidden or past that has bearing on the story.

4. What is necessary for the story to develop.

5. What is withheld from the story, or is being taken away.

6. The pivotal aspect or key of the story.

7. What needs discipline or limiting for success. This position is also governed by the emotions.

8. What needs relaxing to flow. This position is also governed by the mind.

9. The reason or dynamic behind the answer.

10. The answer.

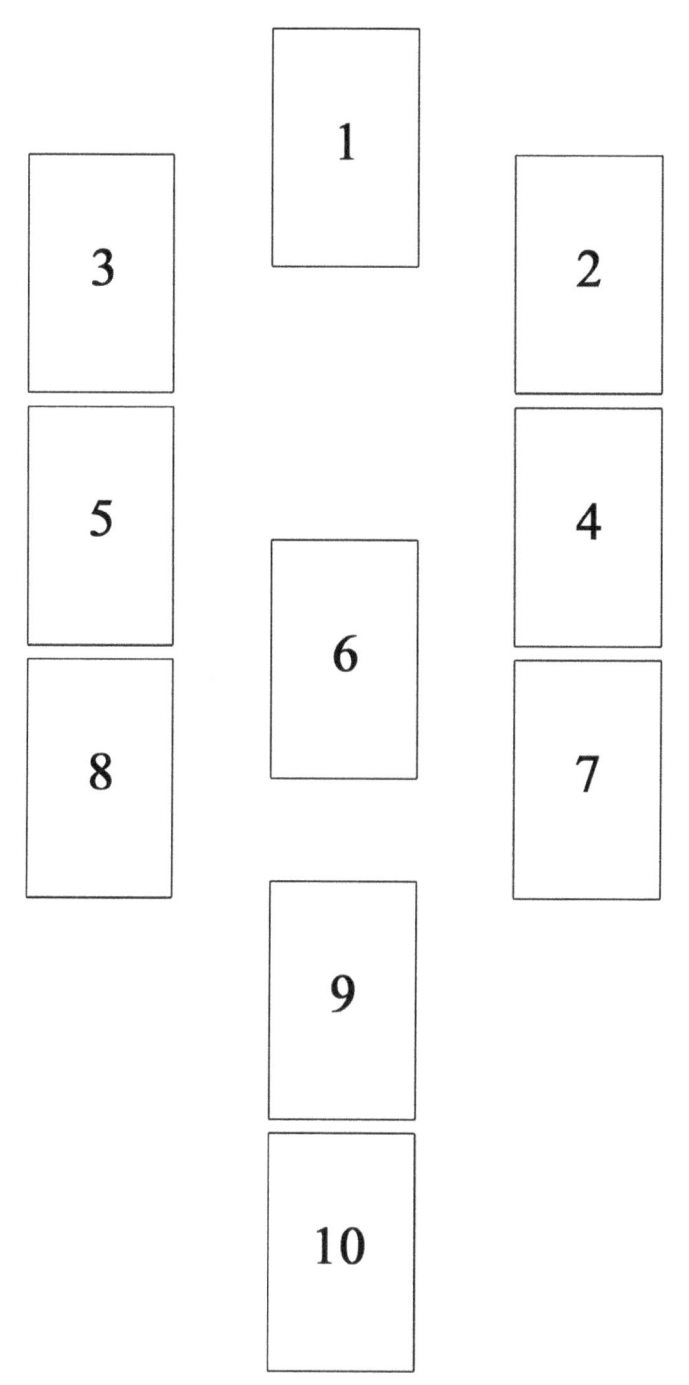

Figure 6.2: Tree of Life layout

6. Layouts

Overview layout

This layout is good if you want a general overview of a person's life over a set time, usually twelve months, but it can be used for any set time period.[1] It uses a lot of cards and has thirteen positions so that you can extract as much information as possible.

It can be simply used with the thirteen positions, or if you need a lot of information then you can use the split deck method.

The split deck method is where you separate out the Major Arcana cards from the minor ones. First you shuffle the major cards while asking your question, and lay them out in the thirteen positions. Then you take the minor cards, shuffle them while asking the same question, and lay them out in the same way, on top of the major cards, but leaving a bit of space so that you can see which major card is under each minor card.

The two cards in each position are read together. The major card is the cause/power behind the situation; the minor card is how that power will manifest. We will look at this closely in the interpretation of layouts chapter.

1. Home/family. This is your ground zero. It is your home, your close community that you identify with, your bloodline, and so forth.

2. Relationships. This is not just love relationships, but includes close friendships and important partners, for example a business partner.

3. Creativity. This position represents what is creatively most important for you. If you are a parent, it is usually your children.

---

[1]Check the first chapter on interpreting a reading for more information on timing and time limits.

Overview layout

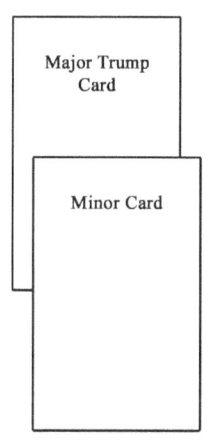

Figure 6.3: Using the split deck method: minor card on top of trump card.

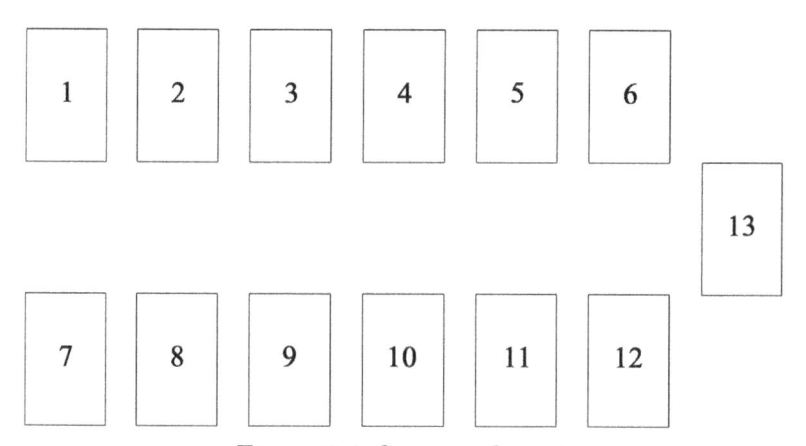

Figure 6.4: Overview layout.

151

6. Layouts

But it is also about what you create and have a passion for: art, computer coding, product design, gardening, dance, etc.

4. Current fate cycle. Fate is an ever-turning wheel. As we go through life, we go from one fate cycle to another. This position shows you what your current fate cycle is.

5. Health. This position shows your overall health for the time span of the reading.

6. Gifts. While fate can hammer us, it equally gives gifts. This position represents the help, resources, support, or protection that fate puts in your path to help you.

7. Conflicts. This position shows open conflicts, which could be personal, interpersonal, situational, or self-inflicted destructive behaviour: whatever is causing disturbance to your equilibrium.

8. Hidden Enemies. Sometimes our friends or colleagues smile to our face while stabbing us in the back. This position also shows hidden dangers: a fraying cable, an unseen danger, and so forth. It is the position of what you are not seeing that holds danger for you.

9. Grinder. This is the position for whatever adversity must not be avoided, but worked through to gain strength, wisdom, or success.

10. Resources. Resources is income, energy, food, etc. This position shows you an overview of your resources for the length of time of the reading—will you have what you need?

11. Unraveller. This position tells you what is your weak spot for the time allotted, and what needs to be identified and voluntarily let go, be it a habit, laziness, procrastination, or something that no longer serves a purpose in your life.

12. Taker. The Taker is a position that shows what will be taken from you for you to move forward on your fate path. It is not about voluntary release like the Unraveller: the Taker position shows what fate will take from your path, be it a relationship, a bad job, or something you are unhealthily clinging to.

13. The Road Ahead. This position shows the overall short-term future for the time span of the reading. It can also indicate the direction your fate is taking, including and beyond the reading's time limit.

Event layout

This layout is good for a forward view of how a particular event will play out. If the subject has triggered, or is intending to trigger, an event—leaving a job, moving house, separating from partner, etc.—then this layout will give insight into how it may play out, and how it will affect the person asking the question.

It can also be used to assess the likely outcome of a choice: how things will play out if some action is taken. This gives the person asking the question a chance to look at different potential choices, to see how each one could play out.

1. The current situation.

2. What is now past that contributed to the situation.

3. What triggered the current situation.

4. What the situation gives you.

5. What the situation takes from you.

6. How the situation will unfold.

7. The conclusion of the situation.

6. LAYOUTS

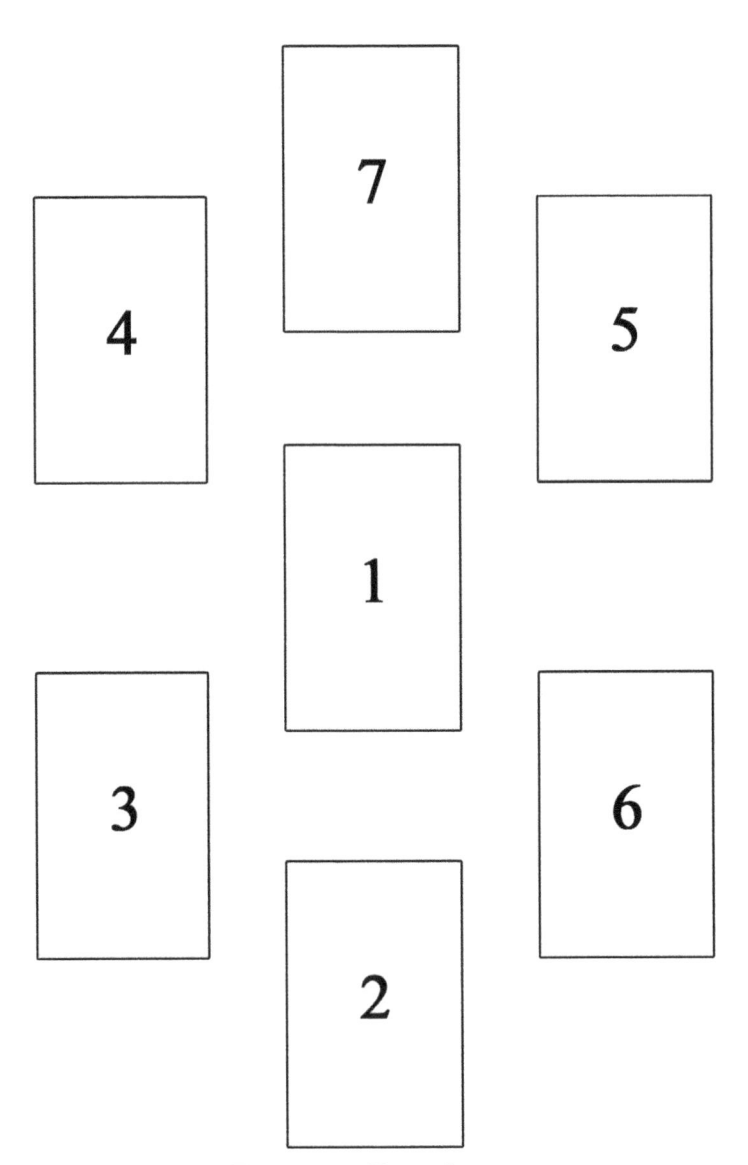

Figure 6.5: Event layout.

Event layout

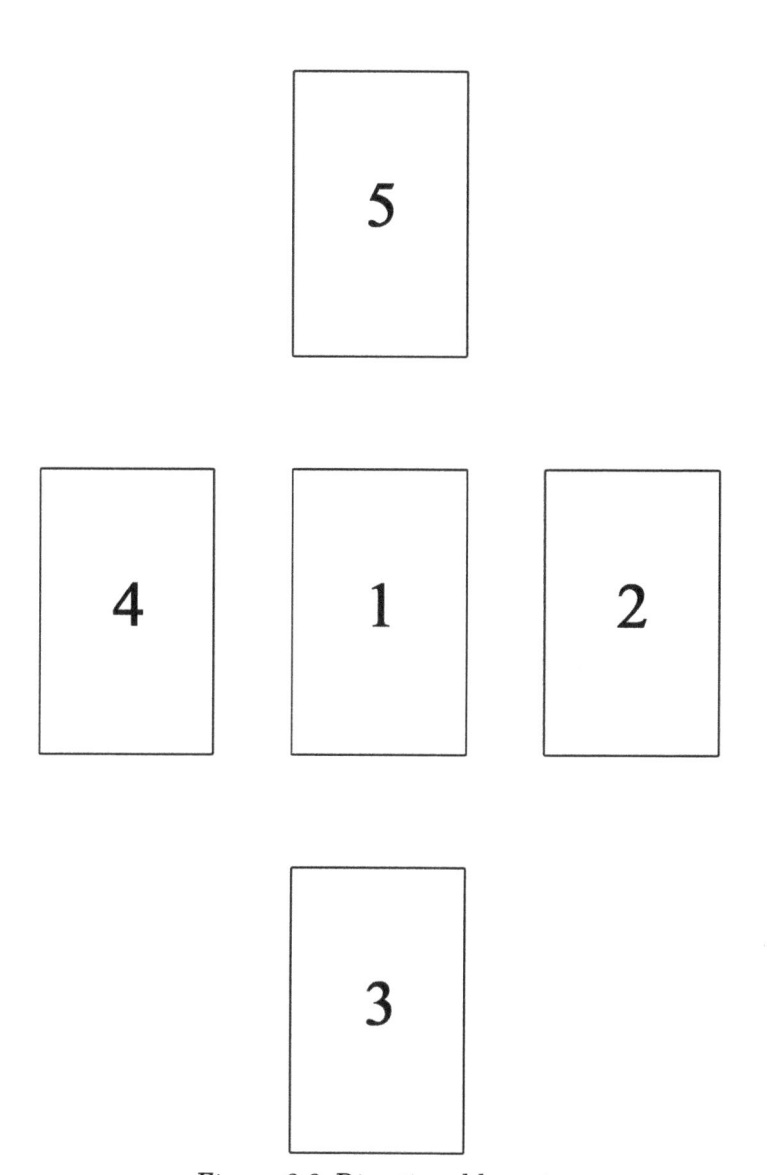

Figure 6.6: Directional layout.

6. Layouts

Directional / location layout

This layout is useful if you need to find something that has been lost. I have used it to locate lost children, pets, and keys, among other things. It is based around the compass directions, and can be used repeatedly to narrow down a search area. It can, however, be a laborious job to locate something in this way.

1. Centre

2. East

3. South

4. West

5. North

Have a map of the area you will search beside you. Divide the map up in your mind into the four directions, or draw out a simple grid. If the search is in a building, draw a map of the building and mark the approximate compass directions: east, south, west, north.

The question must not be vague, and must be to the point: something like "show me in which direction, within a radius of a hundred metres, I would successfully find my passport." You are looking for a success-type of card to show in the reading. If no success-type card appears, then widen your radius.

Assuming the reading indicates east, you would then take the area of the map that you defined as its eastern section, and repeat the process by dividing that section into the four directions, shortening your search radius accordingly. Keep going like that until you have a searchable area. Then search carefully. I once lost an iguana outside and used this process to find him. I got the radius down to twenty square feet, but I could not find him until I looked very carefully indeed: he had blended himself into a bush. So search carefully and thoroughly.

Resources layout

This layout looks at your outer and inner energetic resources. It is a useful tool when you are not sure where you should be focusing your energy, or if you feel that part of your life seems blocked or on hold. This can often come about if one aspect of your energetic resources is depleted or overstocked, or if one resource needs to be put on hold so that energy can support another inner resource currently in more critical need.

The layout reflects the magical principle of personal energetic resources. You have various 'pots' that hold inner energy that enable a resource to be accessible to you. Sometimes one 'pot' or the other has a more urgent need that you are not aware of, and trying to push against a limited resource can end up depleting you further.

The layout uses three columns in an arc. The left column is practical, the central column is your core self, and the right column is your spiritual, psychic, inner side. Your inner/spiritual energy for having or doing certain things shifts and changes all the time—it is like energetic weather that is personal to you. By using this layout you can see where your credits and deficits are, so that you can plan accordingly. Make sure you give your question a time span, e.g. "show me my inner and outer resources for the next three months." Remember, the longer the time span, the more general and less detailed the reading will be.

To help you interpret readings using this layout, some explanations and examples of resource readings are included in the interpretation of layouts chapter.

6. LAYOUTS

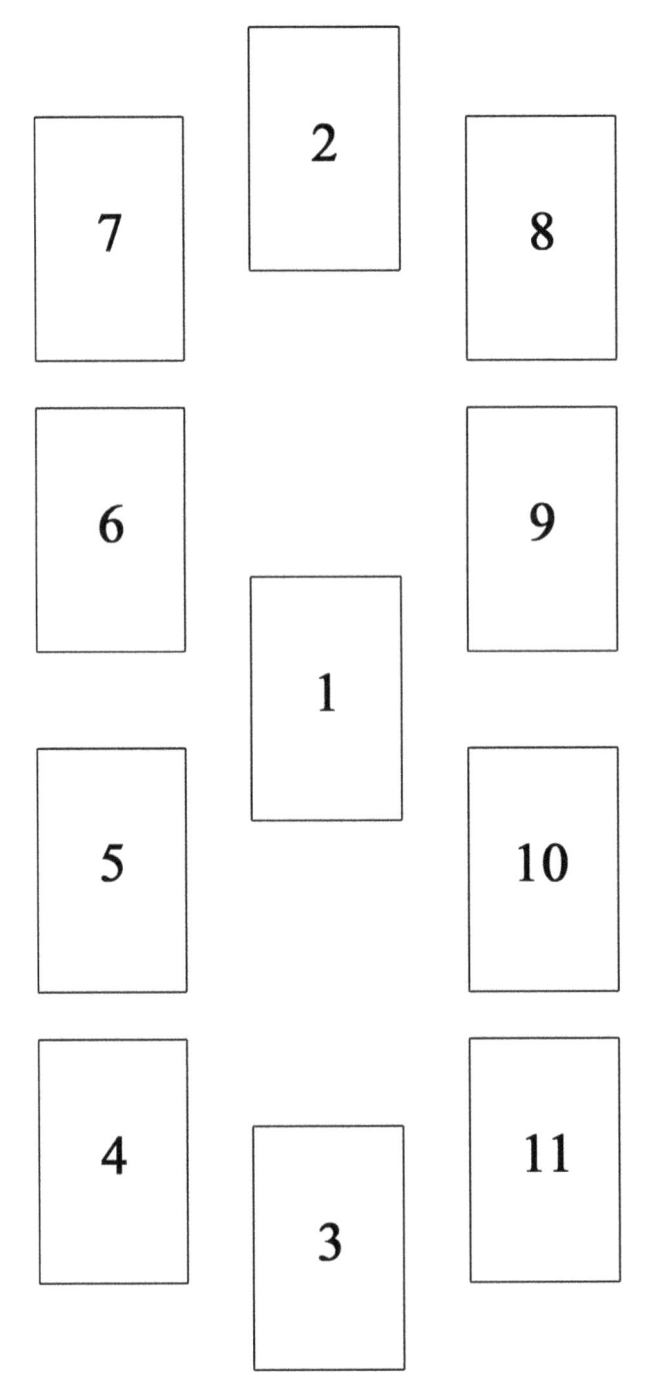

Figure 6.7: Resources layout.

1. Self. How your energetic resources are doing overall.

2. Balance. How balanced you are currently in terms of managing your energy resources.

3. Vital force. Your overarching life force: this ebbs and flows. It is your most important energetic resource.

4. Love and emotions. Emotional stability and love relationships.

5. Money, substance, and property. How your economic resources are doing.

6. Health. Your body's physical health.

7. Creativity. Your creative energy, which can include pregnancies.

8. Communication. Your energy to give and receive clear communications.

9. Intuition. Your energy to tap into your deeper intuition, dreams, and 'inner radar.'

10. Divination. Your energy for clear divination when seeing the future using a method like cards or runes.

11. Magic/mystical. Your energy for studying or doing magical things, or delving into the mystical side of life.

Secondary layouts

Secondary layouts are used a little differently than general reading layouts. In a general reading, each card in each position tells you something. In a secondary reading, only some of the cards and positions are relevant. You do not read the layout as a whole; rather you look for a specific type of card, and the position(s) that type of card land(s) in tells you more about the likely cause, manifestation, or timing of some event.

6. Layouts

Timing layout

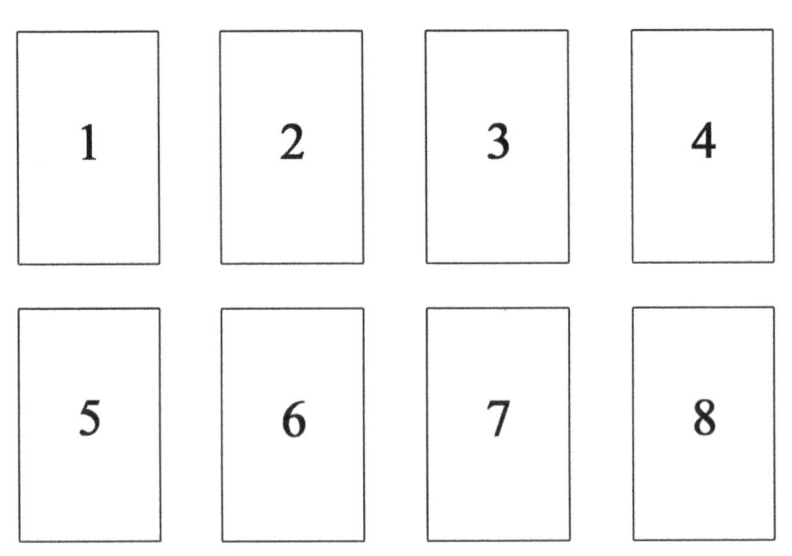

1	2	3	4
5	6	7	8

Figure 6.8: Timing layout.

This simple layout can identify an event's likely timing, or can look at the weeks or months when something may or may not be active. It can be stretched to look something years ahead, but the further away a potential event is, the less accurate it can be: fate can change. So when looking at weeks, it can be accurate, but when looking at years, it gets less accurate unless the fate event is already fixed. Some events are set in a fate pattern years ahead, while some only form a few weeks before an event.

I have recently used this layout to identify risky weeks for my local area during the Covid-19 virus pandemic, and to identify when I would be at most risk of infection should I go out in public areas. Like all readings, you need a focused, specific question if you want an accurate result. For the interpretation method, look at the interpretation of layouts chapter.

The timing layout does not use a magical pattern for its layout; it is simply a time-based sequence of cards. Decide what timeframe you wish to work within: days, weeks, months, or years. I tend to use a unit length of seven: seven days, seven weeks, seven months, and so on. But you can set whatever unit length you want, so long as you do so with focus—and use the same unit length each time: learn to form a pattern of behaviour that becomes your divination method.

I have used weeks in the layout list, but substitute week for day/month/year as needed.

1. The first week: seven days starting from the day you do the reading.

2. The second week.

3. The third week.

4. The forth week.

5. The fifth week.

6. The sixth week.

7. The seventh week.

Manifestation, causation, and solution layouts

The following two layouts are secondary layouts, which means they are used specifically to identify the cause of a potential (and perhaps disastrous) event, and determine useful responses or solutions to it. When a general reading indicates some potentially disastrous event, for instance through the Tower card, but it is not clear what that potential event is about, what caused it, or how it would manifest, then a secondary reading can provide more detail.

6. Layouts

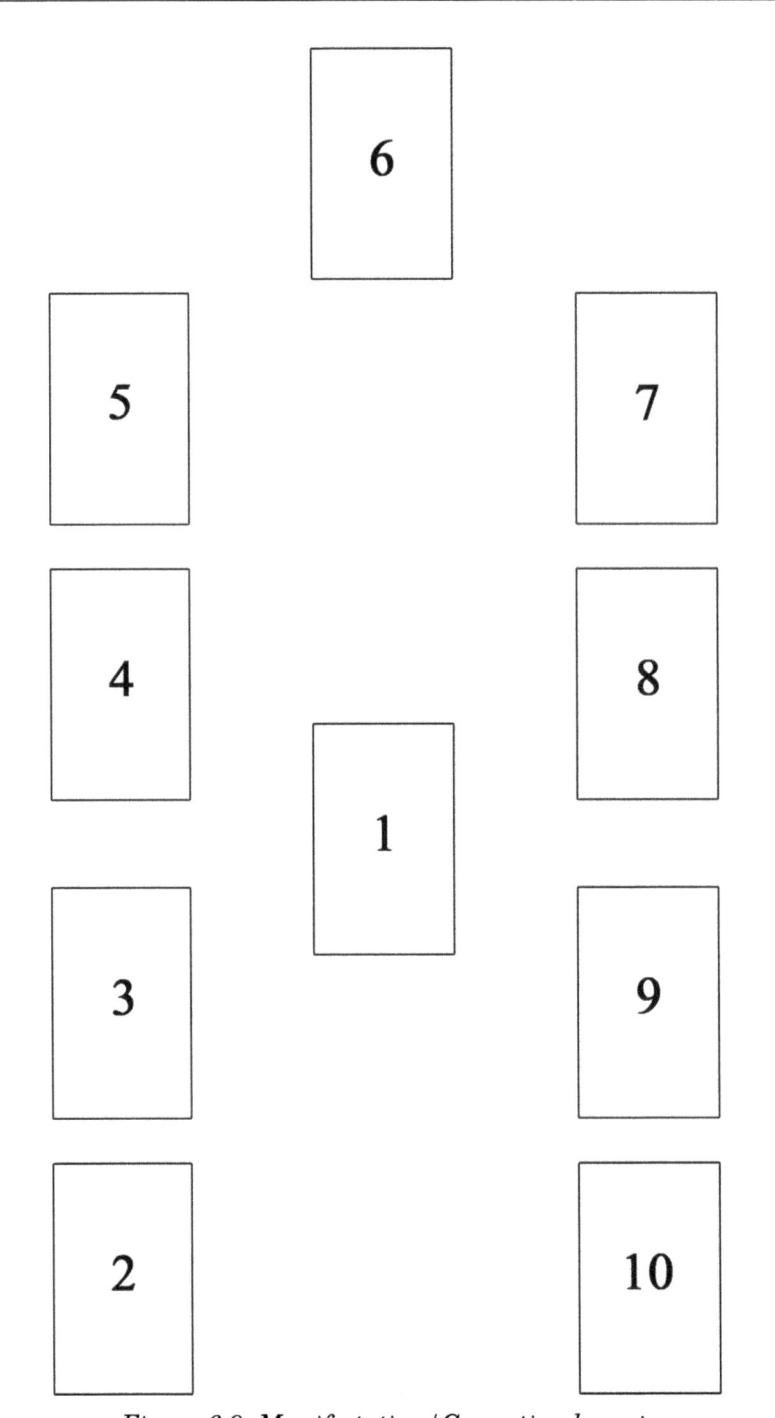

Figure 6.9: Manifestation/Causation layout.

Manifestation/Causation layout

The *manifestation/causation layout* looks at how a disaster on the horizon will most likely manifest: is it an illness? an accident? The layout also includes positions to indicate if the disaster is self-inflicted. When using this layout you are looking for card(s) that mirror the card that represented the event in the general reading. So if this was the Tower, then look for destructive cards. If more than one destructive card appears, then look at any connection or relationships between the two positions the destructive cards fall in. Benign cards indicate irrelevant positions: you do not read them, as they are not what you are looking for.

The *solution layout* includes positions that reflect the type of dynamic approach that would help resolve some issue. In this layout you interpret only the positive, successful, or healing card(s) and their positions, and you would discount any other cards.

Like all readings, how you focus your question is important. The interpretation of layouts chapter contains some examples of how to work with these layouts.

Manifestation / Causation layout

1. The event itself.

2. A natural event (e.g. weather, land slippage, earthquake).

3. An accident.

4. An economic issue (e.g. income, debt, savings, possessions).

5. Illness or injury.

6. A self-inflicted problem.

7. An emotional or mental problem.

8. A relationship issue.

6. Layouts

9. An attack. This could be anything done with aggressive intent to harm you: physical or emotional abuse, theft, fraud, etc.

10. The Scales of Justice (e.g. going to court, legalities, or payback for something).

Solution layout

A problem's solution, while difficult to pinpoint, is usually related to its cause. However, the way that fate works, sometimes the solution can seem unrelated to the problem. This is because sometimes chaos is put in our path as a result of previous actions which created some fateful deficit. Other times, the solution will work itself out, and all it needs is time—sometimes bad stuff happens and it just needs to unfold. Patience is the key to those types of situations.

Other times the solution is staring us in the face but we just do not see it. Maybe the bad argument with your partner that resulted in them walking out is not actually about your relationship, but something else that is happening for you or them. Stress can have a terrible effect on how we handle situations, so sometimes the solution to an issue has longer roots than those which are immediately obvious.

With this layout you are looking for success, stability, or healing cards. The positions in which these cards fall give possible solutions, and the strongest positive card represents the best solution.

1. The event.

2. Passive unfolding. Just let the situation work itself out: let Fate and Time do their jobs.

3. Random action. An inspired or random unplanned act will trigger a solution.

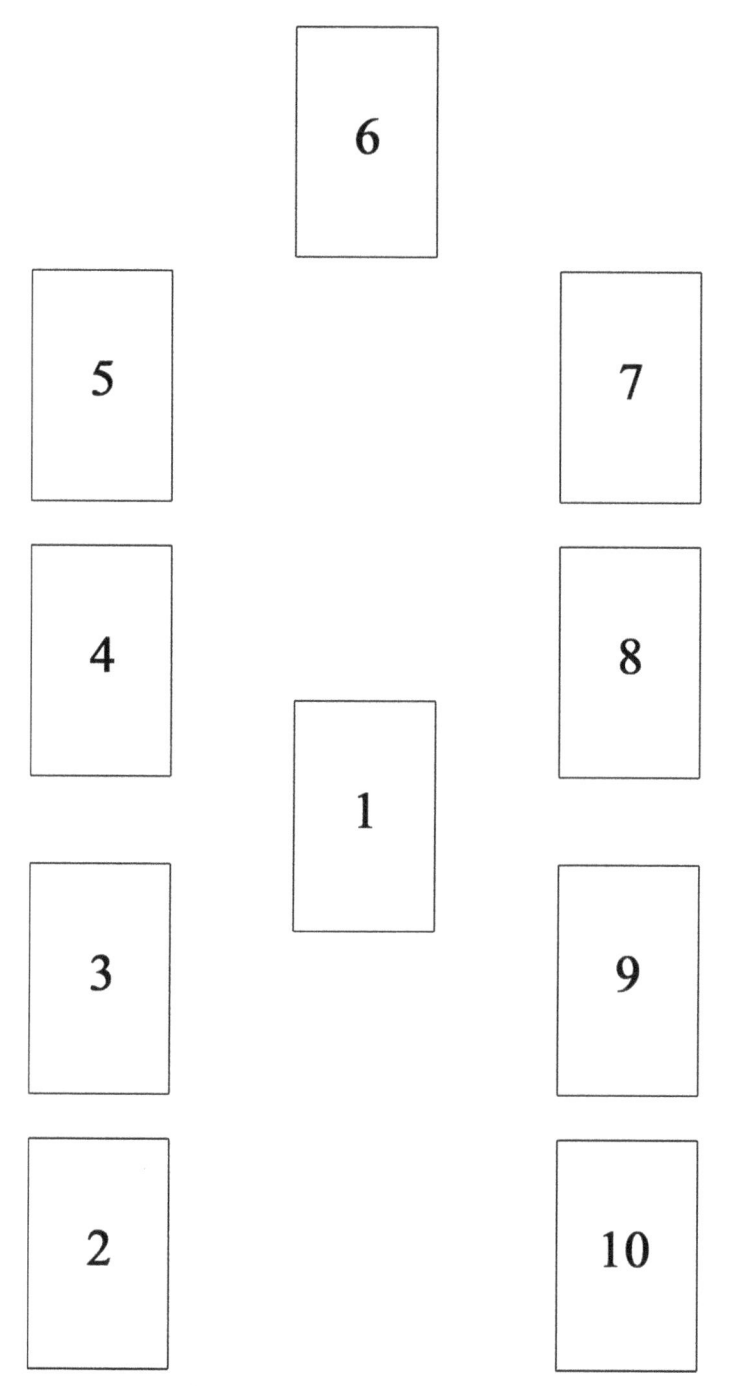

Figure 6.10: Solution layout.

4. Economic. Money or some substance is the solution.

5. Health. Focusing on improving health will bring about a solution.

6. Responsibility. Taking responsibility for an action you caused will bring about the solution.

7. A cool mind. Calm, fair, unemotional negotiation, action, and/or behaviour will trigger a solution.

8. Mercy. Kindness, understanding, and compassion will bring a solution to light.

9. Fight. Fight your corner, stand your ground, and do not give up: this will bring about the solution.

10. Pay your dues. Paying outstanding debt, passing forward your bounty, or returning what does not belong to you will trigger a solution.

Health layout

This layout is only useful for healers and people who know how the body works. It can be used to look at a current health situation to locate the underlying reason(s) for a health issue. It can also be used by healers to track the potential effectiveness of a proposed line of treatment and can flag up any issues that such a proposed line can trigger. So for example, if a healer wanted to use certain herbs on a client, but was concerned about their effectiveness or the client's tolerance, then this health reading could be used to look at the longer term effects of such treatment.

The layout looks at the energy/fate coming into the picture, at health patterns that are forming but have not yet manifested in the body, at how the parts of the body are currently reacting to something, and at the processing of emotions and how these can affect the body's overall health. It also looks at specific layers of the body to help pinpoint the source of some issue.

Caution: using this layout is no substitute for proper medical attention. If you are sick, go see a doctor. This layout can be used to track a recovery or to look at possible complimentary medicines, which should be used alongside medicine from a doctor.

1. The first position shows what is coming into the health picture from a fate/future perspective. What shows here is just beginning to form. It can also show any magical or inner influences. If the only negative influence in the reading occupies this position, then the destructive pattern is still forming and can be obviated or avoided, as it has not yet reached the individual's energy structure: it is not yet 'set in fate.'

2. The second position shows what has formed in terms of fate/future, but it has not yet manifested in the physical body. If there is any energetic or spiritual element to the illness/condition, then it will show here. This position is the threshold between the energetic body and the physical body. Like the first position, things that appear here can be obviated before they manifest in the body; but if left unchecked they can descend into the physical body and cause symptoms.

3. The third position tells us what is physically going regarding the health of the head. This includes the brain, sinuses, lymph glands, endocrine glands,[1] ears, nose, eyes, and the throat (including the thyroid gland) Basically this is everything above the base of the neck.

---
[1]The brain's hypothalamus, pineal, and pituitary glands.

6. LAYOUTS

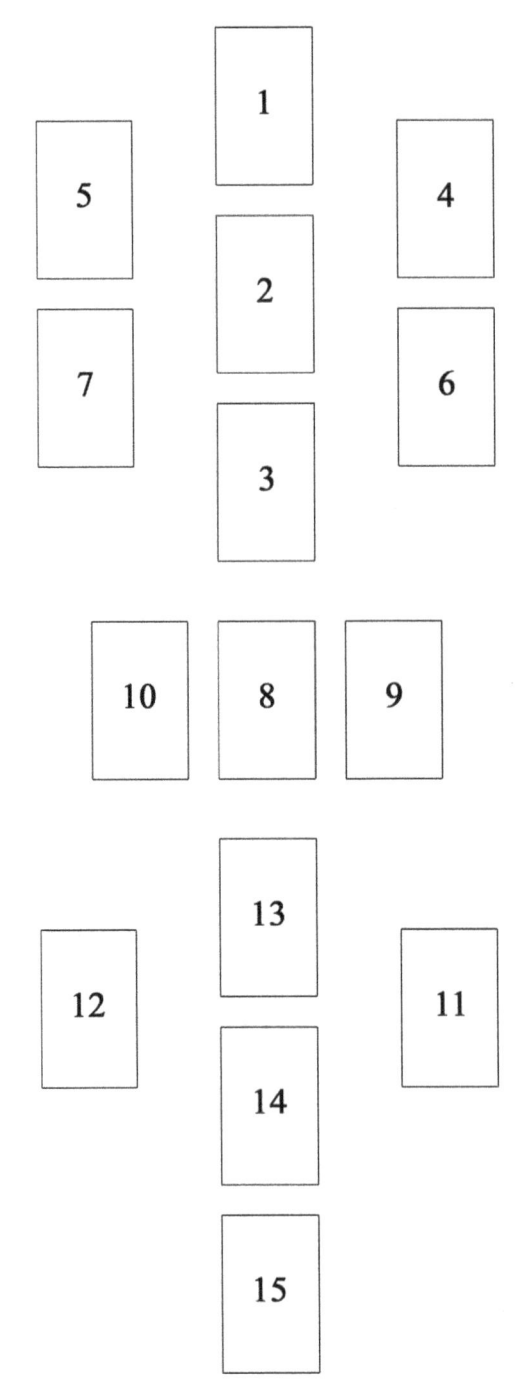

Figure 6.11: Health layout.

4. The fourth position shows the solid energy going in the body. Anything that you are eating, drinking, smoking, or otherwise ingesting will show here, and the type of card that falls in this position will also indicate whether it is affecting you badly or whether it nourishes you.

5. The fifth position shows the state of the emotions: how the person feels, and what their mental state is. Often the emotions can be good indicators of what is going on deeper within the body. The emotions can influence the immune system, and when looking for a treatment make sure that it brings about favourable emotional energies. If a person is in physical pain, it will also show in this position.

6. The sixth position shows what the short-term or primary immune system is currently doing. If it is fighting something or is in overdrive, it will show here. What we put into our bodies directly affects the front line of the immune system, which is why this card sits directly under the 'solid energy' position. Look at the relations between the two cards: if an ingested substance—food, drugs etc.—is contributing to, aggravating, or causing the illness or is affecting the immune system in some way, then both positions four and six will show aggravating or aggressive cards.

7. The seventh position shows the deeper immune system. This system is also affected by emotional wellbeing, which is why card seven sits beneath card five in this spread. This position also shows the secondary immune system that wraps up, locks up, or breaks down threats that have already been overcome. When the querent is already on the winning side of an illness, the aggressive cards will often move from position six—primary immune response—to position seven. This is where disease threats are processed and put into 'sleep mode.' The person's

emotional wellbeing will affect how well this process works, and if they have recently experienced terrible grief, then this area of the immune system can become compromised. This position also tells us how our immune system is functioning. It indicates how well-balanced the immune responses are: if they operating as they should and are not attacking the body itself. With inflammatory diseases, when one is in active mode, it will often show in both immune positions.

8. The eighth position shows the central core of the body, which houses the vital organs: heart, lungs, stomach, pancreas, liver, and kidneys. If there is a problem with these organs, it will show here. If a major aggressive card falls in this position, then the reader needs to do further readings to see which organ has been affected (use yes/no readings).

9. The ninth position shows the male sexual organs, testosterone, and the male bladder. Testosterone is also present in females: if the reading is for a woman and a difficult card turns up in this position, then it will probably be necessary to look in more depth at her endocrine system and hormone balance. If they all look fine in separate readings, then a reading needs to be done to look at her hormonal response to being around males.

10. The tenth position shows the female sexual organs and the bladder. Again, males also have estrogen in their bodies, so if the reading is for a male and a difficult card turns up here, check their hormone system. A difficult card here can also indicate the presence of a member of the opposite sex who is hormonally disruptive.

11. The eleventh position shows the digestive system, and it reveals how the large and small intestines are processing everything

that came in at position four. This area of the body can also be read in conjunction with positions three and five (head and emotions): there is a direct relationship between digestive health and mental and emotional health. For example, neurotransmitters like serotonin play a major part in mood, muscle health, and digestion. Often chronic illness will show causation in positions eleven, three and five. In such cases the solution is in digestive and/or colon health.

12. Position twelve tells us what is happening to us in our sleep and dreams. Our sleep health is often connected to the health of other parts of our body, so if there is a serious sleep issue going on, look also at what is going on in the rest of the health reading.

13. Position thirteen looks at the 'structure and movement' system of the body, which means bone, muscle, and nerves. Any inflammatory reaction, peripheral nervous system disturbance, or bone or muscle impact will show here. If there is a difficult card in this position and in position three (head/brain) then you are more likely to be looking at a nerve problem. If there are fiery cards in this position and in the eleventh position (digestion) then it may indicate an inflammatory disease active with roots in a bacterial imbalance or infection, or an inflammation of the intestine.

14. Position fourteen is the skin. The skin is the most externalized organ and the biggest organ of our body. If the only area that shows a problem in a health reading is the skin, then the situation will likely resolve itself eventually. Usually skin issues beyond injury, infection, and infestation are symptomatic of something else going on in the body, like food allergies or inflammatory diseases.

15. Position fifteen tells us the immediate future of the body's health. If a damaging card turns up in this position, then work still has to be done to help the body come back into balance. Consider this card in relation to the reading's time span: if the reading looked three weeks ahead and the card in position fifteen is a difficult one, then redo the reading with a span of six weeks, to see if the body just needs a bit more time to heal. If at six weeks the card in position fifteen (or other cards) is still difficult, then you need to reassess what action you are taking.

Esoteric layouts

Esoteric layouts are for magicians, mystics, etc. who wish to get an overview of their path or their development; to preview the longer-term implications of some proposed magical working; to communicate with spirits, beings, or ancestors; or to get a look at the condition of a fate pattern to see if they are working in the right way. Esoteric layouts give the magician a deeper look into the past, present, and future so that they can adapt, prepare, or change in order to evolve as a magician and as a human being.

As you work with these esoteric layouts you will start to realize that they mostly work with a similar pattern, which is a magical pattern of existence and contact. It is a pattern used in ritual and in meditation, and it works with the dynamics of life, time, Divine power, inner contact, and magic itself.

One bit of advice I will give people before they dive into esoteric readings, particularly the fate readings: do not do them if you are unable or unwilling to face what they may describe. Deeper magical readings often throw up things we are unprepared for. They can often contradict the narrative we tell ourselves, and if you are too heavily invested in an emotional idea, then facing a different perspective can be disorientating or conflicting.

One of the requirements for being a magician or mystic is the will and ability to *know oneself*. You must face what is there, not what you would like to be there.

Fate pattern layout

This looks at a current fate pattern and gives details about what underlying dynamics need to be worked with, what state that fate pattern is in, and what its highest potential is. People often think of fate as being one continuous path through life: it isn't. A whole life's fate path is made up of lots of smaller paths which magicians call 'patterns.' Each fate pattern has a starting and ending point, and has powers, events, and intersections where the person makes choices and takes actions. These choices and actions decide how the path will reach its destination, and how it will connect with the new pattern that comes next. This dynamic of paths and patterns is the underlying power behind the tarot trump of the Wheel. The Wheel turns and triggers a new fate pattern, or changes the dynamic within the current one.

Using this layout, a magician can get an overview of where they currently are in a fate pattern, what they need to pay attention to, and what they need to let go of; and it gives them an idea of what this cycle can evolve into if they navigate it as best they can. Many people allow themselves to be carried by fate, but a magician is responsible for making the best of each fate path put before them, if they wish to evolve and grow both as a magician and as a human.

6. LAYOUTS

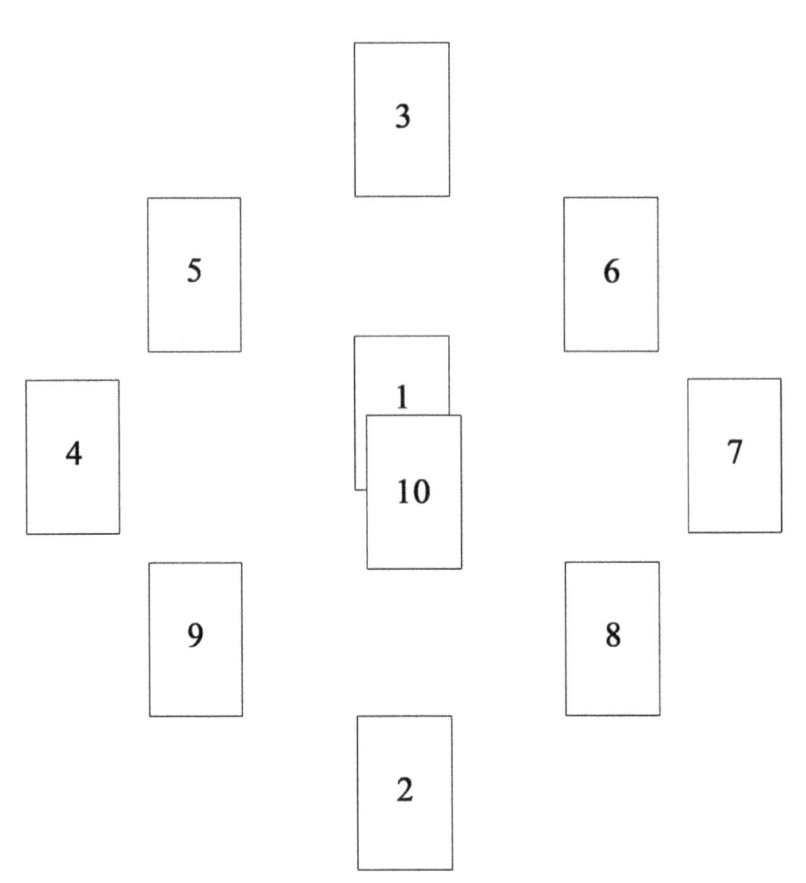

Figure 6.12: Fate Pattern layout.

1. **Current fate path.**

2. **Lessons learned.** What is now left behind that has bearing on the present.

3. **The highest possible potential** for the outcome of this fate pattern: if you get it right, this is what this fate pattern achieves.

4. **Seeds to be nurtured**. what is being planted for the future that needs tending.

5. **Mountains to climb.** Difficulties that must be overcome for success.

6. **What needs releasing.** What you need to let go of to achieve the fate potential.

7. **Harvest.** what have you achieved so far.

8. **The Angel of Severity.** This position tells you what, if anything, in your actions, puts your fate pattern, and thus your evolution, at risk. Anything that shows in this position is deeply connected to your actions, decisions, etc. it is not about anything outside you that you cannot control.

9. **The Angel of Mercy.** This position tells of help to be given to you as a result of your actions, decisions, and reflections so far.

10. **Influence.** This card crosses the first card and shows what is influencing you. Usually it is an inner contact, a being, or a physical teacher. If it is a bad card, then you need to rethink who you take advice from.

6. LAYOUTS

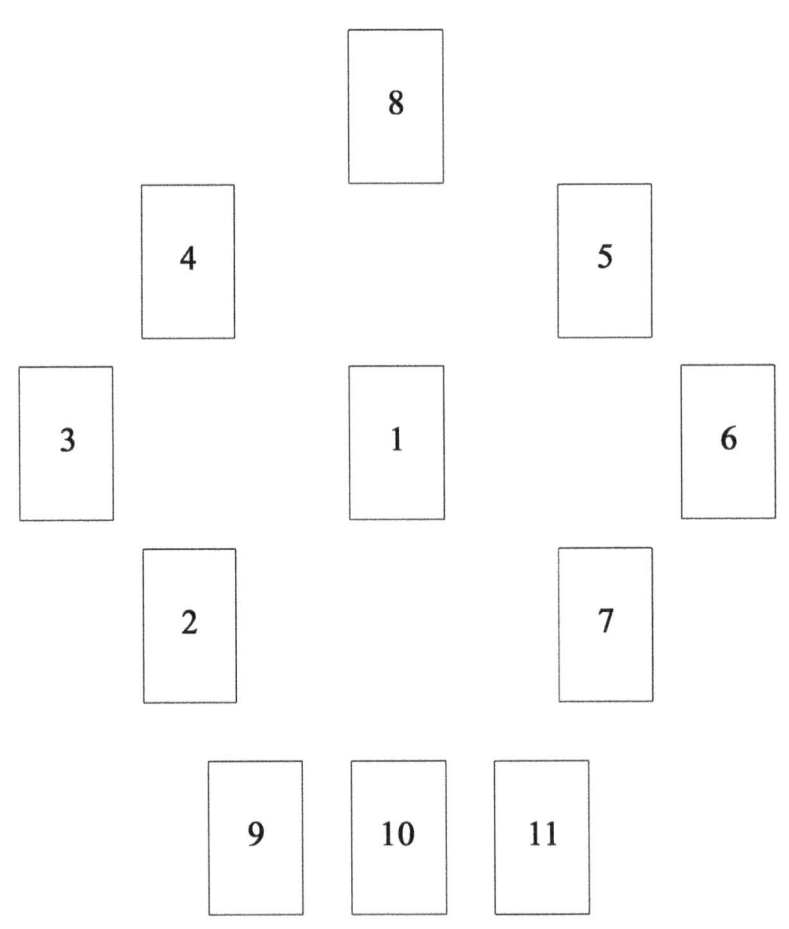

Figure 6.13: Angelic layout.

Angelic layout

This esoteric layout shines a light on you and gives an assessment of your deeper self, as well as your everyday self. It also provides an interface for you to communicate with your personal guardian, also known in magic as the Holy Guardian Angel. The positions are connected to magical tools that are also beings in their own right, and to angelic beings who work alongside the magician or mystic.

If you pay attention then you will notice that the powers and positions are interconnected with the ones in the Fate Pattern layout. Because of this, you can do the two different readings, then compare them. One will tell of the fate path, and the other will tell of the deeper powers that underpin that fate path.

As the angelic layout gives a snapshot of where the magician is in terms of development and magical work, what powers are around them, and what powers are flowing through them, this layout can be used either to get a general sense of where you are at in terms of your development, or to see how a particular magical path or extended working, training, or magical project is affecting you, or will affect you.

It can also be used to look at a particular magical or religious structure: the same angelic patterns flow through religious or magical buildings and temples as through magical or religious systems. The reading will show what power dynamics and potential strengths and weaknesses run through a system, place, or person.

6. Layouts

1. **Self.** The position of the person, place, or system being looked at.

2. **Chesed.** This angelic/Divine power illuminates the path ahead, so in this position it will show if its light is being given, and if so, how the path is forming.

3. **Limiter.** This position shows what is being triggered to slow down or limit the path ahead so that whatever needs to happen, or be learned, can happen. The power of the Limiter is connected to Chesed: it is also connected to the magical sword. It guards and limits so that the magician does not suffer destruction through overgrowth.

4. **Staff.** The staff is connected to the magical staff of the magician. It is a duel serpent power that opens the gates for knowledge and healing. Whatever card lands in this position tells the reader what learning and development is waiting for them to engage and work with. It is the next step on the path that needs to be trodden.

5. **Lantern.** The lantern is the learning and development that has already been acquired, and illuminates the way ahead. It is the human version of the light that the angel of Chesed holds up so that you can see your path ahead. The light in the position of Chesed is the help that Divine fate gives you. The light of the lantern is the light that you have made by way of your development. The two lights should ultimately be balanced as much as possible. When they complement each other, you know that whatever you are doing is serving many good purposes, aiding your path and everything you affect by the nature of your work.

6. **Vessel.** The vessel is a magical tool of harvest and is connected to the magical cup. In the position of the Vessel is work or learning that has been done, and that is currently undergoing threshing so that the grain can be separated from chaff: work or development undergoing maturation. The pure grains eventually become the light of the lantern.

7. **Gevurah.** This angelic/Divine position shows what has been withheld from your pattern, as it serves no purpose and would be detrimental to your future path or development. Whatever lands in this position should not be engaged with or revived; rather it should be left to fall into the past.

8. **Companion.** This is the Sandalphon, the angelic being who guides your on your path ahead into the future. The card that lands in this position tells you, or advises you, about the best way ahead. Whatever type of card lands here, know that the Companion walks that path with you, witnessing what you do, and advising you if necessary.

9. **HGA: what has been.** Through an awareness of what has been, your future is informed. You stand on your past, for good or bad. Positions 9, 10, and 11 should be read together: they are synergetic advice from your guardian angel.

10. **HGA: what is.** The guardian reflects back your true current situation or current self.

11. **HGA: what will be.** The guardian gives you a single insight into what you can be.

6. Layouts

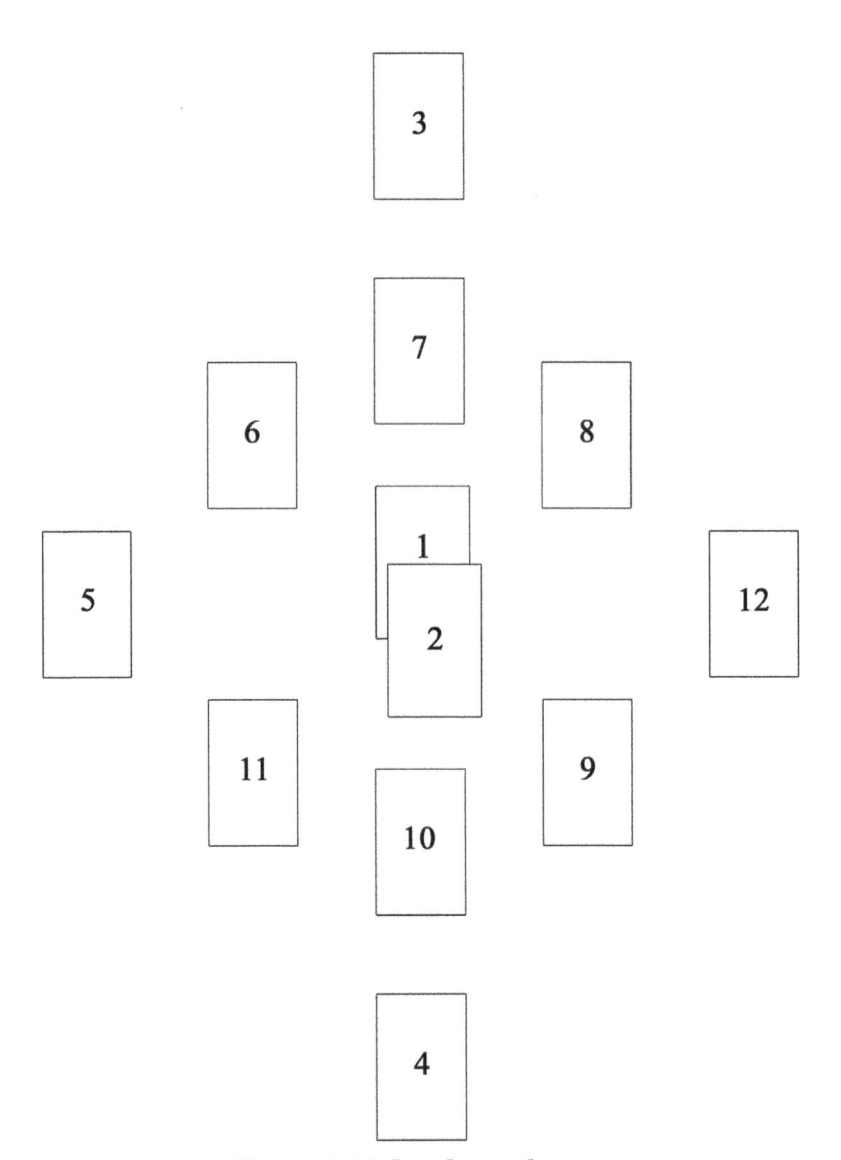

Figure 6.14: Landscape layout.

Landscape layout

I developed this layout in connection with the Quareia Magician's Deck. It shows what is influencing a situation, and what dynamics are at play relating to the past, present, and future. It shows powers and patterns flowing from inner and magical worlds, and how they flow into the everyday life of the subject of the reading. As such, this layout can be used for mundane as well as esoteric readings. Like all readings, it needs a focused question and a time span.

1. **Foundation.** The body, structure, or land.

2. **Union.** The second position, crossing the first, tells us what power or people dynamics we are currently dealing with. It can also show inner contacts you are currently working with or talking to, or it can be a position of relationships.

3. **Star Father.** What is coming in the long-term future and is connected to the question: a pattern that is still being formed in the stars.

4. **Underworld.** What has already passed away down into the depths and will not be coming back. In a magical reading it can also show Underworld influence if the question is about a structure, system, or magical project. But whatever is in this position will not express itself in the living world; rather it is a past that the future is built on.

5. **Gate of the Past.** This is the threshold of what is now in the immediate past. Whatever is in this threshold position has the potential to return at some point in the future, but for the moment it is considered past.

6. **Wheel of Fate.** The current pattern of fate or action that is playing out. This could be a struggle, a cycle of magical work,

a renewal, etc. This is the path you are currently on in terms of fate and its unfolding.

7. **Grindstone.** The hardships and difficulties that must be overcome. On the current path that is indicated in the sixth position, there are bound to be hardships, difficulties, and barriers that must be overcome. These are shown in the seventh position and must be endured if you are to continue in the fate direction you are currently travelling.

8. **The Inner Temple.** What is coming in the situation or fate pattern from the inner worlds or inner contacts. All magical attacks, inner contacts, work programs, inner support, and beings (deities, etc.) who are influencing you will show here.

9. **Home and Hearth.** What influence is affecting your home and/or family surroundings. This position shows what is happening in the home, both on a mundane level and on an inner, magical level. For example, if a magical working is disturbing your house or family, or if there is a problematic spirit in the house, then it will show in this position. Similarly, if there is protection for your home or family it will show here. It can also describe family events that influence the situation being read about. In a magical reading it can also represent a lodge or temple (a magical 'home') or order (a magical 'family'), depending on what the question is about.

10. **Unraveller.** What is falling away or starting to decline. When something is in the process of losing its influence and is breaking up, then it will show in this position. It is travelling towards the Gate of the Past and will finally vanish in the depths. If, however, you do not meet the challenges that appear in the seventh position, then any difficulties indicated here will come right back to challenge you until you get the message.

11. **Sleeper.** Dreams and/or sleep. What your deeper unconscious mind is dealing with, and what is happening to you in your sleep. It can also be a position for visionary work if the question is about a magical working. Often visionary work can affect a magician's dreams, so the two dynamics can be considered together in readings.

12. **The Path Ahead.** The way ahead. The short-term outcome to your question. (For a longer-term outcome, look to position three.)

Map of the Self layout

This is an extensive layout that looks at the different layers of a magical person, structure, or system. Rather than looking at the practical details of the subject, this layout looks at the soul or spiritual expression manifesting in the physical world. It is mostly used to get an overview of the magical life of something, be this a person or a structure (like a temple).

This layout has three layers. The first layer looks at the mundane physical expression, the second layer looks at the magical expression, and the final layer looks at the deeper inner soul. It works in a spiral, answering the question in expanding circles. The positions line up with each other in magical patterns that expose the relationships between the mundane, magical, and spiritual expressions of the subject in question. It is a layout I do not analyze in the interpretations of layouts chapter, as it is up to the magician to figure out how this works. By working with the layout, you will discover its magical patterns and interconnections for yourself: it is a work of discovery.

6. Layouts

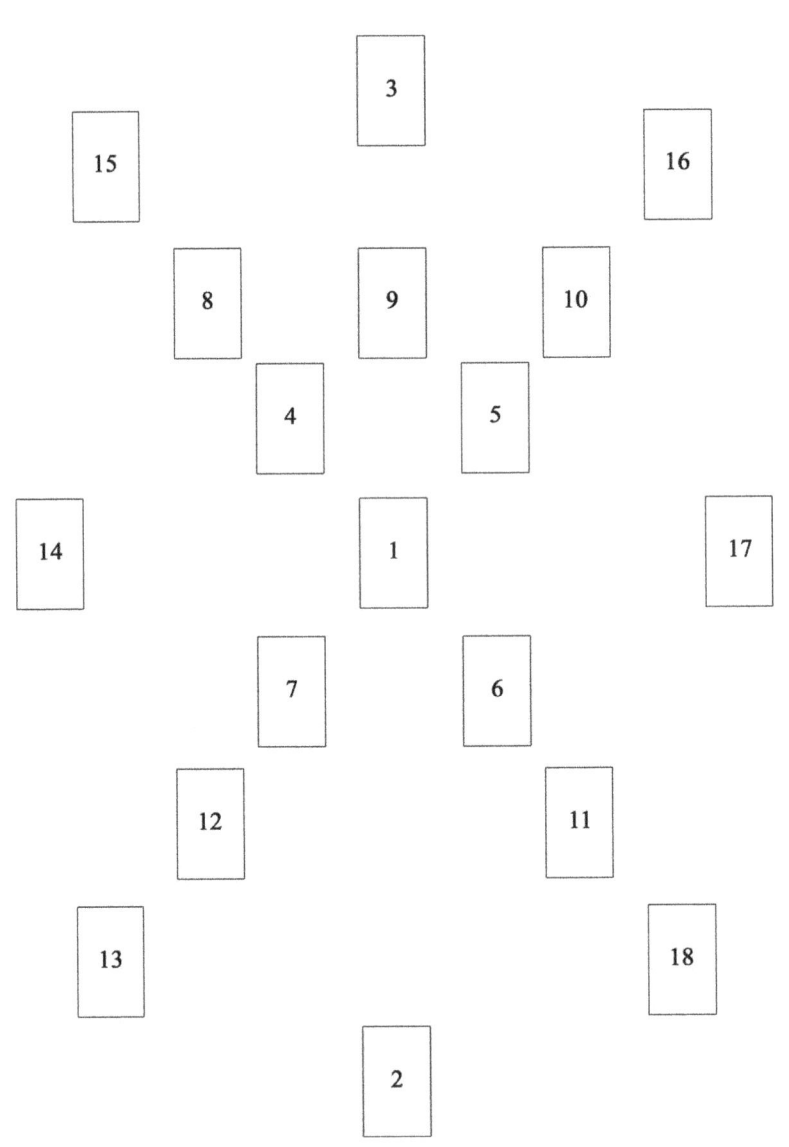

Figure 6.15: Map of the Self layout.

Map of the Self layout

1. **Self.** Ground zero for the question.

2. **Origin.** Where the subject has come from.

3. **Destination.** Where the subject is going.

4. **Mundane positive.** What is contributing to the physical and mundane life of the soul.

5. **Short-term future.** What the short-term, mundane future is for this soul.

6. **Recent past.** What has now passed from the fate of this soul.

7. **Mundane negative.** What is negatively affecting the physical and mundane life of this soul.

8. **Magical or spiritual path.** How the magical or spiritual path that is being walked is serving or influencing the soul.

9. **Magical contacts.** The type of being who is talking to and/or guiding the magician.

10. **Magical future.** Where the current magical path is taking the soul.

11. **Magical adversary.** What power is working against the magician. Every magical path has an adversary to act as a counterbalance to growth. This adversary can never be overcome, but it can be reconciled with, or outlived.

12. **Foundation stone.** What foundation holds up the magical path, and whether it is solid or unstable.

13. **Soul steps.** What overarching lesson or action the soul needs to achieve in this lifetime. While each life has many lessons, jobs, and events, there is usually one overarching theme.

14. **Soul path.** What type of path the soul needs to walk in this life to achieve its aim.

15. **Soul fate pattern.** What type of overarching fate pattern has formed to facilitate the soul's path and steps. The fate pattern creates options of paths, and the paths influence how the steps are taken.

16. **Soul harvest.** What harvest the soul has acquired so far in this life. The harvest is the 'grains' of knowledge and experience that have been acquired so far.

17. **Scales.** What imbalance is still on the scales. What debts and deficits still need to be balanced. These debts and deficits, though in a soul position, relate directly to mundane life and actions which affect the balance of the soul. The balance refers to necessity, the spindle of fate.

18. **Restraint.** What still needs restraint on a mundane and magical level so that it does not undermine what you are trying to achieve in this life. The card that lands here shows your folly that can undo you.

Chapter Seven

Interpretations of Layouts

In this chapter we will look at the layouts described in the previous chapter. We will look at how those layouts work, and how to interpret readings by looking at examples. It is always a good idea when you are learning, or just a reader in general, to record your important readings, the question asked, and your interpretations. (Photographing the reading is a good way of ensuring you record the cards' positions accurately.) Later, as the event read for unfolds, you can go back and look at the reading to see what it was actually saying, and compare this with how you interpreted it. You can learn a great deal from doing this, both about how a deck works and how your interpretation skills need refining. It is something I still do after more than forty years of readings.

Remember, these layouts work regardless of what type of tarot or oracle deck you are using. I have used the Rider-Waite deck throughout this book only because it is the most commonly used deck when people first start working with tarot.

The way I will approach this chapter is to first show the reading and a short summary of general meanings, then I will do a complete answer which looks at the layout in more detail, and looks at the variables of meanings for interpretation that can crop up, based on the question posed. There will also be a technical look at the layout itself for readers who are more esoterically or magically inclined.

7. Interpretations of Layouts

Along with looking at a layout in action and interpreting it, I will also do a 'panicked' commentary for some of the layouts. When a question is emotionally loaded and it is about ourselves or something dear to us, it is easy to panic if difficult cards come out. If emotions get in the way of a reading, we can interpret a card as meaning 'a plague' when it is actually saying 'a bad cold'. Conversely, it is also easy to make light of a warning or danger, so we will look at that too.

I will also finish each analysis with a short brief on how I would relay that reading to the person who is asking the question.

Mundane layouts

The first part of this chapter gives worked examples of the layouts that can be used to investigate mundane matters. I have also given a technical overview of the esoteric and magical aspects of the layouts for those who study such things. For each example I also discuss the dangers of reading it in a panicked way, and what advice you could potentially give if you are reading for someone else.

Simple yes/no layout

QUESTION

"Will I lose my job in the next three months?"

BACKGROUND

The person has been furloughed due to the Covid-19 pandemic and is worried about losing their income.

Simple yes/no layout

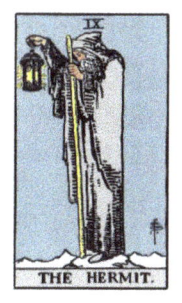

Figure 7.1: Simple yes/no reading

189

7. Interpretations of Layouts

Position meanings

1. What the question is about.

2. Relevant past. What is in the past that led up to the event in question.

3. Difficulties to be overcome.

4. Help you are given.

5. Future of the outcome. What the answer will lead to.

6. The answer.

Reading results

1. Nine of Coins. The question is about financial stability.

2. Eight of Coins. The relevant past is the trade and work of the person. They have worked hard and diligently. This will have a bearing on the future. It also shows the furlough. Their work is recent past.

3. Ace of Swords. This card can either be referring to the pandemic itself or being furloughed. Its position underneath the eight of coins is the relationship between what is in the relevant past that will affect how the difficulty is overcome. In this case, diligent work will help overcome the difficult situation.

4. The Hermit. Introspection and utilizing past experience and wisdom will help the person get through the bad situation.

5. Wheel of Fortune. This card, along with The Hermit, are the two trumps that appear in the reading. They hold the most power and importance, so they have the most bearing on the answer. The Wheel says, change is coming. In context of the question, it is likely the person is going to change jobs.

6. Nine of Swords. The answer is suffering and upset. As a direct answer to the question, yes it is likely that the person will lose their job over the next three months.

Complete answer

The Wheel and the Hermit work together: past knowledge and experience will bring a change of fortune. That is strengthened by the Eight of Coins in position two, the relevant past. The past work experience and knowledge of the person will come to fruition in a new job that is forming in their fate, and it will be connected to their past jobs and work skills. So while the short-term answer is bad, the outlook in general is good. They will lose one job but gain another one. And as the future outcome is a good trump card, it is likely that the new job will be much better than the old one.

Observations for esoteric study

The two bottom positions, 3 and 4, are the two 'legs' the reading stands on. The difficulties to be overcome are weighted in balance to the help and resources the person has to overcome such difficulties. This connects in magic to the Grindstone of the left foot and the Threshing Floor of the right foot. The difficulties that life throws at us are balanced against our wisdom gained from past experience. The more difficulties we successfully overcome, the more knowledge and wisdom we gain to help us overcome new difficulties.

The two top positions, 2 and 5, are the polarizations of fate and time. What has happened in the past and how we dealt with it has direct influence over the way the fate path unfolds in the future. Looking at the two positions together will tell you a lot about how the future fate path will unfold, and if some rebalancing is going on for the fate of the person.

7. Interpretations of Layouts

Positions two and four can also be read together. Position two tells you what happened in the past that will have some bearing on the future, and position four tells you what they learned and gained from that past experience. Both of those have a direct influence on how the card in position five will manifest.

Panicked reading

If the reader simply looks at the difficulties to be overcome, the initial answer and the future outcome, then they will panic. The Ace of Swords, Nine of Swords, and Wheel of Fortune would likely be read as saying "it's a really bad situation, you will lose your job, and your fortunes will change for the worse." However, approaching it that way ignores the past that is the foundation of the future—and the past in this reading is hard work (Eight of Coins) and wisdom from experience (Hermit). Those two gifts have a direct bearing on how the Wheel of Fortune turns, and what it brings.

Whenever there is a panic with a reading, it pays well to look at the whole reading to see what past experiences will directly influence the future. And the key to that is the title of position two: *relevant* past, not just past. That position outlines how the future will unfold *based on* the foundation of the past that the future stands on.

Interpretation and advice to the client

Yes, it is likely that you will lose your job. However, there is something else lining itself up for you, and it is something where your skills and experience will get you the new job. My advice would be to start looking for a new job now, while you are furloughed, and look in areas of work not just in your present capacity or role. Also think about past skills you have gained, and how those skills could also get you a job. By starting to look now, before you lose your job, you will help the doors of fate to start opening, and new paths to start forming for you. I would also advise you to rein in any spending and to save if you can, so that if there is a time lag between losing your job and gaining another, you have something to keep you afloat.

Tree of Life layout

QUESTION

"I am stuck in my job, but I want to get a better job prospect. I was thinking of going back to university and doing an MA in my speciality. But that could mean a lot of extra work and would cost me a lot of money, which I don't want to waste. My question is: would going back to university at UC Davis and doing an MA in Veterinary studies be a good idea for my long-term future?"

Note: notice in the question it was not a random MA, but a specific one that the client was thinking about. Specifics are important: the name of the university and the specific MA will get a more accurate answer. However, note that the answer will be specific to that course and that university. If it was a more general question (not listing the university or specific course, just an MA) and you got a positive answer, then yes/no readings could follow, looking at the various course and college choices open to the client.

POSITION MEANINGS

1. What the story is about.

2. What positive, giving aspect helps form the story.

3. What is hidden or past that has a bearing on the story.

4. What is necessary for the story to develop.

7. INTERPRETATIONS OF LAYOUTS

Figure 7.2: Tree of Life reading

5. What is withheld from the story, or is being taken away.

6. The pivotal aspect or key of the story.

7. What needs discipline or limiting for success. This is also a position governed by emotions.

8. What needs relaxing to flow. This is also a position governed by the mind.

9. The reason or dynamic behind the answer.

10. The answer.

READING RESULTS

1. Seven of Cups. What the story is about. Searching for the hidden jewel: looking for a new horizon, but not sure which option to choose, or not seeing all the options.

2. The Lovers. The story involves making an agreement or partnership with something—the university?

3. Knight of Coins. The relevant past is based on the client's experience as a vet tech, a junior working with animals.

4. Two of Wands. What is necessary for the story to form is to look carefully and thoughtfully, and to look at different options ahead.

5. The World. This option would mean having to withdraw from the world for a while, which means less socializing, less going out, and no holidays. It could also mean that the course would be remote, online, and not in the world, or that would be the option offered to the student.

6. Judgement. The whole story hinges on an important decision or judgement: being accepted, or not, to the university.

7. Interpretations of Layouts

7. The Chariot. The choice of university, should they be accepted, would involve a lot a travelling or commuting. This could also mean a broadening of perspectives and innovative thinking.

8. The Hierophant. Don't approach the application or the study in too rigid a way. For the application to be a success, it needs forward thinking and innovation with a loosening of intellectual rigidity.

9. Three of Swords. Either a separation of dreams, or a separation from family.

10. Three of Cups. Celebrating success.

Complete answer

The first three positions tell us a bit about not only the situation, but the person. The first card, Seven of Cups, tells us that on a deeper level this person really doesn't know what they want, but at least having a focus and making a decision (the Lovers) moves them away from a weaker past and towards a stronger future. It is also possible that the Lovers card indicates a possible relationship tied in with the decision: if the person is thinking of starting a family, or wanting to find someone to settle down with, that might be the driving force behind the initial decision.

Often readings will show the underlying dynamic behind a question before the client themselves is aware of it. The next three cards, (positions 4, 5, 6) tell us about the pivotal power necessary to drive this situation. The central pivot of the reading is Judgement, a major decision. In this case, because the client is asking about going to university, Judgement in the centre refers not only to their choice and decision, but also to whether or not they will be accepted on the course.

That acceptance would be dependent on the careful thinking and weighing up of what exactly they need and where to get it from. The World in a withheld position is most likely saying that acceptance by the university would be dependent on either it being a remote, online course, or the client being willing to be not 'out in the world' in the study. Putting those three together, I would interpret them as saying that the university would base their decision on the careful forward thinking that is put into the application and the rationale behind why the client wishes to do it, as well as how well they can demonstrate that they can do a remote course while holding down a job and financing themselves. That means that the university would want to see a higher quality application, above and beyond what the client is currently thinking.

The success of the application, the course, and the future ahead needs forward thinking, innovation, and evolution through hard work and focus (Chariot in a position of discipline) as well as a loosening of rigidity of thinking and approach (the Hierophant in an unravelled position). It is possible that the current thinking or methodology in the university has moved on and evolved from when the client was last in a study situation.

The three of Swords in the ninth position could have a few different meanings dependent on the client's individual situation. The ninth position in this layout potentially has a wide range of meaning, from family, home, and tribe, to dreams andwishes, to what is forming in the inner consciousness and fate. The interpretation would be dependent on the client's situation. If they are in a family situation (partner or living with parents) the course may lead them to leave that situation, perhaps to study; or the success of the course would lead them in a different direction away from home. But it could also indicate that the client wishes to separate themselves from their old life by doing the course.

7. Interpretations of Layouts

Because the Lovers featured so strongly at the start of the reading, I would guess that if they are chasing the degree to solidify or find a lasting relationship, it will actually have the opposite effect: the three of Swords is separation. And yet they would be happy with the outcome.

The outcome as three of cups is a success: they would be accepted and it would most certainly be a good idea for the long-term outcome of their future. Note that the degree outcome itself is a minor card: success and celebrating. But the true strength in the reading are the two cards in position seven and eight. The course would mature and drastically challenge the person's way of thinking and how they approach the subject matter. Both cards are trumps, and hold the most power over the lower part of the reading that deals with the outcome.

From this I suspect that they would successfully get the MA, but then move away from the subject matter altogether and find a career path that is better for them, that they had not even thought about yet. But doing the course is a vital step in that process: without doing the course, their prospective good future cannot form.

Observations for esoteric study

The Tree of Life layout operates in three parts. The first three cards tell the story of the question itself, the middle three tell you the central dynamics of the situation, and the last four cards tell you how the answer forms, with the final card being the answer.

The layout also works in three columns with the central column being about how the situation forms and then expresses itself. The column to the right contains the loosely positive forward action cards that carry the story forward, and the column on the left shows loosely past, withheld, and then 'tightly wound' dynamics (that need to loosen). The two opposing sides create a tension that allows the central power to flow down the Tree and keep everything stable.

The top three and middle three cards are also the more powerful underlying reasons, dynamics, and powers behind an action, whereas the last four are how those powers manifest themselves in a practical and personal sense. We often have less power or influence over the top and middle part of the tree, as those positions, mostly, are affected by the flow of fate. But the three cards before the final answer card are very much about how we deal with the situation, and we have total power over that. If any of those positions (7, 8, or 9) are destructive cards, those are ones we can change by changing our approach.

Panicked reading

A lot of inexperienced readers would focus on seeing Judgement in the centre and the three of swords in position nine, and would read that as a failure for an answer. It is surprising how many readers fail to look at the actual outcome card, and instead focus on destructive ones further into the reading.

With the Tree of Life layout, as with any other layout that has a defined 'answer' position, it is wise to remember that the answer card is literally the answer. The rest of the reading tells how that answer would come about, and what potential difficulties will be encountered. If the answer is good but how it gets there appears to be too destructive, then it means that the actual fate is going in the right direction, but you may need to rethink how you approach getting to that actual fate.

Interpretation and advice to the client

I would advise the client that if they take more care with the application process by updating their current understanding of the

7. Interpretations of Layouts

university and of what the admissions office want to see in terms of strong applications, then there is a strong possibility they will be accepted, and that it would be a successful outcome.

I would also suggest that they seriously think about how they will approach study and their future in general. They will get on the course and have a successful outcome, but that this qualification is not potentially pointing to a path in the specific sector of work they have in mind. Rather, it appears to be preparing them and giving them skills for something potentially different in the future, something that would be better suited to their needs and fate path.

I would also advise that while they may feel that relationships and family are major factors for consideration, ultimately they have to focus on the right path in life for them as an individual. If the relationship or family is meant to be, then it will blend well. If it isn't then there may be changes ahead, but there is no indication that those changes would be bad, just different.

Overview layout

QUESTION

"Show me my life events and what I need to know for the next twelve months."

Note that the question not only asks about life events in a twelve month period, but also includes what the person *needs to know* for that twelve months. Sometimes there are things that crop up in our lives that are not events, but are undercurrents building in our lives, or parts of our lives that we are not paying attention to that are important that we address in a timely manner.

Overview layout

Figure 7.3: Overview reading

This layout can be done with one card in each position, or using the split deck method. To illustrate how to interpret a split deck, I will use that for the reading.

Position meanings

1. Home, family. This is your ground zero. It is your home, your close community that you identify with, your bloodline, and so forth.

2. Relationships. This is not just love relationships, but close friendships and important partners: a business partner, for example.

3. Creativity. This position is for what is creatively most important for you. If you are a parent, it is usually your children. But it is also about what you create and have a passion for, such as art, computer code, product design, gardening, or dance.

201

7. Interpretations of Layouts

4. Current fate cycle. Fate is an ever-turning wheel, and as we go through life we go from one fate cycle to another. This position shows you your current fate cycle.

5. Health. This position shows your overarching health for the time span of the reading.

6. Gifts. While fate can hammer us, it equally gives gifts. This position can represent help, resources, support, or protection that fate puts in your path to help you.

7. Conflicts. This is open conflicts. The source of the conflict could be a person or a situation, or it could represent some internal conflict or self-inflicted destructive behaviour. It represents whatever is causing disturbance in your equilibrium.

8. Hidden Enemies. Sometimes our friends or colleagues smile to our face while stabbing us in the back. It can also be a position where a hidden danger can show, like a fraying cable, an unseen danger, and so forth. It is the position of what you are not seeing that holds danger for you.

9. Grinder. This is the position for whatever adversity must not be avoided, but worked through to gain strength, wisdom, or success.

10. Resources. Resources is income, energy, food, etc. This position shows you an overview of your resources for the length of time of the reading: will you have what you need?

11. Unraveller. This position tells you your weak spot for the time allotted, and what needs to be identified and voluntarily let go, be it a habit, laziness, procrastination, or something that no longer serves a purpose in your life.

12. Taker. The Taker is a position that shows what will be taken from you so you can move forward on your fate path. It is not a voluntary release like the Unraveller: the Taker position shows what fate will take from your path, be it a relationship, a bad job, or something you are clinging to that has become unhealthy for you.

13. The Road Ahead. This position shows the overall short-term future for the time span of the reading. It can also indicate the direction your fate is taking including and beyond the reading time limit.

READING RESULTS

1. Judgement + Six of Cups. A decision will needed to be made about the home and/or family this year. The six of Cups shows that while the subject is happy in their home and/or family, this is most likely an illusion of happiness rather than seeing what is actually there.

2. The Fool + Nine of Wands. Foolishness in a relationship that causes difficulties and conflicts.

3. Hermit + Two of Swords. Introspection and wisdom expressed through debate or writing.

4. Emperor + Eight of Coins. The dominant fate cycle for this time period is one of leadership and productive work.

5. High Priestess + Nine of Coins. The health for this timeline is good. This person cares for their health, and enjoys the fruits of good health.

6. Temperance + Five of Swords. The gifts that fate gives in this time period are tempering and protection from unbalanced

7. Interpretations of Layouts

forces. Minor upsets and disappointments protect from much bigger problems manifesting.

7. Hierophant + Four of Swords. Conflicts with rigid, narrow-minded individuals or organizations are best handled by withdrawing, stepping back, and keeping one's silence.

8. Chariot + Three of Swords. There is a possibility that the person's car or mode of transport has some hidden problem to cause it to cease functioning. Because position eight is hidden enemies, be careful to check that your car or travel mode has not been tampered with.

9. The World + Five of Cups. Beware of complacency. When we have all we need, it is easy to want more or to be disappointed in what we have. It is important in this time cycle to learn to be happy with what you have, and not wish for better or more.

10. The Sun + King of Cups. Economic success, possibly connected with a boss or older man who is firm but kind.

11. The Lovers + Four of Wands. What can unravel your success this year is celebrating a partnership or agreement and thinking everything is fine: it needs work. Do not rest on your success, it will be your undoing.

12. The Star + Page of Coins. What will be taken from you, or will not get off the ground this year, is a new project or idea that possibly gets to the early stages but will go no further.

13. The Magician + King of Swords. Your fate path is leading you to take control and organize yourself, because you will be challenged to defend yourself by a person or an organization.

Complete answer

This twelve month reading appears to be strong in terms of economic viability, work and health, but weak in terms of family and relationships. It shows a lot of complacency from current and past success, and it is a complacency that could be the undoing of the person's future. At some point within the next twelve months or just after, the person will be challenged either legally or within a company structure to account for themselves and their actions.

Let's look at this reading in detail, as it uses a lot of cards, and it can be useful to see how they interconnect and support each other.

The first pair of cards is in the position of home and family. It shows a weariness of home life and the forces behind that aspect of the person's fate are pushing them to make a decision. When you look at the home and family, also look at the relationships and conflicts positions to see what is happening there. Sometimes the cards in position one can refer to the home's physical structure, rather than to its inhabitants or the person's family. If everything else looks good in the other positions that deal with people and connections with people, then it is more likely that any bad card in position one refers to problems with the actual house, home, or community where the person lives.

In this reading, most of the cards in positions that refer to people are weak or problematic. So it is possible that while the person's fate cycle looks good financially, their personal life looks like a bit of a struggle. The relationships position has the Fool and the Nine of Wands, and the conflicts position that sits under the family/home position has the Hierophant and Four of Swords. This appears to be telling a story in which the person is either not in a relationship (the Fool can count as zero/no/none) which they find difficult, and they are in conflict with a rigid member of the family (a parent?)

7. Interpretations of Layouts

but feel they cannot stand up to them (Four of Swords) so they are thinking about leaving the family home (Judgement/Six of Cups). I also found it curious that in the position of hidden enemies—which can also mean hidden things that can harm you, not necessarily an actual enemy—there sits the Chariot and the Three of Swords. And the hidden enemies' position is underneath the relationships position: they are both intimately connected. This person would not be the first to have their tires slashed or brake line cut by a disgruntled lover.

The Lovers in position eleven, which is what unravels your stability, as well as the four of Wands, could point to the person wanting a relationship or taking a lover, and that potentially becomes their undoing. That would make me look back at the relationship position and it's cards: the Fool and the Nine of Wands. Is this person having an affair that will be their undoing? The Lovers can be about business as well as relationships, and as this reading has a strong economic element, I would tread carefully over deciding what type of union this card is referring to. If it was imperative to know, then I would do a further reading using a yes/no layout.

I found the polarity between position three, creativity, and position nine, the Grinder, interesting. In position three we have The Hermit and Two of Swords, and in position nine we have the World and the Five of Cups. The creative impulse in this person is measured, thoughtful and reclusive, and expresses itself through words (Two of Swords) or through weapons (literally picturing two swords as weapons). Opposing that in the Grinder is disaffection with the world.

I then looked at the outcome in position thirteen, which is the Magician (control) and the King of Swords (harsh rule, legalities, or a man like a seasoned warrior). If there were a few dangerous cards in the reading, I would suspect and worry that this person, while seeming to have everything going for them on the surface, was harbouring a dangerous disaffection under the surface. This could out itself through conflict or attack. However, there is little evidence of such underlying violence in the reading, so I would propose that the Hermit/Two of Swords is about a person who writes as a way of release from a successful but ultimately dissatisfying life that they wish to change.

Looking at the overall themes of the reading, which are economic and business success, but failure in relationships and disappointments or loss in creativity/new projects, I would assume that the outcome, position thirteen, points to the person deciding to take control of the unhealthy sides of their life, and that the Judgement/decision they make in their family/home position expresses itself through the merciless cutting of ties (King of Swords). The fate cycle that they are on is very much about power and money, so that will unconsciously drive their decisions, and anything that gets in the way of that will be attacked or dispensed with.

Observations for esoteric study

The top six positions have direct relationships with the six positions beneath them. If you are using the split deck method, the two cards in the same position are really cause (trump) and effect (minor card).

When you look at the relationships between the two layers of positions, it starts to give insights into how certain areas of our lives can influence others. For example, in position one and position seven we learn about how our connection and identification with a family, group, organization, or tribe is most often the cause of conflicts in our lives, either directly or indirectly.

It also highlights how our upbringing can affect how we deal with conflicts, and how we manage ourselves in groups. When you look at the group of four positions: one, two, seven, and eight, we see an even tighter orbit of cause, origin, and the expression of conflicts, adversaries and so forth. This is the expression of polarity within every living thing: we organize ourselves into 'packs' and identities that prop up our sense of self, which helps us to navigate our way through life.

The next grouping of four positions, position three, four, nine, and ten, tell us about how our fate works, and whether or not we are resourced to fully participate actively in that fate pattern. These four positions work in an X shape: three and ten, and four and nine. Three, creativity, and ten, economics, express the instincts of every living thing at its deepest level of understanding: procreation and food sources. Creativity and economics are the modern human expressions of those base primal instincts. When something goes wrong with either one of those two dynamics, it can send even the most level-headed person into a tailspin, as both are driven by the most primal urges for survival within us.

It is worth keeping that underlying dynamic in mind should difficult cards come up in those two positions. Regardless of how mundane or esoteric those cards are, they will potentially trigger the primal instinct in a person. Then, logic usually goes out of the window, and it is up to the reader to gently nudge the person away from a panic reaction and towards a logical one.

With the second arm of the X we have position four/fate cycle, and position nine/Grinder. Where the first arm of the X is about pure primal instinct, the second arm of the X is about engaging and understanding fate, and thus knowing yourself. One arm is mundane; the other is esoteric. The fate cycle itself is expressed in position four. It is connected to the Grinder, which expresses what the person needs to do or overcome to achieve the best possible learning and development from that fate pattern.

Each turn of the wheel of fate brings with it challenges that can toughen and strengthen us, and knock a layer of bullshit out of us. If we are aware of those challenges and engage with them consciously to overcome them to the best of our ability, then we have a good chance of drawing the best possible outcome from that fate pattern. If we ignore those challenges then we learn nothing, and we can end up in the same situation over and over again. This is not because we have some master of fate wagging a finger over us, but because by engaging with the challenge, we learn the skills and build the strength which makes us less likely to be confronted with the same messy challenge again. Eventually we learn to spot old troubles coming and know from experience what to do about them. The two positions tell us how the person will be challenged by that fate.

The last cycle of four in the pattern are positions five/health, position six/gifts, position eleven/Unraveller, and position twelve/Taker. This is an interesting orbit of dynamics that has more under the surface from an esoteric point of view than is at first apparent. Health is a major resource, but it can be adversely affected, often unknowingly, by one's inner resources. Again, this orbit of four works in an X shape: position six/gifts and position eleven/Unraveller reflect how incoming resources—gifts and help—can unravel our stability if not approached wisely.

Position five/health is often interdependent with position twelve/Taker. This reveals the dynamic in which when our fate resources are needed to uphold our health, which is a major necessity, it can often be at the expense of something else. What is not necessary is cut from the fate pattern or let go of to allow the resource energy to flow to the health. When you put the four positions together, you get a pattern where the health can sometimes be energetically dependant on the person's energetic handling of incoming resources that are given (not

7. Interpretations of Layouts

earned). If the person clings to more than is necessary (greed) it can begin to unravel them.

This in turn can affect their inner energetic health, which at times can also affect their physical health. If they voluntarily release/give up/give away their excess, then the Taker (a fate dynamic) does not need to take it. This halts the unravelling process which stabilizes the health. The ability to give and release is heavily entwined with a person's physical, mental, spiritual, and energetic health.

The two rows of cards can also be viewed as two parallel columns of positive (top row) and negative (bottom row), and can show the polarity of balance between the two in a person's reading. The tensions and interplay between the two culminate in the last card which is the sum total expression of cause and effect.

Panicked reading

I think there is little in this reading that would cause someone to panic, except maybe the last position, the outcome or overall path for the year, which is The Magician and the King of Swords. I can already hear the question that is put to me so many times when people terrify themselves with readings: "am I going to be cursed or magically attacked?" Even if the reading was for a magician (which it was not) those two cards do not indicate any such attack.

The King of Swords often frightens some beginners, yet it can often mean an older man of sharp mind, or a lawyer, a judge, and so forth. The only possible bad interpretation I would see from that reading is Judgement in the family position and the King of Swords as the outcome. This could potentially be talking about family court proceedings or a divorce case, particularly with the Fool in the second position of relationships.

Any bad or destructive cards have to be read in context of the life of the person, their current fate path, the context of the question, and the interplay between the cards themselves. A single bad card surrounded by good cards is an isolated incident, and bad cards that are minor cards are outweighed by good trump cards.

However, it is wise to not downplay disasters when you see them in readings. The whole point of readings is not to reassure someone, but to give them a 'heads up' about what is beyond their line of vision on the horizon. If you see a potentially disastrous situation, then it would be wise to do timeline readings, yes/no readings, then an overview of two years instead of one. That will give you a better idea of just how damaging it could potentially be, how long it will take to recover from, and if there are actions and changes the person can make to modify or avoid the situation.

Interpretation and advice to the client

My advice to this person would be, do not be complacent. Your finances will be fine, but don't expect that tap to flow indefinitely. I would also suggest that the person sort out whatever is going on at home in a clear, honest way with integrity: letting it just drift along will cause major problems for the future. I would also suggest that if they are tempted to have an affair or are hiding a relationship from their family, then such an approach is likely to lead them down a difficult and potentially destructive road.

I would outline to the client that overall the reading shows that they have reached a place in life where they are financially secure but it is not enough: they want something else. If they do not approach that dissatisfaction with intelligence and care, then they are likely to get themselves in a mess. Their fate is currently on a path of health, power, and financial stability, which gives them the chance to make changes to the other areas of their life that are not working so well. It would be wise to take that opportunity to actively address family, relationships, and emotional issues properly to avoid the outcome being about legal conflict, harshness, and control.

It would be much better to transform that fate path through proactive, balanced, and fair actions so that the fate outcome of the Magician and the King of Swords can express through creativity: through the writing, communication (King of Swords), and systematization (Magician) of something. A perfect fate expression would be giving talks on how to approach financial success, as the person appears to have a good grasp of money, work, and power.

Event layout

QUESTION

"How will this divorce play out for me?" (The person is female.)

This simple layout can help a person not only to know what is coming, but it also gives insight into the underlying issue which caused the event. This can help the person gain a more balanced view of what is happening, why, and where it is going.

POSITION MEANINGS:

1. The current situation.

2. What is now past that contributed to the situation.

3. What triggered the current situation.

4. What the situation gives you.

5. What the situation takes from you.

6. How the situation will unfold.

Event layout

Figure 7.4: Event reading

7. Interpretations of Layouts

7. The conclusion of the situation.

Reading results

1. The Magician. The situation is about control, or a controlling person.

2. The World. The world that the person enjoyed no longer exists.

3. Page of Wands. Small, angry annoyances triggered the event.

4. Six of Cups. The event will provide the chance to move on.

5. Nine of Cups. What is taken away is comfort and stability.

6. Eight of Swords. It will happen by pain, constriction, and feeling helpless.

7. Queen of Coins. The conclusion of the event is stability and strong autonomy.

Complete answer

This woman wants to know how her divorce will play out, and the reading gives a few interesting insights. As she is asking, and it is her divorce, the first card shows her part in the current situation. The Magician tells a story of control and order, of trying to form something that they have power over. If she filed for divorce, then that is what this card is saying. If she didn't file for divorce, then it is likely that her need for control and order was a major factor in triggering the divorce.

What is now past (position two) is her world. Even though the divorce is in the early stages, the world she inhabited with her partner no longer exists. The house, car, and so forth may all still be there, but the actual day-to-day world that she identified with has now gone and cannot be returned to.

Event layout

The trigger for the divorce, the Page of Wands, tells of either a child or an energy of small but continuous aggravating exchanges. The pages in general are difficult to read, as they can mean so many different things depending on context. In this context it could be a literal child, either a love child from outside the marriage who has come to the attention of one of the partners, or feuding between the partners over a child.

The Page of Wands in the context of this layout and question can also refer to small but ultimately destructive undermining behaviour, like nagging, putting the other partner down, and temper tantrums. A Page can mean 'small,' 'less,' and Wands are fire: so it is something small that ultimately burns away this couple's love and daily life. Small but continuous comments and actions that challenge or undermine another person will eventually damage a relationship. If you then look back at position one, the Magician, then you will start to see a pattern of control, order, and potential nagging or constant undermining.

The divorce gives this woman a chance to move on, often with a feeling of defeat. It is common for marriages to last far longer than they should, with both parties suffering needlessly. The whole idea of breaking up a marriage can be horrifying for people, but once it is done, they often find a whole new world ahead of them. When I see the Six of Cups in the fourth position in the layout, this is the dynamic I am seeing: moving on with a sense of defeat, yet this is a gift as yet unrecognized.

What is taken away from the person is shown in position five, the card of which is the Nine of Cups. The stability and sense of emotional security that comes from the relationship is destroyed by the divorce, which is no surprise, but it also points to a deeper sense of emotional wellbeing being damaged. When we draw our deeper

215

7. Interpretations of Layouts

emotional stability from something outside ourselves, be it a partner, a child, or a job, then we are vulnerable to having that stability destroyed at some point. This will eventually force us to abandon seeking stability outside of ourselves. For this reading, I would say, after looking at all its cards, that the divorce is simply an outer symptom of a much deeper change that is going on.

The 'how it will happen' position has the Eight of Swords, which is a difficult card. The good side is that it is a minor card, but that still doesn't take away from the pain and struggle this card can represent. Whenever a reader is in doubt over the meaning of a card, it is good to refer back to its actual image, and that is particularly true of this card. The person is bound up, blindfolded, and surrounded by Swords. In this position with this question, it shows that the divorce would not unfold in the way the person thinks it will.

The first card, the Magician, suggests that this person is used to being in control. The Eight of Swords takes that control away completely. They are helpless, suffering, and surrounded by threat. In terms of fate, this is what is really necessary for this type of person in this situation: where a person's tight control has begun to destroy something, fate will teach you what it feels like to be on the other side of that tight control, to see if you get the message. Some do and learn from it and adapt their behaviour; others fall into victimhood and blaming others.

It is likely that in this divorce, the settlement will not be what the person wanted, and things will come out in the proceedings that take the power away from this person: a good lawyer may take them apart. It is also a warning card: everything in life is affected by how you stand before life's challenges and how you deal with them. If you act with integrity, then it is irrelevant how others behave or what nasty things are done to you or said about you: your integrity is not dependent on what others give to you, it is about how you are as a human being. That strengthens you in the face of injustice, and helps you face your own injustice. This card in this situation binds and blinds the person *so that they can truly see.*

Let us see what this person potentially does in that situation. The outcome is the Queen of Coins. She is a lesser version of the Empress, and she is about autonomy, strength, creativity, and self-sovereignty. Once the divorce is done, the person will have a strong potential for really stepping into her own power, a power that is not dependant on controlling others, and which indeed is not dependant on others at all. She finally finds herself and becomes secure in that self. The Queen of Coins also indicates financial stability: not only will she find herself, but she will no longer be dependent on others for her resources.

It would appear that this person, through the suffering of her divorce, will learn a great many lessons; and though the situation will initially force her into a sense of defeat, this will actually be an evolutionary step that will bring her into a better place materially and within herself. The warnings of the reading are clear though, and it is up to the reader to outline those warnings: when it turns bad, do not lash out, but keep honest and always act with integrity. It is also important not to try and control the situation, but to be balanced and fair. By doing so, she will shed a skin and grow into a new and better one.

OBSERVATIONS FOR ESOTERIC STUDY

The pattern of the layout has a central column that tracks the event through time: present, past and future. Magically that would be a directional flow from north/past through the centre/present, to the future/south. How that flow of fate and time presents itself expresses

7. Interpretations of Layouts

is through an X pattern, something you should be familiar with by now.

Position three/trigger is diagonal to position five, which represents what is taken away. Something that no longer serves a person's life or personality is brought to the surface usually though a trigger or series of trigger events. It is interesting to note magically that cause and effect are not always what they seem. It would be easy to say that the Page of Wands was the cause and the consequence is that the Nine of Cups is taken away. That would be logical.

However, fate is not often that tidy and obvious. From a magical perspective, looking deeper beyond the surface, a different picture can emerge. If a person has become so settled in a situation that they are starting to 'rot,' i.e. they are no longer evolving but are simply kicking back and enjoying the ride, then at times fate can trigger to kick you out of that comfort zone and push you back on the path through life.

Though at a mundane level the Page of Wands is identifiable as the trigger, at a deeper level it is the *symptom*: often the cause is what is to be taken away. The person became too comfortable and was becoming stagnant, which made them feel irritable. That dynamic made them snap at their partner a lot, which eventually degenerated into fights. The real cause was the comfort and stagnation, and that is what the divorce situation will take away from this person's fate.

The other arm of the X consists of position four/what it gives, and position six/how it will happen. Again, the dynamics between the two positions flow both ways in terms of cause and effect. Position six, how it will happen, shows what level of necessity flows to release what is given in position four. If the card in position six is a really tough one, as in this reading, then it shows the level of impact needed to push the person forward. The more dug in they are in terms of their lack of development, the more fate needs to kick them to get them out of their comfort zone and move them forward. So looking at position six in relation to position four will tell you a lot about the deeper underlying issues within the person that fate is attempting to remedy.

Panicked reading

In the reading the Eight of Swords is in position six, the loss of emotional stability in position five, and the loss of the world in position two. This is enough to panic most people who look at such a reading. However, as with all panic readings, it is wise to step back and look at where fate is taking you, what it gives you, and why it is happening.

That enables a person to understand that these painful life events are part of life's normal progression, and as in all panic readings, it is wise to look at the actual outcome. If a person can see the difficulties and, instead of panicking, they prepare to mitigate the worse of the event by adapting their behaviour, then the fear of disruption that causes the panic will be taken away. People do not like change, but change is a necessary part of life. The more we learn to change in a balanced way, the less it will threaten us when it turns up again.

Interpretation and advice to client

My advice to this woman, based on the reading, would be: "Things are not going to play out how you expect, and it could be a difficult time for you. But the whole situation will lead to a much better path ahead for you. You will come more into your power, and this will not depend on anyone else. The future shows you secure in your self-power and content with it: it is important to keep that in mind as you go through the divorce because how you handle the twists and turns of the divorce proceedings will have a direct effect on how strongly you come out the other side of it.

7. Interpretations of Layouts

"I would seriously suggest the following: plan for financial loss in some areas of your life. They are not devastating, but they will be cumbersome if you do not prepare for them. When the divorce gets to the stage of negotiating terms and conditions, do not try to control the situation, do not get aggressive or fall into the blame game, and do not try to go beyond what is fair and honest.

"It is likely that the other party in the divorce will be aggressive and will not play fair, but do not get sucked into that as a battle. This part of life, in terms of fate, is about learning to let go. Let go of control, and let go of belongings, even if it means settling for something that is unfair to you. By doing this, you will release the pressure that has been building up within you, and it will cut away all those energetic ties that have been aggravating you at a deep level.

"As a result of letting things go, the fate incident of binding and suffering will manifest in lesser ways that are easier to cope with, and faster to recover from. Through loss in this situation, you will gain in the longer term. You will find your feet, have everything that you need, and will be emotionally and energetically in a much better place. It is better to lose wealth and lose face, but gain stability, strength, and necessary resources, than to win the fight but end up emotionally, mentally, physically, and energetically drained and battered. Fighting this battle would literally put you in the Eight of Swords: in suffering, bound up, and isolated. Walking away from the fight, or just accepting the terms, will give you a new stability and the resources that you need.

Directional layout

This is a simple layout so there is no need for any complex explanations, esoteric overviews, etc.

QUESTION

"I lost my wallet somewhere on my property. If I look carefully within a two hundred foot radius, where and in what direction will I successfully find it?"

POSITION MEANINGS

1. Centre
2. East
3. South
4. West
5. North

READING RESULTS

1. Five of Swords
2. Justice
3. Six of Wands
4. Page of Coins
5. Four of Swords

7. INTERPRETATIONS OF LAYOUTS

Figure 7.5: Directional reading

Complete answer

The reading throws up two possibilities: the Six of Wands, which can be read as a victory card, and the Page of Coins, which can be read as something small with Coins. As the two cards are in directions that are next to each other, south and west, it is possible that the two cards refer to the wallet being in southwest.

Personally I would start by looking in the southwest, and if I didn't find the wallet there, I would then concentrate on the south, as the Page of Coins is the stronger indicator of a wallet. However, because the question asked about success, the Six of Wands/west could also be the stronger indicator. As you can see, it is not always straightforward with such a reading, but you can focus on each option by using yes/no questions: "will I find my wallet if I looked in the southwest area of the two hundred foot radius?"

It is also wise to remember, when doing something like this, not to assume that the wallet is lying on the ground. Within the set search radius, if there is a car, an outbuilding, or part of the house, then those need including in the search.

Here is an example of a reading for the same question which would show that the wallet is *not* within that radius:

1. Ace of Wands

2. Five of Coins

3. Knight of Cups

4. The Fool

5. Ace of Swords

The wallet is in none of those directions. So the radius would either need stretching out, or the person would need to rethink where they

7. Interpretations of Layouts

lost it, or whether it could have been stolen. Again, to narrow those possibilities down, one would use a yes/no layout to rule out certain possibilities.

Resources layout

Question

Show me this person's overall resources for the next three months.

I used the word 'overall' in the question so that the reading would not show a temporary dip in resources, say for a week, if that was going to happen in the three month period. What I want is an overview of the resources for the whole of that three month period, as the person is about to embark on a three month trip abroad to study cultures in third world countries.

Position meanings

1. Self. How you are doing in terms of energetic resources overall.

2. Balance. How balanced you are currently in terms of managing your energy resources.

3. Vital force. This is your overarching life force: it can ebb and flow. It is your most important energetic resource.

4. Love/emotions. This is emotional stability, love relationships.

5. Money, substance, property. How your economic resources are doing.

6. Health. The physical health of your body.

7. Creativity. Your energy to create, which can include pregnancies.

8. Communication. Your energy to give and receive clear communications.

9. Intuition. Your energy to tap into your deeper intuition, dreams, and 'inner radar.'

10. Divination. Your energy for clear divination. Seeing the future using a method like cards or runes.

11. Magic and mysticism. Your energy for studying/doing magical things or delving into the mystical side of life.

READING RESULTS

1. Eight of Coins. Things are working as they should.

2. Two of Swords. Balanced and communicating.

3. Four of Wands. Celebrating, happy.

4. Nine of Coins. Contentment.

5. The Moon. Unseen factors; no clear thinking.

6. The Hermit. Withdrawn, experience and wisdom.

7. Eight of Wands. Fast-moving energy.

8. Nine of Swords. Suffering.

9. The World. Solid success and the power of nature.

10. Page of Wands. Weak, communication.

11. Five of Swords. Disappointment, defeat.

7. Interpretations of Layouts

Figure 7.6: Resources reading

COMPLETE ANSWER

The insights are to be looked at in the context of the question and taking into account the further information that they are about to travel for three months in foreign countries while studying. What a person will be doing tells you what resources they will need, and if those will be lacking then you can offer advice on how to bolster or work around any weak resources. The person is a graduate student but is not involved in magic or divination in any way.

The first card, which is the self and the body as a complete unit, shows the Eight of Coins. This says, "everything is working as it should be." So there appears to be no hidden illness or physical condition that would cause problems for the trip. The resources that show in the 'self' position are the energetic resources that uphold the day-to-day function of the body.

The second position shows the overall balance of the person. It is a good card, again a balanced number, and is basically saying "yes, we are fine thanks." But the Two of Swords is a minor card and a weak number. So while this person is not lacking all resources, they are not strongly resourced either.

The third position, which is the vital force, is the most important resource position of all. The vital force is literally the life force of the person, and if that is weak or damaged then it will undermine everything else. It is the foundation that they stand on in terms of energetic and physical health. The card that fell in this position is the Four of Wands. It is not a bad card, but in terms of power it is weak. This tells me that in this period, the person will be operating on a functioning vital force, but it is not a strong one. Should they get a sudden infection or have a serious accident, and not have proper medical care nearby, it could become a serious situation.

The fourth position is the Nine of Coins, which is happiness and contentment. It is a substance card, being the element of earth, and says "yes, this area of their life has a lot of good fate energy behind it." Position five is economic resources (money, property, substance), and the card in that position is The Moon. The Moon is very much about shades and shadows, about not seeing clearly, and about hiding from oneself or fooling oneself. It is where someone is driven by their emotions and lack of self-knowledge, and to have it in the position of money resources is worrying with respect to the adventure they are about to embark on.

It is likely that they are unaware of the various costs that could be incurred on such a trip if they are not properly prepared. It could also indicate that they are pretty bad with money in general and do not plan well: that they just let money flow through their fingers. It could also point to the other end of the spectrum: that they are so wealthy that they do not need to think about money at all, and they have no idea how much they actually have.

Position six is health, and in that position we have the Hermit. When looking at resources, always look at position six, one, two, and three together: this will give you a strong overview of the physical health of the person in general. The Hermit is not a good card to have in a health position. It is not a bad card in itself; it is just that the good qualities that the Hermit brings are not strongly or directly relevant to good health. Often a deep thinker has weak health: that is the price they must pay, from the point of view of their inner resources, for having such an abundance of mental and spiritual energy.

I would read this card in this position as saying, there is something deep and long-term (The Hermit is a deep and long-term card) in this body's health that needs careful and close inspection. If I were to give a slogan to the Hermit, it would be "think carefully." With such a card I would not expect hidden conditions like cancer or any other debilitating illness; in light of the other cards in the key positions, I would expect something more like a hidden condition that has not yet fully developed, or an inherently weaker immune system. The other thing that it could be, going by the vital force card as well as the health card, is a latent condition that does not show up in normal conditions, but appears once the body is put under unusual stress.

From looking at the overall reading and bearing in mind that they are about to be physically and emotionally stressed in ways they have not even thought about, this person needs to plan ahead for their trip and make sure they have proper health insurance, a list of doctors in the areas they will visit, and full vaccinations for any diseases in those areas. They should also plan for having low energy at certain points on their trip.

In position seven we have creativity. The card in the creativity position is Eight of Wands, which is a high energy and creative card. In light of the question, and the state of the overall health and vital force of the person, I would advise them not to do any art, dance, or creative pursuits in that three month period. Why? Because it is a strong resource, and it is not vital for their survival. If they do not use it, it can be drawn on by the weaker areas to bolster available energy. That is how these inner fate and vital resources work. If a critical 'pot' is getting low, full 'pots' in other areas of the life will be drawn on to replenish the weaker vital pot.

Position eight is communications, and the card in that position is the Nine of Swords. This is a bad card to have there. Swords/air is the natural element for words and communication, and the Nine of Swords is a hostile, aggressive card. The person will not have the fate resources to communicate well, and if they are going to foreign countries where language and communication will be vital, that does

7. Interpretations of Layouts

not bode well. Resources like creativity and communication are about inherent abilities, but those abilities need fuel to bring them to the fore.

Seeing that card in that position, I would advise them to make a serious effort to learn some basics of the language before they go, and also to have a guidebook containing useful phrases. Relying on technology when going to a third world country is not always wise. Also, making the effort to learn at least something of a language shows respect to the people of that country. Either way, I would warn them that it is likely they will have language difficulties that could put them at risk. To have a bad card in that position not only says that they do not have the ability or resources to bluff their way through language situations, it also says that the fate pattern they are currently in has little buffer or protection in terms of communications. So they need to be prepared for language issues to become a major issue that may threaten their overall safety or health. I would also advise against getting into arguments or using condescending language, as that would likely trigger someone to attack them.

Intuition and inner sight is strongly represented by the World in position nine. This strong card, which is a trump, is about as good a card as you can get in this position. Their inner radar is much resourced by the world around them. *They are deeply in touch with nature,* which is a necessity when it comes to intuition. In the world around us, everything is communicating all the time, from plants and trees to birds, animals, and even landmasses. This person has a strong intuition, and in this trip, that facility will be strong and healthy.

This can make up for the poor communication resources. The person's inner radar will help them navigate difficult situations, smooth over ruffled feathers in bad communications, and will also help them stay safe if they listen to their intuition. I would advise them to listen to their own intuition and to trust it when they feel threatened, lost, or afraid.

Position ten is the position for ability to use divination in one form or another, and the card in that position is the Page of Wands. If a person does not have a natural ability, then high resources in this position would help them to be basically proficient when necessary. When a person has a high natural ability but the current resources for divination are poor, that is a warning to back away from divination for a while. There is not enough gas in the tank to fuel readings. People who start using tarot do not realize for quite some time that it takes a lot of energy to do readings, and it is easy to get badly drained if it is not approached properly.

Looking at this person's layout, the strong card in intuition tells me they have a natural facility for inner sight, which makes them perfect for divination. However, their divination resources are low, so if they used divination, it would drain them badly during this time. Looking at this reading, there is a reason for that pot of resources being low, which I will discuss in the technical breakdown. Luckily, this person is not interested in using divination.

The final position, number eleven, is the position for magic, mysticism, and religion. The card that falls in this position is the Five of Swords. This position tells us about the deeper underlying need or ability of the person to connect with something greater than themselves. It is not about playing at, or dogmatically following, a religion or magical path, but the energy that is supplied to uphold a person when they are walking a more mystical path, or are spiritually engaging with something to connect with the Divine.

For this person, the card is troubled. The Five of Swords is disappointment, a sense of defeat and loss. This energy is low and turbulent, and thus this is an area of their life that they would be wise to stay clear of during this three month period. Again because of the frail state of their health and vital forces, I would advise against going into temples, churches, or engaging with religious activities. The person has strong natural inner senses which are well resourced, and such people are often drawn to mystical practices and religions. However, because there are also turbulent/weak cards in the positions of health, communication, and vital force, partaking of such activities that have an already turbulent energy pot will potentially drain off energy from the vital force and health.

They are too poorly resourced at the time of their trip to cope with the inner patterns and energy tangles of such religious and mystical places and activities. It is better they focus on the reason for the trip and keep their mind on the study they will do without getting sidelined into religious practices. The other important point to make about this card and situation is that a lot of third world mystical, magical, and religious practices involve spirits and magical patterns, particularly in indigenous communities. As this person has strong natural inner sight, it will make them visible to those spirits and could put them in danger. They do not have enough energy resources in that part of their energy 'pots' to navigate such threats.

Observations for esoteric study

When this layout is closely looked at, besides giving a snapshot of a person's energetic resources, it can also tell us a lot about how those resources balance each other and interconnect.

When you look at a person's resources through a reading, there are two ways of looking at them. One is to look at the overall resources that are theirs for their lifetime: their natural pots. The other way is to look at how those pots operate within a given time span. Make sure that you are clear, when doing such readings, which you are looking at. If you are looking at a specific time limit, it can also, by the nature of the pots, show you long-term patterns that go beyond the time limit you have set: the baseline natural lifelong pattern can show. However, when you do a lifelong reading to overview the resources, it will not show how those resources ebb and flow over time, as happens naturally with life events.

Energetic resources are not the same as the body's fuel system (food, etc.). The inner energy resources are a non-physical resource that connect the body and the spirit, and they uphold that connection as the person navigates their way through fate in their life. If something specific is coming up in the fate of someone, and it is important that they navigate that event and survive, it is the inner resources that uphold the person through that event. Fate brings the situation, and the inner energies support the body and spirit through that fate. So being able to track inner resources is important, and it can also give a deeper insight into the underlying features of a particular fate pattern or event.

The layout itself is like a set of justice scales, with a fulcrum in the middle, and equal pots on both sides. Those pots/positions are deeply interconnected and often when a vital pot is getting low, another will lend its resources to the low pot. Knowing that, you can identify which part of your energetic activity you need to back off from in order for those resources to be used elsewhere. Let us have a look at the relationships between those pots.

The central line, the fulcrum, is about the critical resources without which we cannot hold onto life. The resource of balance is a foundational resource without which everything else spins out of control. It is like the central controller for the energy system. It is this resource pot that directs and organizes all the other resources, sending excess from one pot into another that is critically low. If the

7. Interpretations of Layouts

balance pot is in a bad way, then it is advisable for the person to withdraw from all energetic activity as much as possible and to work on rebalancing. This can be done through meditation, rest, and being out in nature.

The central card of the self sits below the controller, and is the basic control panel that the controller (balance) works on. If both the self card and the balance card are poor or bad, the root cause is usually the controller. Without a solid controller energy, the day-to-day running of the body starts to get out of sync, and things start to spin out of control. If you are familiar with car mechanics, the controller/balance is akin to the timing mechanism in a car. If the timing belt on a car is sagging, then the engine itself will eventually be damaged.

Vital force sits below the controller and the control panel, and is really the power source for everything. Without a vital force, the body starts to die. However, the vital force does go up and down, so it is important not to terrify yourself if you see a bad card in the vital force positions. The time to worry is if the vital force position is constantly showing bad or poor cards over a long time. If that is the case, something is draining it off, which can be poor physical health, drugs, fate, or constantly using up too much of the other resources. Most of the time it is situations where you can intervene by changing your behaviour.

However, if nothing changes it, and no credible options for change show in the reading, then it is time to look at the fate of the person themselves. It may be that unfortunately they are in a fate pattern that is talking them towards their death. If that is the case, then the magician can use divination to see if that is the end of their measure (i.e. that it is a set fate pattern that cannot be changed), or if can it be avoided, changed, or modified to make sure they survive whatever is walking them towards death. With death fate patterns, even sudden accidents will often show as weak, damaged, or absent vital force in a resource reading, often months or even years before the event.

There are some longer-term situations that can drain off the vital force for a prolonged time, but then it recovers: it is wise to be aware of that before you terrify yourself or others. For example, writing the Quareia training course was a heavy physical and magical job that took three years. During that time, my vital force became seriously depleted, as it was such a tremendous inner and magical burden. I had a lot of illnesses, injuries, and energetic exhaustion as I wrote the course, and for a couple of years after. However, I was aware in advance that this would be the case, and I adjusted and adapted my life to compensate. Now my vital force is strong and fine. So be aware that a person's vital force can bottom out for quite some time if they are doing something that is a huge energetic burden. The trick is to see if their vital force will recover, which you would establish through a yes/no layout with a time limit.

Those three critical positions hold everything up. To the left we have the resources that are about everyday life, and to the right we have the resources that are more about the person's inner, hidden world. But they interconnect and uphold each other in ways that can produce interesting insights into how the outer and inner worlds of a person operate together. In the layout they interconnect both diagonally and as 'shoulder partners' i.e. the pot next to them.

Position four, relationships, and position eight, communications, are connected. All the left and right pots have diagonal connections where things flow back and forth as necessary. For example, if someone is fated be to an important communicator, then it is likely that even if their relationship pot is strong, they will not have good relationships. That resource will be used as a backup for the communications resource. Why is communication so important that it has its own pot? Because communication and utterance is the basis of our inner existence. It is what sets us apart from most other creatures. Many mystical texts from around the world touch on this in various ways. The most well-known one, in the West, is the beginning of the Gospel of John: "In the beginning was the Word." One could write a whole book on just the resource of communication: suffice to say that it is far more important, from both an inner and outer perspective, than most people realize.

The opposing diagonal dynamic can also be true: if they have strong communications and strong relationships resources, but their fate is to have a deep and abiding relationship and family, then their communications resource will be constantly low as its resource is channelled to the family.

The trick, really, in all these interrelationships, is to find a balance between the two pots if fate allows for it, so that neither aspect draws much on the other. This is fine for an ordinary life, but if someone's fate is to achieve or do something extraordinary or intensely focused then one pot *will* feed the other.

The next pairing of resources is position five, money, and position nine, intuition. The same dynamic applies: if a person is fated to be wealthy for some reason, then their intuition—even if it is naturally strong—is likely to be drained off to some extent to support their wealth pot. I have come across wealthy people who do have good intuition, but then in their resources reading there is often another pot that is constantly kept drained. It is usually the pot next to the hardest working one. So for example you may have a fate picture of a wealthy person who also has great intuition, but their communication skills will be terrible and they will have no luck in relationships.

The next connection to look at is position six, health, and position ten, divination. These two pots are important to keep an eye on if you use divination regularly, as excessive divination can impact the body. If you read professionally, fate will at some point start to draw on your health pot to prop up any deficit in your divination pot. This is why professional tarot readers often suffer health issues in the long term, particularly chronic fatigue.

Position seven, creativity, and position eleven, spirituality, are a diagonal pair that fascinate me a great deal. I have spent my life around artists, performers, priests, magicians, and mystics. I have seen the resource pot dynamic between these two pots play out over and over again. When looking at them in terms of their overarching lifelong resources, I have often found that brilliant artists have difficulty reaching deeply into mysticism and magic. They are often deeply interested and aligned to such things, but actual depth of practice eludes them. Similarly, people who are adept in the long-term practice of magic, mysticism, or religion (actual long-term practice, not study) often find it hard to creatively externalize their experiences through art.

I have also found that there is often a direct energetic correlation between positions eleven and five. Those who are deeply embedded within mystical or magical work at a highly active practical level often find that their wealth resources are fed into the pot of mystical/magical resources. Usually they have, or attract, what they need in terms of monetary resources, and no more. These deeper dynamics are really too complicated to outline in a few sentences how and why they work: that would need a whole book to examine properly.

If you are a magician or occultist and you spend some time looking at the interrelationships between these resource pots, you will find all sorts of interesting connections and balances that will give you insight into how fate, action, and energy work together. These insights cannot be gained simply from looking at the layout pattern, however:

7. Interpretations of Layouts

you would need to track the readings, over time, of various different types of people and see how their fate plays out.

The one bit of advice I will give to any magician is do not try to magically interfere with these pots of resources. This is something I explored in my earlier days, and I ended up nearly killing myself.

The resource pots are finely balanced, both in terms of overall lifelong resources, and in terms of short-term fluctuations. An astute reader or magician can spot where it is necessary to back off one type of activity to shore up another, but trying to directly magically move resources from one pot to another will kick off a chain reaction that can be difficult to stop. They do not work as individual units, as I found out, but as complex interdependent energy sources that constantly flow in multiple directions. Interrupting that flow using magic, to force everything into one pot or another seriously, undermines the balanced foundation, the controller, so the chances of everything spinning out of control are massive.

But learning to watch how your inner resources ebb and flow, as well as observing your fate patterns and how they unfold, can teach you a great deal which will inform your magical practice.

Panicked reading

The biggest potential for a panic in this reading is to assume that the Two of Swords in the vital force position means that they have little vital force. That would be unnecessary: the time to panic is if you see the Fool in that position, as it means there is little, if any, vital force left. In such a case you would need to identify if that situation is temporary or not, and to identify why it should be so, and to see if there is anything you can do in your life to change it.

The other source of panic would be the Moon in the financial position. But it is important to remember that you can survive a financial drop, even if it means losing your home, etc. If you have your health and central control all working, then you have the opportunity to work with fate and rebuild a more sustainable way of living.

All panic readings come back to common sense and learning not to be emotional when you look at such things. Focus on the question and the answer card, then think carefully about how the pattern plays out in relation to everyday living.

INTERPRETATION AND ADVICE TO THE CLIENT

The first thing I would suggest to this person is that they make sure they have really good travel and health insurance before they go on this trip, that they get all the necessary vaccinations, and that they take all important medicines with them if that is possible. I would point out the health weaknesses of the reading, and suggest that they plan for things going wrong with their health, but let them know that if they are prepared and insured, all will be well. I would also suggest that they visit their family doctor and ask them to pre-prescribe some emergency medicines to anticipate the most likely health issues that could arise for all the countries they intend to visit on their trip (i.e. a broad spectrum antibiotic, etc.).

I would also point out that communications may be a major issue on this trip. This could come down to a lack of language capacity, and/or a loss of their phone or laptop, leaving them with no way of communicating with people. So it would be wise to have a good phrasebook handy, plus a backup phone or pad, and to plan ways of dealing with any loss of communication equipment. A bit of pre-trip research on the internet will tell them where they can get replacements, at what cost, and what the address and contact details of the agent or store is.

7. Interpretations of Layouts

It would also be important to discuss with them the need to stay clear of getting drawn into the magical or mystical side of the cultures they will study beyond superficial observation and understanding. In this time period, their energy resources could be drained off or could get hit by delving into these areas of the cultures. It would be wiser to keep things on an intellectual and social level.

They have the resources they need to accomplish this study trip, but to avoid disaster, they really need to plan carefully and make provision for things going wrong. Even if they have spent a lifetime travelling without worry or preparation, now is not the time to do such a thing.

Timing reading

I have used weeks in the layout list, but substitute week for day, month, or year as needed. I used eight cards, one for each week, to look at a two-month period. Remember, with a week-by-week reading, the first card is seven days starting the day you do the reading.

Question

"What weeks would not be safe for this person to leave home with respect to the early days of the 2020 Covid-19 pandemic? They are older and have medical issues, but not enough to be considered a member of the high risk group."

Position meanings

1. First week.

2. Second week.

3. Third week.

4. Forth week.

5. Fifth week.

6. Sixth week.

7. Seventh week.

8. Eighth week.

Reading results

1. First week. The Chariot. Travel.

2. Second week. Queen of Cups. Happiness.

3. Third week. The Moon. Something unseen.

4. Forth week. The Emperor. Structure, officialdom.

5. Fifth week. The Devil. Temptation.

6. Sixth week. Ten of Wands. Burden.

7. Seventh week. Nine of Swords. Suffering.

8. Eighth week. Temperance. Bring balance.

Complete reading

Remember always to interpret the card meanings in relation to the subject matter and question. Each card has various meanings, but in such a specific context, those meanings narrow right down, which enables you to grasp straightforward answers.

Week one and two look fine: they are both good cards. The Chariot is a literal thumbs-up, indicating a good time to travel to the city. The third week the situation starts to change: the Moon represents, among

7. Interpretations of Layouts

Figure 7.7: Timing reading

other things, not seeing something, or something being hidden or its understanding being confused. A virus is unseen, and in the early stages of a peak, many people can be infectious without appearing ill. This is the most dangerous part of a pandemic when the virus has a longer incubation period. The infection is spreading without public awareness of the situation. So that card starts the period of "stay home."

The next card is the Emperor, which is likely when the government or health authority realizes the virus is spreading unchecked and brings in restrictions of some sort.

Position five, the Devil, is a card that is likely to confuse many people in a reading like this, as we are asking about safety and the spread of a virus. In a health-related reading, this would be considered a more dangerous card, as it can indicate a lack of regulation along with imbalance and temptation. From seeing that card following the Emperor, I would presume that the government advice was insufficient, and that a lot of people would be tempted to carry on as normal. Again, like position three, it is a warning of hidden risk.

When the Devil is looked at in context of the two cards that follow it, the Ten of Wands and the Nine of Swords, we can see that it represents a major warning about the chance of infection being high. The Ten of Wands represents fire at its strongest for a minor card, and the Covid-19 virus triggers high fevers and high levels of inflammation. When you have a card that is a lot of fire in a health reading like this, it is saying "high fevers, you will get sick." The Nine of Swords is a suffering card and a strong negative card, so again it says "you will get sick."

The last card is Temperance, which shows the start of the rebalancing process. However it is just the start, and under such circumstances it would probably be wise to do a further eight week reading to see what continues on from Temperance. However, Temperance is literally 'tempering a situation,' so it could be taken as advice that it would be safe to go out if absolutely necessary and if you 'temper' your usual behaviour. In this instance that would mean wearing a mask and gloves, using 99% alcohol hand wash, and being extremely careful in what you do, where you go, and what you touch.

INTERPRETATION AND ADVICE FOR THE CLIENT

While this is not a layout that needs esoteric analysis, we should consider how to condense the reading its meaning can be relayed to another person in a way that they would understand. Under such potentially dangerous conditions, particularly if the person you are reading for has medical conditions or is older, it is wise to err on the side of sensible caution without going so far that they would ignore the reading's advice as too troublesome.

I would tell them that during week one and two it would be okay to go out, so long as they were sensible and cautious. Week three and four they should only go out if it is absolutely essential, and then they should take all possible precautions including masks, gloves, and hand sanitizer, and that they should sanitize their shoes, bags, and keys before reentering their home. As soon as they are home they should go straight to the bathroom, take a shower, and change their clothing.

Weeks five, six, and seven they should stay home, go nowhere, and have no visitors. Week eight looks better, and to be on the safe side, if they do have to go out, they should do it towards the end of the week, not at the beginning.

Manifestation / Causation layout

QUESTION

"In a twelve month overview reading for person X, the short-term future showed the Tower. How will that disaster/Tower manifest itself in this person's life/fate?"

Causation readings are usually done when something dramatic has shown up in a general reading. It is often wise, before doing a causation reading, to do a yes/no type of spread, or extend the timing of the overview reading to see if they survive the event.

This is often best done without explaining to the client/person what you are doing. If they are potentially not going to survive, then you will need to think carefully about what to tell them. You can do far more damage than good to a person by giving them a full account of such a reading. The job of the reader is to give the person options, not to terrify or depress them.

Manifestation/Causation layout

Position meanings

1. The event itself.

2. Natural event: weather events, land slippage, earthquakes, etc.

3. Accident.

4. Economic. Income, debt, savings, possessions.

5. Illness or injury.

6. Self-inflicted.

7. Emotional/mental.

8. Relationship.

9. Attack: anything from a physical or emotional abuse to theft, fraud, etc. Anything done with aggressive intent to harm you.

10. Scales of Justice: courtroom, legalities, payback for something, etc.

Reading results

1. Ten of Wands. Heavy burden.

2. Four of Swords. Seclusion.

3. Seven of Coins. Job well done.

4. Five of Wands. Argument.

5. Ten of Swords. Defeat.

6. Temperance. Restoring balance.

7. Knight of Wands. Young, creative person.

8. Five of Swords. Disappointment.

7. Interpretations of Layouts

9. Page of Earth. Small child.

10. The Fool. Foolishness or nothing.

Complete answer

Bearing in mind the question, we are looking for a card that would mirror the Tower, or has enough of a disastrous energy to it that it could identify what form the Tower would take.

When looking at something specific like this, do not fall into the common trap of looking for a trump card that outweighs the importance of the minor cards. In a question like this, it is wise to remember that besides the Tower, there really aren't many ways for the trumps to identify disaster. There the minor cards come into their own.

Remember the dynamic of cause and effect discussed in the interpretation chapter. We know from the person's overview reading that there is a Tower (cause): what we are now looking for is the *effect*: how will that tower play out? That dynamic is usually expressed through a minor card.

The first card, which is the event itself, shows the Ten of Wands, which is a heavy burden indeed. It is a lot of fire: too much for a person to handle, hence my key word of 'burden.' So the minor card that would identify the cause of the trouble through its position needs to have the same level of strength, burden, and disruption. It needs to weigh in against the Tower and the Ten of Wands, as they are both about the event itself and its strength, energy, and effect on the person.

The second card in the position of a natural event is the Four of Swords, which can be a minor illness or a withdrawal into seclusion. That is a weak card and does not show disaster. The third card in the position of accident is the Seven of Coins, which is not a suffering

Manifestation/Causation layout

Figure 7.8: Manifestation / Causation reading

247

7. Interpretations of Layouts

card. The fourth card, which is in the economics/financial position, is the Five of Wands. This shows some conflict, but again is not anything like the suffering represented by the Tower or the Ten of Wands.

The fifth card is the Ten of Swords, which has fallen in the position of illness. This is a strong enough card to be the indicator card. Indeed, the Ten of Swords is the minor card equivalent of the Tower. But just to be sure, we will look at the other cards.

The sixth card, in the self-inflicted position, is Temperance. Temperance is a good card and is about balancing, so that trump is not our indicator card. The seventh card is the Knight of Wands in the position of emotions/mental health. That combination is a possible indicator: the knight of Wands is not in full maturity and is full of fire. Its falling in a position that indicates mental/emotional health makes it a possible indicator card, but it is not as strong as the Ten of Swords.

The eighth card, in the position of relationships, is the Five of Swords. This is about failure and disappointment, but it is not strong enough a card or situation for the Tower. The ninth card is the Page of Earth in the position of 'attack,' so unless you were going to be licked to death by your cat, this is also not the likely candidate. The final card is the Fool in the position of balance. Though this trump is stronger than a minor card, the Fool, in this context, means zero: no, nothing.

So we are left with two possibilities: the Ten of Swords in the position of illness, and the Knight of Wands in the position of emotional/mental health. Of these two I would presume that the Ten of Swords is the more likely candidate, but there is also the interesting possibility that they are both right.

Think about it this way: an event is the Tower. The general effect of that event is the Ten of Wands, burden. The Ten of Swords also came up in the position of illness. Now, that position does not indicate mental or physical illness, just illness. The Knight of Wands in the

248

seventh position, emotional/mental health, could represent someone losing control emotionally or mentally.

If the person is prone to mental health issues, then it may be possible that the illness indicated could also cause mental or emotional issues for them. Some physical illnesses can do that, particularly with difficult diagnoses like cancer.

Interpretation and advice to the client

The reading shows that the disaster on the horizon is a health issue or illness that could also be stressful emotionally. The next step would be a solution layout to ascertain what would be the most productive way for them to prepare, and how to deal with the issue once it arrives.

It would also be a good idea, once we have more information from the solutions reading, to look at whether it is necessary for them to go through this situation or whether there are ways to avoid it or mitigate its effects. (You would use a landscape reading for that.)

Solution layout

Question

"What would be the best, most successful approach for the person (who I just did the causation reading for) to navigate the potential illness that has shown in their causation reading?"

This reading would be put alongside the causation layout so that one can see the direct correlations between the two. A good way of doing this is to compare the result with a photograph of the previous layout. Remember, we are looking for a success card that, through the position it lands in, would tell us the best approach to the situation.

7. Interpretations of Layouts

Position meanings

1. Event.

2. Passive unfolding. This means let fate and time do their jobs. Just let the situation work itself out.

3. Random action. This means an inspired or random unplanned act will trigger a solution.

4. Economic: money or substance is the solution.

5. Health. Focusing on improving health will bring about a solution.

6. Responsibility. Taking responsibility for an action you caused will bring about the solution.

7. Cool mind. Calm, fair, unemotional negotiation, action, and/or behaviour will trigger a solution.

8. Mercy. Kindness, understanding, and compassion will bring a solution to light.

9. Fight. Fight your corner, stand your ground, and do not give up: this will bring the solution.

10. Pay your dues. Paying outstanding debt, passing forward bounty, and/or returning what does not belong to you will trigger a solution.

Reading results

1. Eight of Swords. Trapped in suffering.

2. Six of Wands. Victory.

3. Two of Coins. Balance of resources.

Solution layout

Figure 7.9: Solution reading

251

7. Interpretations of Layouts

4. The Magician. Control.

5. Eight of Cups. Moving on.

6. Seven of Wands. Getting the upper hand.

7. The Lovers. Union, agreement.

8. Three of Coins. Work/payment.

9. King of Cups. Kind man.

10. Five of Coins. Poverty.

Complete answer

The first card in the 'event' position represents the situation that needs a solution. In this position we have the Eight of Swords, which is trapped in suffering. This is the illness itself. The second card, the Six of Wands, representing victory, is in the position of 'passive unfolding.' It indicates allowing this situation to play out without interfering too much: i.e. take the medicine given, and let your body deal with it. That is a potential answer card to the question, but let us continue and see what the rest of the reading says.

In position three (random act), we have the Two of Coins, balance. This card is weak and has little correlation to the situation. In position four, which is money, we have the Magician. The Magician is a controlling card, not necessarily a success card, so that is also not what we are looking for.

In position five (health) we have the Eight of Cups. Because this is a question about an illness, we have to pay careful attention to whatever falls in this position, even if it is not the answer card. The Eight of Cups is about the conclusion to a past event that now needs moving on from. If we read that together with the only successful card we have so far seen, which is in the position of passive unfolding, then it starts to tell us a story about this illness. It is something that appears necessary to go through, to let unfold, as it allows something no longer valid to fall away and be moved on from. It may also be that through victory in overcoming this illness, the person will gain better health.

In position six, which is the position of self responsibility, we have the Seven of Wands. This is about gaining the upper hand in a conflict or difficult situation. It is not a card of victory, but means "keep at it and you will succeed." In position seven (coolness of mind/emotions) we have the Lovers, which has no direct bearing on success, and in position eight (understanding/kindness) we have the three of Coins, which again is not strong nor about success. In position nine (fight your corner) we have the King of Cups, and this combination again has no direct correlation either to the question at hand nor to success. In position ten (pay your dues) we have the Five of Coins, which means poverty, lacking, or loss.

From looking at the various cards in the positions, the only one that truly jumps out as a clear success card is the Six of Wands. Sixes are very much to do with the past and how the past affects the future; and the Six of Wands is about success after struggle.

Observations for esoteric study

While this layout has no esoteric pattern, the causation and solution positions directly relate to each other. Looking at the readings them side by side can offer a lot of insight beyond the simple answer that you are looking for.

Interpretation and advice to the client

The best approach the person can take to this oncoming health disaster, is to not try to avoid or dodge it, and not to throw everything they have at it in terms of money, struggle, and so forth. It is a fate

7. Interpretations of Layouts

event that has some bearing on the past and needs to happen to clear the way for a new fate to begin to unfold. The advice of the cards is to make sure you are prepared to take some time off work and all that entails, and not to flood your schedule with heavy work months in advance.

By the look of the various cards that came out in the outcome reading (Tower), the causation reading (Ten of Swords), and positions two and five of this reading, this is not going to be like a few days in bed with a bad cold. Whatever illness is coming will challenge the person a fair bit. It could be on the scale of a bad dose of influenza, or even a broken leg: injuries show up as illness and health issues. It is the health aspect of an accident that causes the issue, not the accident itself.

Using a timing layout could probably narrow down the month it would be most likely to happen, and when that time comes, the subject of the reading should just rest up, take any medicine the doctor gives them, and let their body go through the experience. With the victory card coming in a passive position, it is extremely unlikely that this illness will seriously damage them; it is more likely to be something that just needs going through. It may try their patience and be unpleasant, but it is serving a purpose, and just going through it appears to be important not only for their recovery, but also for their health fate pattern for the future.

Sometimes painful and annoying illnesses help us later in the future to avoid other diseases, or they prime our immune systems to work better in the long term. It could also be a fate situation in which they are at home being pretty badly sick so that fate can pass something their way that would not be possible if they were at work.

Health layout

This health layout is meant to be an adjunct to allopathic medicine, not a replacement. It is meant for healers, herbalists, etc. to get better insight into what is happening in the body. If you do not understand the anatomy, physiology, and functions of the body, then this layout will be useless to you. When there is illness, the person should always go see a doctor.

QUESTION

"This male person is feeling exhausted and depressed. What in their health is causing this situation?"

POSITION MEANINGS

(A more in-depth description of each position can be found in the layout chapter.)

1. The first position shows what is coming into the health picture from a fate/future perspective. What shows here is just forming, and can also show any magical or inner influence.

2. The second position shows what has formed itself in terms of fate/future but it has not yet manifested itself in the physical body. If there is any energetic or spiritual element to the illness/condition, it will show here.

3. The third position tells us what is physically going regarding the health of the head. This includes the brain, sinuses, lymph glands, endocrine glands,[1] ears, nose, eyes, and the throat (including the thyroid gland) Basically this is everything above the base of the neck.

---
[1] The brain's hypothalamus, pineal, and pituitary glands.

7. Interpretations of Layouts

4. The fourth position shows the solid energy going in the body. Anything that you are eating, drinking, smoking, or otherwise ingesting will show here.

5. The fifth position shows the state of the emotions: how the person feels, and what their mental state is. If a person is in physical pain, it will also show in this position.

6. The sixth position shows what the short-term or primary immune system is currently doing. If it is fighting something or is in overdrive, it will show here.

7. This position shows the part of the immune system that educates T and B cells, and the part of the immune system that wraps up, locks up, or breaks down threats that have already been overcome.

8. The eighth position shows the central core of the body, which houses the vital organs: heart, lungs, stomach, pancreas, liver, and kidneys. If there is a problem with these organs, it will show here.

9. The ninth position shows the male sexual organs, testosterone, and the male bladder. Testosterone is also present in females: if the reading is for a woman and a difficult card turns up in this position, then it will probably be necessary to look in more depth at her endocrine system and hormone balance.

10. The tenth position shows the female sexual organs and the bladder. Again, males also have estrogen in their bodies, so if the reading is for a male and a difficult card turns up here, check their hormone system.

11. The eleventh position shows the digestive system, and it reveals how the large and small intestines are processing everything

that came in at position four. This area of the body can also be read in conjunction with positions three and five (head and emotions): there is a direct relationship between digestive health and mental and emotional health.

12. Position twelve tells us what is happening to us in our sleep and dreams.

13. Position thirteen looks at the 'structure and movement' system of the body, which means bone, muscle, and nerves. Any inflammatory reaction, peripheral nervous system disturbance, or bone or muscle impact will show here.

14. Position fourteen is the skin. The skin is the most externalized organ and the biggest organ of our body. If the only area that shows a problem in a health reading is the skin, then the situation will likely resolve itself eventually.

15. Position fifteen tells us the immediate future of the body's health.

READING RESULTS

The interpretation of the card meanings is focused on bodily health and functions: this is reflected in the choice of words used for each card meaning.

1. Four of Cups. Balance of emotions and fluids.

2. Five of Coins. Deficit of substance.

3. Eight of Swords. Trapped, suffering, unable to access something.

4. Page of Wands. Small irritant (fire).

5. The Moon. Unbalanced emotions, something unseen.

7. Interpretations of Layouts

Figure 7.10: Health reading

Health layout

6. Four of Swords. Resting withdrawn.

7. The Magician. In control, doing its job.

8. Two of Wands. Watchful waiting.

9. Knight of Coins. Health and solidity.

10. Page of Cups. Small, fluids.

11. Ten of Wands. Aggressive inflammation.

12. Ace of Swords. Issues with airflow, sharp pain, loss of ability.

13. The Chariot. Free movement.

14. Ten of Cups. Happiness, all is well.

15. Knight of Swords. Defending or attacking.

Complete answer

Background: this male person has been suffering from fatigue and depression for some time and is considering the doctor's offer of antidepressants. First through, with their doctor's approval, they want to explore any alternative natural treatment or adjusting of lifestyle to see if that would help. If it doesn't, they will take the medicine. The reading is done on the request of a herbalist who is helping the person, to make sure there is not some serious underlying health issue that needs immediate medical attention, and to make sure that any herbal treatment will not make the situation worse.

The first step for the herbalist would be to get an overview of what is potentially happening in the body. This is done by first looking at each card in each position, then looking at the relationships between different areas of the body.

7. Interpretations of Layouts

The first two cards, which show incoming fate, are okay. The second card does, however, show a potential for 'loss of substance.' This could be loss of weight or some deficit slowly getting worse. It is not a serious card, but one to refer back to depending on the rest of the reading.

The third card, in the position of head, neck, brain, etc., is the Eight of Swords. This is not a good card to have in this position. The reader physically looks at the person's head and face, and sees no physical issue, like an issue with their teeth, jaw, or mouth. As the person is fatigued and depressed, this card points to two possibilities: either the thyroid gland in the neck is running slow, or there is something happening with the neurotransmitter balance in the brain (serotonin etc.) which can cause depression. Also fatigue can be a symptom of depression, but it is a symptom of a lot of other things too.

The fourth position, which is everything that goes into your mouth, shows the Page of Wands. This literally means 'little fire'. There is something that the person is taking into themselves that is an irritant to their system.

The fifth position is the Moon. In this position this card can indicate either mental health issues or depression. As the person is depressed, this card is confirming that. The sixth position represents the first line of the immune system that triggers the first wave reaction to an infection, (sneezing, fever, etc.). The Four of Swords says that the immune system is not in reactive mode.

Position seven has the Magician, which is about control and function. Position seven covers things like the function of the thymus gland (which matures T and B cells which then fight infection) and the part of the immune system that is the clean-up crew. The Magician shows that this part of the immune system is functioning well and is in control. Going by the cards in positions six and seven, whatever is happening to this person, it is not an infection.

Position eight is the central critical organs (heart, lungs, stomach, liver, kidneys, and pancreas), and they look fine. The Two of Wands is 'watchful waiting' and shows that the system is functioning: there is no disaster or anything serious happening there. Positions nine and ten, the male and female hormonal and genital systems, both look normal and nothing there indicates a hormonal imbalance (low testosterone in a male can trigger exhaustion and depression).

Position eleven is the 'food processing unit' i.e. the intestines/colon. In this position is the Ten of Wands. For this reading, this is the jackpot: the likely cause of the issue. Ten of Wands is a lot of fire, which tends to mean a lot of inflammation or a high fever. Seeing as there is no infection in this reading (position seven, the primary immune system, is quiet) the only other thing it could be is inflammation. We will come back to this.

Position twelve is sleep and dreams. Here we have the Ace of Swords. With Aces, even though their number is one, their value is the same as ten. Ace of Swords in a sleep position can mean a few things: not sleeping well, nightmares, or breathing issues at night. Talking to the subject will be able to pinpoint which one it is. In this case the person was not sleeping well.

Position thirteen is the Chariot, which is movement. This position is about bones, muscles, and nerves, so everything there is working just fine. Position fourteen, the skin, is the Ten of Cups. This can indicate excessive sweating, but mostly its says "yes, everything here is happy." Position fifteen, which is the short-term future, is the Knight of Swords. This indicates things like unrest, fighting, irritation, and so forth. This is saying that whatever is going on in the body will slowly become more aggressive.

So what is happening in this body? The main card that stood out was the Ten of Wands in position eleven, in the intestines. This directly links to the stomach (position eight) which is fine, so the stomach is not affected, and to position four. It also links to what is taken into the body, which is the Page of Wands, a small irritation. We also have a troublesome card in position three, which is the head and neck, and a problem card in position five, the Moon. If there was no issue in position four then I would suspect the thyroid, but having a small irritant in position four indicates that something the person is eating, drinking, or otherwise ingesting is irritating the intestines. It is not food poisoning, as the central organs, which include the stomach, look fine.

I strongly suspect that the person is eating something that they are intolerant to or which is aggravating their intestines, which can cause an inflammatory situation in the bowel. When the intestines are constantly exposed to an irritant, it can trigger irritable bowel syndrome (IBS). Sometimes the IBS comes first, and certain foods cause it to flare. Either way, there is a clear connection in this reading between what goes in their mouth and how it affects their gut. Why is that important for someone who has depression? There is a complex relationship between serotonin (which affects our moods) and the gut. I don't know enough about medicine or biology to fully understand that relationship, but it is a known dynamic that often inflammatory bowel situations can also affect energy and moods.

The other mind/mood/gut connection involves bacteria in the gut, and the balance of those numerous bacteria directly affect our immune response and our moods/emotions/sleep.

The key appears to be the diet. Everything that goes into this person's mouth needs to be looked at carefully, and a process of elimination worked with to identify what causes irritation and what doesn't.

OBSERVATIONS FOR ESOTERIC STUDY

The interconnections between these card positions are mostly more about how the body works, and how the different systems of the body affect each other. So there is more biology to this layout than esotericism. However, there are some things that are worth noting for magicians and esotericists, as they have a direct relationship with magic and magical practice.

The first two cards are about formation. The first card shows the unfolding of fates and tides in their early stages: what is starting to form as a fate path, but has not yet completed its inner formation nor locked into an inner pattern. That means that when a magician looks at this reading, the first card tells them what powers are flowing around this person, waiting to form—first as a fate pattern, then as a physical pattern. If a bad card lands here and the rest looks okay, there is a strong possibility of illness forming for the future. At this stage of formation, it can be negated by changing the approach to health, for instance by shifting the diet.

For a magician whose body has been impacted by inner magical work or when there is a dangerous tide of fate building up, so long as there is something in position two to block the flow of that fate, you are protected, but it is something you would need to keep an eye on.

Position two, in Kabbalistic terms, is synonymous with Yesod, the ninth Sefirot, where formations prepare to manifest in the physical sphere. This is also the area/position which magicians call the inner landscape. This is not a psychological landscape (a common misconception) but the inner pattern that the outer body is connected to. Before something forms in the physical body, it appears in the inner landscape. In such a position, the illness or event first forms an inner fate pattern before it finally expresses itself physically, and as such it can be stopped and reversed before it physically manifests.

7. Interpretations of Layouts

If you have a 'guarding' card in position two, then whatever calamity expresses in position one will be unable to move down into position two to draw closer to you.

Position three includes the thyroid gland, which can often be affected by large magical impacts. So if you are doing a heavy round of magical work, or have been hit by a magical impact by accident, as a side effect, or as an attack, and a bad card is in position three, then suspect a thyroid impact. This can be confirmed or discounted by doing a Tree of Life reading to look at the general health of the gland.

Another position of interest to magicians is position eight, which includes the heart and stomach, two organs that can take impact from magical work. The heart and heart spirit can be affected by magical attacks or by magical actions that are heavily unbalanced, and the stomach can be affected by taking in magical information, contact, or work that must be energetically 'digested'. The inner energetic body and the outer physical body mirror each other and can sometimes overlap. This means that, for example, taking in magical patterns or knowledge from an inner contact or being can trigger the physical body to act as though it has eaten something that it cannot cope with. Stomach aches or bowel disturbances can happen.

Often these disturbances follow a physical pattern, so the intake of difficult energy would show issues in position eight and position eleven. In such cases there is no outer physical cause; it is a physical reaction to an inner power. However, it is always wise to first always assume there is a physical cause, to make sure that you do not ascribe energetic blame to something that is actually a physical illness.

Positions five and twelve also work together, and from a magical perspective what happens in the dreams can affect the heath of the emotions. When you see bad cards in both these positions and the rest of the body looks healthy, it is likely that you are either battling something in your sleep, or being drained in your sleep by some being or person.

If as a magician you are working in different areas of magic, it can be interesting to do health readings every few weeks to see how the energy of your magical work is processed through your body. This can teach you a great deal not only about how your body processes magical energy, but also how to uphold and support the body when you are doing intense work. By tracking the effects, you can see areas of health that you can support by adapting your diet, sleep patterns, or placing protection around you while you sleep, and supporting your body with herbs when it gets impacted. If you know the root of the problem, then you can work out how best to resolve it.

Panicked answer

When people look at their own health using a health reading, even doctors can panic and think the worst. But it is important always to put things in perspective and approach such readings with logic and not emotion. For example, in the above reading, someone who is depressed and had noticed that they also had intestinal issues, might immediately think 'bowel cancer.' And of course, occasionally this can indicate the start of such a terrible disease.

The way to put such things into perspective is to do a second health reading looking at what the overall health would look like over a six month period if the person adapted their diet and was more careful about what they put into their body. Usually the inflammation cards should have dropped down in intensity (so lower-numbered irritant cards) or have cards that show regeneration, balance, or calm. If the picture still looks the same (but no worse) then it would be time to repeat the health reading with the same timeline and look at if you got medication from the doctor. If it still is no better, or has increased in ferocity, then it would be wise to have a stool sample done or a colonoscopy to see if there are early signs of bowel cancer.

In any difficult health reading, first always stretch the time span forward to see if a situation resolves over time, which most do. And if no options looked at in readings seem to work, then a visit to the doctor is important. Ignoring health issues out of fear is just stupid: just because you ignore something does not mean it will go away.

But always, in any difficult health reading, first think of the most common reasons for issues, things that you can do something about like changing diet, stopping drugs, getting exercise etc.; and look at how changing how you tend to your body changes the longer term picture of the readings.

Interpretation and advice to the client

My advice to this person would be to work with their herbalist and educate themselves on things like food intolerance, Crohn's disease and colitis, IBS, and IBD. I would suggest that they work out exactly what it is they take into their body, i.e. everything that goes into their mouth (solids, fluids, smoking, etc.) and start to cut things from their diet. Learning how to do this properly and over what time span is important so they can more easily identify the culprit/s. It takes time and patience but is worth it.

I would also suggest that they make sure they still have a wide variety of different fresh foods, as that helps the bacterial balance in the gut, which can mitigate inflammatory conditions. I would suggest that they practice semi-fasting, i.e. not eating after a set time in the evening or before a set time in the morning, so that they fast for a minimum of twelve hours, and preferably fourteen hours, in every twenty-four hours. This enables the digestive system to rest, repair, and recharge. Overeating, and/or eating poor quality or highly refined food, is a major cause of a lot of bowel inflammation.

Esoteric layouts

The second part of this chapter is aimed at magicians and esotericists who can use these layouts as part of their magical practice. Because they are magical layouts and not used for everyday mundane readings, I have not included panic readings nor interpretation/advice for clients, as it is not necessary.

Fate pattern layout

QUESTION

"Show me my fate over the next five years if I do nothing to intervene in my current fate path."

Fate patterns are cycles that occur throughout the life of the individual. Some fate patterns are short, lasting a couple of years, and some can span decades. Keep this in mind when you use this layout. You can, if you need to, use a timing layout to track the probable length of a particular fate pattern.

POSITION MEANINGS

1. The current fate path.

2. Lessons learned. What is now left behind that has bearing on the present.

3. The highest possible potential for the outcome of this fate pattern. If you get it right, this is what this fate pattern achieves.

7. Interpretations of Layouts

Figure 7.11: Fate pattern reading

4. Seeds to be nurtured. What is being planted for the future that needs tending.

5. Mountains to climb. Difficulties that must be overcome for success.

6. What needs releasing. What you need to let go of to achieve the fate potential.

7. Harvest. What have you achieved so far.

8. Angel of Severity. This position tells you what if anything in your actions puts your fate pattern and thus evolution at risk. Anything that shows in this position is deeply connected to your actions, decisions, etc.: it is not about anything outside you that you cannot control.

9. Angel of Mercy. This position tells of help that will be given to you as a result of your actions, decisions, and reflection so far.

10. This card crosses the first card and shows what is influencing you. Usually it is an inner contact, a being, or a physical teacher. If it is a bad card, then you need to rethink who you take advice from.

READING RESULTS

1. Queen of Coins. Maturity and stability.

2. Four of Coins. Clinging onto things.

3. The Emperor. Power and responsibility.

4. Seven of Cups. Unseen Mystery.

5. Eight of Coins. Craft and creation.

6. Three of Coins. Wages and earning.

7. Two of Swords. Balance of thoughts, words and ideas.

8. Five of Wands. Conflict.

9. Two of Coins. Balance of substance.

10. Four of Cups. Dissatisfaction, complacency.

7. Interpretations of Layouts

Complete answer

The current fate cycle that this person is on is one of maturity and stability, so it is likely that they are in their mature years. What has passed them, what lessons they have learned that are relevant to the future, is to not cling to things. They have learned to let things go: they no longer cling to things. This is a healthy dynamic for magicians, as clinging to things like belongings, position, wealth, etc. creates stagnation in the magical path, which blocks potential evolution through the twists and turns of fate.

The highest potential they can reach in this fate pattern over a five year period is a position of power and responsibility. Fate holds a potential for them of leadership, and as it is the Emperor, regardless of whether this person is male or female, it will be a position of mundane leadership, not for example a magical, mystical, or religious position of leadership.

Position four, seeds to be nurtured, is the Seven of Cups, which in a magical reading is about the unseen Mysteries. This card in this position is saying that a seed for the long-term future, a seed which is connected to mysticism or the deeper aspects of magical evolution and learning, has been planted in the fate of this person, and needs careful nurturing. It will flower once the fate stage of the Emperor has reached its peak. What is seeded in a fate pattern is often nurtured through that fate pattern and will flower in the next fate pattern. Each cycle of fate seeds the next one, and a fate pattern can run for a couple of years right through to a couple of decades depending on the individual's overall fate and the choices they make.

Position five has the Eight of Coins, which is about working at one's craft. In this position is shows that the craft/skills of the person, whether mundane or magical, will be hard work for the person, but ultimately productive. Through the application of discipline to their craft, this person will forge a solid future in leadership.

What needs letting go of, in position six, is the card the Three of Coins. The Three of Coins is about earning wages, bringing in income, and being productive. This is an interesting contrast to position five, which is about one's craft. In the past it appears that this person clung to substance and/or money. Such clinging often comes from fear of being without. Positions five and six in this reading are saying "don't worry about the income; focus on the work."

Position seven is the person's harvest so far, what they have learned and achieved up to this point in time, and the card here is the Two of Swords. They have learned to balance their communications and their conflicts, and it is possible they have learned to write or communicate to a wider audience. Through this process they have learned valuable skills and wisdoms that will stand them in good stead for the future.

Position eight is an angelic position. That doesn't mean it is a guardian angel or a being you can talk to: it is a power dynamic that upholds balance in all things, and this particular power dynamic does it through limitation, withholding, and loss. Everything that grows needs to die at some point, and in position eight, the card that lands here shows what is being limited and is dying off so that the person can grow and evolve.

Whatever lands here is a weakness that needs strengthening through limitation, and is something that can undo the individual if they do not keep it in check. The card that landed here is the Five of Wands: conflict. This is saying that excessive conflict—and how the person deals with it or triggers it—may be their undoing. So it needs to go. If the person actively works to limit conflict in their life, then the angelic power will step up and join in their effort using limitation, diverting conflict where it is not useful until eventually, and as a result of both human and angelic efforts, that dynamic dies away, and slowly ceases to exist in their pattern.

Position nine is the angelic power that gives what is needed for things to evolve and grow. In this position is the Two of Coins, which is essentially money in, money out: the balance of income and payments. This is about necessity: *you will be given what you need and no more.*

Position ten, which crosses the first card and influences you for good or bad, has the Four of Cups: dissatisfaction and/or complacency. When we have more than we need, we become picky about what we want and what we do not want. A person who is never hungry will become a picky eater, for example. In this position, that influence is about learning the dynamic of necessity and learning to recognize the difference between wants and needs.

Looking at the overall reading, we start to see a theme. This person is still learning about power and resources, about what is truly necessary and what is not. The fate pattern they are currently in is teaching them about these dynamics by putting certain situations in their path to highlight the differences between what is truly important and what is not. The best they can achieve from this learning cycle is to become a leader who has power over resources, over people, and over properties. To achieve that power in a truly balanced way, first they need to learn about handling conflicts, how to communicate, how to recognize true need over want, and how to judge fairly. Those skills are first learned by us through our own life challenges, so that our knowledge can come from direct experience.

Coming into that power of the Emperor is a temporary thing, and that is also an important lesson for this person to know. There will come a time when it is no longer right or enough for them (dissatisfaction), and they will yearn for something deeper and more meaningful to them. That is the seed that was planted in position four, which will eventually flower once the person has crossed the threshold from one fate pattern to the next.

OBSERVATIONS FOR ESOTERIC STUDY

The fate pattern layout works loosely with the magical directions of east, south, west, north, and centre. New fate pattern formations come in from the east, which is position four, and go out in the west, position seven. Time runs north to south, with position two being in the north and position three being in the south. The centre is the individual in the present time: they are travelling from the north/past into the south/future.

Positions eight and nine are the two angelic powers present behind the right and left shoulders of the person. These two powers are worked with magically as distant helpers, and their powers are similar to two sefirot in Kabbalah: Chokmah (left) and Binah (right). In their most reductionist terms, these are 'give' and 'take' powers that are beyond humanity (hence angelic). They are impersonal powers that flow from the Divine source in the process of creation and destruction, and are what is necessary for the growth and evolution of any living thing.

In popular Kabbalah left is Binah and right is Chokmah, but that is because the person is mirroring the Tree of Life. Magicians, particularly mystical magicians, do not mirror the tree: *we are the tree*. The Tree of Life is a map of creative power that runs through every living thing, and in this layout some of the Sefirot powers are present, showing the flow of creation and destruction through time into manifestation (the south). All that creative and destructive power manifests through patterns of time, substance, and fate.

7. Interpretations of Layouts

Similarly, positions four and position seven are mirrors of sefirot powers: they are what fate brings and takes according to our individual fate, and how we have handled what fate has thrown at us. Positions four and seven are loosely connected to Chesed (four) and Gevurah (seven). Chesed brings creation into seed and Gevurah limits that growth.

Positions five and six are connected to the sefirots Netzach and Hod. Netzach (position five) is a power that is about discipline and working hard to perfect the gifts fate has given you, while Hod (position six) is about letting go of whatever is no longer necessary for you. In totally reductionist terms, Netzach is tightening and training, and Hod is loosening and relaxing.

If you step back and look at the pattern in magical terms, you can see the powers of creation and destruction, expansion and contraction, and forward momentum, all of which are dynamics that are necessary for fate to flow through. We start at one, the present, we stand on the past, two, and we are going into the future, three. That establishes the time flow. Then the pattern flows from the east (dawn/Chesed/left) and circles around the directions until we end up in the northeast (position nine/Chokmah/right) which is the moment just before dawn: potential, expression, decay, death, rebirth. The gifts given in position nine are the fertilizers that feed the seedling in position four so that the fate cycles can continue to turn. The whole cycle is constantly moving and renewing itself, just as the acts of creation and destruction are constantly expressing themselves.

By working this pattern, it is much easier to dig deep into looking at fate patterns, as the layout mirrors and flows with key powers as they interact with each other. The more you look at this simple pattern, and look at the various relationships between the two, the more it will give you unorthodox insights into the sefirot and the natural paths that flow between them.

Angelic layout

QUESTION

"Show me the inner magical health of our magical temple."

POSITION MEANINGS

1. Self. The position of the person, place or system being looked at.

2. Lightbearer. This angelic/Divine power illuminates the path ahead for something, so in this position it will show if that light is being given, and if so, how the path is coming into formation.

3. Limiter. This position shows what is being triggered to slow down or limit the path ahead, to enable whatever needs to happen or be learned. It guards and limits so that you do not suffer destruction through overgrowth/expansion.

4. The Staff. The staff is connected to the magical staff of the magician, and is a duel serpent power that opens the gates for knowledge and healing/medicine. Whatever card lands in this position tells the reader what learning and/or development is waiting for the magician to engage and work with. It is the next step on the path that needs to be trodden.

5. Lantern. The lantern is the learning and development that has already been acquired, that illuminates the way ahead. It is the human version of the light that the angelic power the Lightbearer holds up so that you can see your path ahead. The light in the position of the Lightbearer is the help that Divine fate gives you; the light of the lantern is the light that you

7. Interpretations of Layouts

have made yourself through your development. The two lights should ultimately be balanced as much as possible. When they complement each other, you know that whatever you are doing is serving many good purposes: your path, and everything else you affect through your work.

6. Vessel. The Vessel is a magical tool of harvest and is connected to the magical cup. In the position of the Vessel is work or learning that has been done, and that is currently undergoing threshing so that 'the grain can be separated from chaff': the work or development that is undergoing maturation. The pure grains eventually become the light of the lantern.

7. Binder. This angelic/Divine position shows what has been withheld from your pattern as it serves no purpose and would be detrimental to your future path or development. Whatever lands in this position should not be engaged with or revived; rather it should be left to fall into the past.

8. The Companion. The Companion is the Sandalphon, the angelic being who guides your future path ahead. The card that lands in this position tells you or advises you about the best way ahead. Whatever type of card lands here, know that the Companion walks that path with you, witnessing what you do, and advising you if necessary.

9. HGA. What has been. With awareness of what has been, your future is informed. You stand on your past, for good or bad. (Position 9, 10 and 11 are three cards that are read together and are collective advice from your guardian angel.)

10. HGA. What is. The guardian reflects back to your true current situation or current self.

11. HGA. What will be. The guardian gives you a single insight into what you can be.

Reading results

1. Knight of Cups. Young, hopeful, and possibly naïve.

2. Two of Cups. Relationships, balance of emotions.

3. Six of Coins. Payment of what is due.

4. The Star. Early new beginnings.

5. Justice. Balance of the Scales.

6. The Devil. Temptations, unbalanced emotions.

7. Four of Wands. Celebrations.

8. The High Priestess. Wisdom and knowledge.

9. Ten of Swords. Defeat.

10. Strength. Power.

11. Two of Swords. Just balance.

Complete answer

The Knight of Cups in the first position tells us that the subject of the reading, the magical temple, has reached adulthood but has not yet fully matured. It is a power of good nature, of trusting, but it is still somewhat naïve.

In the second position is the card the Two of Cups. This position tells us what light is being shone to bring the future path of the temple into illumination. The Two of Cups is about favourable relationships and balanced emotions. It means that the future path of this temple

7. INTERPRETATIONS OF LAYOUTS

Figure 7.12: Angelic reading

will blossom through balanced relationships not only between its members, but between the temple and its inner contacts. The inner magical and outer physical structure of the temple, combined with its members and its inner contacts, are collectively one 'being,' and the future of this temple is reliant on good, balanced interactions and relationships between all its components.

In position three we have the Six of Coins, which is about dues being paid, and giving where it is needed. It is financial and material necessity. In the position of the Limiter this card is both a gift and a warning. It is saying that it is important for the temple as an organization to understand that whatever is necessary will come to it in terms of resources, but that these should be used and given away only when necessary. This is teaching the temple about resource management, and while the lessons are applied, the temple will have what it needs; but if it squanders those resources, then the Limiter will trigger and will stop those resources flowing.

In position four, the Staff, we have the Star. The next step for the temple is therefore to engage the power of the Star, which in this position means developing something new by bringing through inner and outer work that will eventually blossom into a whole new magical structure, system of working, or knowledge. The position of the Staff is a bridge to the future, and the Star is new beginnings.

In position five we have Justice. Position five shows the skills, knowledge, and wisdom that have already been learned: such learning will be vital for the future path of the temple. By identifying what falls in this position, the temple as an organization will know *what is their guiding light* for their future: by following the principles of the card that falls in this position, the organization is far more likely to achieve its long-term goals to the best that fate decrees.

In position six we have the Devil. Position six is the Vessel, which is about the harvest of the magical temple to date. With a card like the Devil, we can see that there is something in the harvest that is potentially poisonous to the organization. This would indicate that some practice, some inner contact, a member of the temple, or an activity or action by the group or an individual, is poisoning the inner structure of the temple. Something is seriously not right and needs adapting, adjusting, or cutting away. It would be up to the leader of the temple to use divination, meditation, and common sense to identify

7. Interpretations of Layouts

what, exactly, in the recent or current situation is out of balance, and to deal with it.

In position seven we have the Four of Wands: socializing, parties, and celebrations. The position shows what is being withheld and needs to be let go of and fall away into the past, as it is detrimental to the future. This card in this position most likely refers to group socializing, or where magic and socializing have been mixed together. Sometimes that works okay, and a lot of the times it doesn't as it allows for power struggles and personality clashes. In a magical gathering, it also allows for the parasitic infection of a group.

In the eighth position we have the High Priestess. This position is the Companion, the guiding light and inner advisor to the temple. While ever the temple activities are in balance, the power of the Companion will guide and teach. If the temple spins out of balance, then the first power to withdraw is the Companion. The High Priestess is a power of deep mystical knowledge and wisdom: a powerful companion indeed. So it is well worth it for the magical temple group to make sure that this guide is not lost.

Positions nine, ten, and eleven are read together, and are essentially what was, what is, and what will be. These three positions are where the guarding angelic being of the temple (or person, if the reading is about a person) reflect back to the reader these three dynamics of past, present, and future, to give them a clear view without self-delusion. The three cards that came in these positions are the Ten of Swords (what was), Strength (what is), and the Two of Swords (what will be).

The past history of the temple or its formation was unbalanced and had a pattern of suffering or defeat. It is likely that this temple had a difficult and hostile birth, but through that difficulty and how that difficulty was approached, it gained a powerful strength. This is mirrored in the card landing in position five, the Lantern. This represents the pearls of wisdom we have acquired, which in this reading is Justice: the magical sense of balance, necessity, and truth. Strength in the face of adversity, not giving up on one's ethics, and staying with truth all build inner and magical strength.

The future, the Two of Swords, is communication. Either the temple will be involved in work that involves communication with various beings, or it will become a teaching temple.

Observations for esoteric study

This layout is a well-formed, well-used magical pattern that involves the magical tools, the magical directions, and angelic inner contact. The magician is in the centre, standing facing south (position eight is south). Behind them is the north, and to their left is east and so forth. You can overlay the pentagram pattern over this layout, as the pentagram is the pattern for 'human.' If you get the proportions right, you can draw first this layout pattern as points, then put the pentagram over the top, and the end of the left arm of the pentagram should touch the Limiter position.

The Limiter and Vessel positions are your sword and cup. The Staff and Lantern are the two deeper, more powerful magical tools that are gained through your development and evolution. When you step forward from magic to mystical magic, the sword and vessel become passive tools and the Staff and lantern become the active, contacted tools. This is illustrated in the trump card the Hermit.

The angelic powers that work with and through you are the angelic powers of the Lightbearer and the Binder: expansion and contraction. The Lightbearer mediates the light over your left shoulder to illuminate the way ahead, while the Binder mediates the powers of the dark over your right shoulder. One gives light, the other takes it.

7. Interpretations of Layouts

The positions of Lightbearer and Lantern are directly connected: both give light, but the light of the Lightbearer is the mercy of the Divine, while the Lantern is the light you have generated from your own development and evolution. The positions of Binder and the Staff are similarly connected.

The Binder is the angelic power of Divine Strength, the strength that can take away light, life, and action from someone or something. The action of this angelic power in the magical pattern is similar to the concept of the Sword of Damocles. The more power and responsibility a person has, the thinner the thread is that holds the sword over their head. The Staff is a contacted tool that is a being in its own right, and is the power of two serpents. They teach and heal, or they strike and attack. If that tool is misused, then it will attack you. But if it is worked with properly, then it will work with you to teach and guide you as you walk the path illuminated by the Lightbearer.

Landscape layout

Question

"I feel my magical work has stalled. Show me what is happening in my life that has caused this slump in my magical work."

Position meanings

1. Foundation. The body, structure or land.

2. Union. The second position, crossing the first, tells us what power or people dynamics we are currently dealing with. It can also show inner contacts you are currently working with/talking to, or it can be a position of relationships.

3. Star Father. What is coming into the long-term future connected to the question: a pattern that is still being formed in the stars.

4. Underworld. What has already passed away down into the depths and will not be coming back. In a magical reading it can also show Underworld influence if the question is about a structure, system, or magical project. But whatever is in this position will not express itself in the living world: it is the past that the future is built on.

5. Gate of the Past. This is the threshold of what is now in the immediate past. Whatever is in this threshold position has the potential to return at some point in the future, but for the moment it is considered past.

6. Wheel of Fate. The current pattern of fate or action that is playing out. This could be a struggle, a cycle of magical work, a renewal, etc. This is the path you are currently on in terms of fate and its unfolding.

7. Grindstone. The hardships and difficulties that must be overcome. On the current path that is indicated in the sixth position, there are bound to be hardships, difficulties, and barriers that must be overcome.

8. The Inner Temple. What is coming into the situation/fate pattern from the Inner Worlds or inner contacts. All magical attacks, inner contacts, work programs, inner support, beings that are influencing you, deities, etc. will show here.

9. Home and Hearth. What influence may be affecting your home and/or family surroundings. This position shows what is happening in the home, both on a mundane and an inner/magical level. For example, if a magical working is

7. Interpretations of Layouts

disturbing the house/family, or if there is a problematic spirit in the house, then it will show in this position. Similarly, if there is protection for the home/family it will show here. In a magical reading it can also represent a lodge/temple (home) or order (family) depending on what the question is about.

10. Unraveller. What is falling away or starting to decline. When something is in the process of losing influence and is breaking up, it will show in this position. It is travelling towards the Gate of the Past and will finally vanish into the depths. If, however, you do not meet the challenges that appear in the seventh position, then any difficulties that show in the tenth position will come right back to challenge you until you get the message.

11. Sleeper. Dreams and/or sleep. What your deeper unconscious mind is dealing with, and what is happening to you in your sleep. This can also be a position for visionary work, if the question is about a magical working. Often in magical readings, visionary work can affect the magician's dreams, so the two dynamics can be read together.

12. The Path Ahead. The way ahead. The short-term outcome to your question. (For a longer-term outcome, look to position three.)

Reading results

1. Two Swords. Justice, balance.

2. Ace of Coins. Shield or block.

3. Justice. Equal power, true justice.

4. Ten of Wands. Burden.

5. Knight of Coins. Hopeful naïveté.

6. The Moon. Unclear sight, something hidden.

7. The Tower. Destruction.

8. Temperance. Protection and nurturing through balance.

9. The Hermit. Wise seclusion, introspection.

10. Death. The end of something.

11. Nine of Swords. Suffering.

12. Nine of Wands. Survival.

COMPLETE ANSWER

The question was to look at why a person's magical work had stalled and why they felt unable to progress. The first card, which is you, is the Two of Swords. This is a lesser version of the Justice trump, and shows that your body and mind are healthy, so it is not a health issue. Crossing you is the second card, which shows what you are interacting with. This is the Ace of Coins.

In magic, the Ace of Coins can often indicate a shield or at times a block, or a stone/substance that you are working with. Looking at the overall reading in context to the question, it is immediately obvious that the Ace of Coins in this instance is a shield or block to stop you doing magical work. All magical energy and contact has been blocked from flowing to you.

In position three, the long-term future is the card Justice. The theme of balance and rebalancing reoccurs in this reading in different ways. So in the long-term future you will be back on track with your work, and in a far better and more balanced place to do it.

In position four, what has fallen deep into the past and will not return, is the Ten of Wands: burden. Because this is a magical reading,

7. INTERPRETATIONS OF LAYOUTS

Figure 7.13: Landscape reading

I would guess that you have completed a cycle of fate or magical work that was a tremendous burden to you, which has pushed you to your limits. But those times are now past and will not return.

In position five, the recent past, we have the Knight of Coins. This is a card of a personality that is adult but young, often idealistic, but practical and hardworking. Through work or fate a burden has now passed, and you have matured and moved forward a step in your development. However, the recent past could be revisited, which means that the maturity is not yet totally solid: it is possible for some of that less mature personality to leak back into your life if you are not careful or put under stress. It is a bit of a warning. Don't look backwards and fall into old ways; move forward and apply what you have learned.

In position six, the position of the Wheel of Fate, is the Moon. This is saying that your fate is hidden within moonlight. You are going through a fate period where you need to be hidden, not seen in full, or alternatively *you* are not seeing clearly and being easily fooled. Sometimes it can be both. The rest of the reading needs to be looked at to ascertain the full meaning of this card. It can also indicate mental illness; however that is not indicated in the rest of this reading. We will come back to this card.

What needs to be overcome in this fate pattern is indicated by what card falls in position seven, and here we have the Tower. There is some major disaster that you must get through to survive, and you will learn many lessons as you navigate your way through this situation. The card is a trump, and there are a few trumps in this reading, which tells us that this situation is strong and fateful.

In position eight, which is what flows from the Inner Worlds into your life, we have Temperance. This is a protective power that balances things out, that ensures what is needed flows to the person

7. Interpretations of Layouts

or situation. Going back to the Moon in position six, we can now see that the fate cycle of the Moon was not referring to mental health. If it were, then position eight would have a type of card that blocks or shuts your inner aspect down. When someone who is active in magic goes through a mental health crisis, often the inner worlds/inner contacts close down and present a block to protect the magician from further harm. Sometimes, if you were practising unbalanced and unhealthy magic, we would see conflict cards in this position, or indications of parasitical spirits. But what we are seeing is a power that tempers and balances. This tells us that whatever the Moon is about, it is not about you yourself. Something is happening around you in terms of fate that you need to be hidden from.

In position nine, Home and Hearth, we have the Hermit. And this ties in nicely with the Moon, the Tower, and Temperance. The Hermit, yet another trump card, is saying that you need literally to be a hermit. You need to be normal, mundane, stay close to home, and not participate in anything magical at all. The Hermit is divested of magical tools and has only his staff and lantern to guide him. He has withdrawn from everything and stands alone on the mountain with only his gained wisdom to light his way. Looking back over the cards so far, there is a dangerous situation unfolding (Tower) and you have been stalled and blocked (Ace of Coins) so that you can be hidden in the moonlight and shadows. The inner contacts and spirits are providing guardianship and protection (Temperance) and you need to be mundane and thus invisible (Hermit).

In position ten, what is falling away/being unravelled from your fate is Death. Whatever fate situation you are going through, one of its potential paths is death. However, by being protected, shielded, hidden and withdrawn, you will still go through danger, but your chance of death is being unravelled from your fate pattern.

The Nine of Swords in position eleven is in the position of dreams and visions. The Nine of Swords is a card of suffering. Looking back over the whole reading again, I see that that the fate pattern is something that is not particular to you; rather it is something bigger that is happening around you that you need shielding from. This card in this position tells me that the sleep/dreams will be influenced by whatever destruction is going on around you. This is a dynamic that I see often. In such situations, the person can be shielded from the worst of the disaster, but they usually cannot be shielded from it all, and often it is best not to be fully shielded anyhow. And this is reflected by the Tower in position seven. You have to overcome some aspect of the disaster that pertains particularly to your development. Seven is a magical number and indicates the trials and lessons necessary for evolving beyond the mundane. The safest way for you to have to overcome this Tower is through disturbed sleep, nightmares, and so forth. Your deeper spirit will navigate the disaster through the dream state, which will in turn teach you how to overcome inner danger.

Position twelve is the short-term future, and the card in that position is the Nine of Wands: survival. If you look at the imagery of that card, you see someone who is battered and exhausted, but who has survived. So you will emerge from this disaster in one piece, exhausted, but a lot wiser and stronger because of it. That is mirrored by the card Justice in position three. This card is saying that once you have got over your trials and the sense of being battered, then the strength, wisdom, and knowledge that you will have gained from the experience will bring you into balance, and your 'scales' will be healthier for it. Justice and the scales of justice are connected to the magical harvest that becomes the light in the lantern (like in the Hermit). In magical terms, it is saying that this trial that you must survive will take you on your next step in your magical and mystical development.

7. Interpretations of Layouts

Observations for esoteric study

This layout works through oppositions and tensions. The far future and far past are 'above' and 'below,' while the recent past and near future are behind and forward. You are in the middle, standing within a pattern of time.

The cycles of fate are balanced across from the mundane physical life (home and hearth), as it is in the physical world that the wheels of fate turn. The Inner Temple, which is your inner spirit world, is balanced across from the dreams/visions, which is where your inner spirit works.

The Grindstone and the Unraveller oppose each other on either side, with you in the centre facing your road ahead: the short-term future. The Grindstone is the necessary work and struggle needed to build strength, skills, and knowledge, and the Unraveller is what is falling away and does not need any further engagement with. Power in, power out.

If you keep looking at and working with this pattern, then you will discover other interconnections and relationships between the powers playing out, which will give you further magical insight.

Map of the Self layout

This layout is not to be used lightly, and should be approached with thought and care. It is also not one that a non-magical person should mess with, for misinterpretation and panic could adversely influence the decisions and actions the person takes as a result of this reading.

From a magical perspective, it is also not helpful for me to do a ˙mple reading. This is one of those magical layouts that you will ˙ to work out for yourself. The struggle of understanding and

Map of the Self layout

interpreting this layout brings with it a layer of learning that can unfold for you over some time.

If you look carefully, you will notice that some of the dynamics in the previous esoteric layouts also appear in this one. This layout is a deeper layer of the earlier ones, and an expansion of them. If for example you look at the angelic layout, then look at this one, you will (eventually) see how the angelic layout sits on top of this one. Indeed, you can read the position meanings together, and that will give you a deeper understanding of both layouts.

What I can do is give you some things to think about as you look at this reading. Here are the position meanings again from the layout chapter:

1. Self. Ground zero for the question.

2. Origin. Where the subject has come from.

3. Destination. Where the subject is going.

4. Mundane positive. What is contributing to the physical and mundane life of the soul.

5. The short-term future. What the short-term, mundane future is for this soul.

6. The recent past. What has now passed from the fate of this soul.

7. Mundane negative. What is negatively affecting the physical and mundane life of this soul.

8. The magical or spiritual path. How the magical or spiritual path that is being walked is serving or influencing the soul.

9. Magical Contacts. The type of being who is talking to and/or guiding the magician.

7. Interpretations of Layouts

10. The magical future. Where the current magical path is taking the soul.

11. Magical adversary. What power is working against the magician. Every magical path has an adversary to act as a counterbalance to growth. This adversary can never be overcome, but it can be reconciled with, or outlived.

12. The foundation stone. What foundation holds up the magical path, and whether it is solid or unstable.

13. Soul steps. What overarching lesson or action the soul needs to achieve in this lifetime. While each life has many lessons, jobs, and events, there is usually one overarching theme.

14. Soul path. What type of path the soul needs to walk in this life to achieve its aim.

15. Soul fate pattern. What type of overarching fate pattern has formed to facilitate the soul's path and steps. The fate pattern creates options of paths, and the paths influence how the steps are taken.

16. Soul harvest. What harvest the soul has acquired so far in this life. The harvest is the 'grains' of knowledge and experience that have been acquired so far.

17. Scales. What imbalance is still on the scales. What debts and deficits still need to be balanced. These debts and deficits, though in a soul position, relate directly to mundane life and actions which affect the balance of the soul. The balance refers to necessity, the spindle of fate.

18. Restraint. What still needs restraint on a mundane and magical level so that it does not undermine what you are trying to achieve

in this life. The card that lands here shows your folly that can undo you.

OBSERVATIONS FOR ESOTERIC STUDY

This layout has four layers:

1. The self. This layer has three cards: who are you, where are you from, and where are you going?

2. The mundane. This layer has four cards and is about the balance of tensions in your mundane life within the current fate pattern you are in. What is positive, what is negative, what is flowing away, and what is flowing to you in terms of time and fate.

3. The magical. This layer has five cards, the number of the human and the magician. This looks at the magical path you are walking, how it is serving you or holding you back, and how healthy or not it is for you in terms of your overarching soul development. The dynamics and situations that appear in layers two and three are changeable. If they look unbalanced or unhealthy, and if they are not serving your development at a deeper soul level, then they are things that you can change. These are the smaller paths, side channels, and potential dead ends within your overarching fate pattern that can be intentionally changed. Don't try to make these perfect . Sometimes difficult or stupid paths can take you places you need to go, but if they show that you are on a path that is degrading or blocking your evolution and development, then think about changes that need to be made.

4. The Soul. This layer has six cards, and shows you the path your soul is taking through this life. It also reveals what still needs working on at the time in your life when you do the

reading. Anything that shows as needing further development can be addressed by making changes in the magical layer. The mundane and magical layers are the active ones that trigger steps within the path, and the soul level reflects how (or not) those changes have brought the soul path into focus.

Use this layout as though you were taking a photograph. It is done without a time limit, as it gives you a snapshot of where you are in your fate and development, and where you are going. Just like a photograph, it fixes in time how things look: ten years later, when you look back at a photograph, your appearance may have changed considerably, but it is still you. Similarly, the mundane and magical layers change constantly, but the soul layer is still you.

And just like a photograph that is not staged or digitally enhanced, it will give you a clear image of what things look like—and it can sometimes be a shock to see that. But in later years when you look back and are no longer emotionally invested in yourself at that time, then you will see what was good, what was not, and how far you have come.

I would not use this layout for a personal reading more than once every five years or so. To do this layout frequently will not only entangle and block your development, but it will also leave you open to becoming parasited and obsessed with controlling your fate. It is a very useful tool, but one that should only rarely be used.

> I am a skilful lector priest who knows his utterance, and I know all the skilful magic by which one becomes an Akh in the necropolis.
>
> — Tjetu[1]

---

[1] Simpson 1980, fig. 15.

Bibliography

Brown, R. (1885). *The Phainomena or 'Heavenly Display' of Aratos: done into English verse*. London: Longmans, Green, and Co.

Callataÿ, G. de (2005). *Ikhwan al-Safa': A Brotherhood of Idealists on the Fringe of Orthodox Islam*. Makers of the Muslim World. Oxford: Oneworld.

Clough, A. H. (1860). *Plutarch's Lives: The Translation Called Dryden's: Corrected from the Greek and Revised*. Vol. 1. Philadelphia: John D. Morris & Company.

Colson, F. H. (1939). *Philo Volume VIII*. Loeb Classical Library 341. London: Harvard University Press.

Creech, T. (1700). *The five books of Mr. Manilius containing a system of the ancient astronomy and astrology : together with the philosophy of the Stoicks / done into English verse with notes by Mr. Tho. Creech*. London.

"Pontifex Maximus" (1997). In: *The Oxford Dictionary of the Christian Church*. Ed. by F. L. Cross and E. A. Livingstone. 3rd ed. Oxford: Oxford University Press, p. 1307.

Damrosch, D., N. Melas, and M. Buthelezi (2009). *The Princeton Sourcebook in Comparative Literature: From the European Enlightenment to the Global Present*. Princeton and Oxford: Princeton University Press.

Durant, W. (1928). *The Story of Philosophy: Lives and Opinions of the Great Philosophers*. New York: Simon & Schuster.

Evelyn-White, H. G. (1950). *Hesiod: The Homeric Hymns and Homerica*. Loeb Classical Library. London: William Heinemann Ltd.

Faulkner, R. O. (1985 [1972]). *The Ancient Egyptian Book of the Dead*. Ed. by C. Andrews. Revised edition. London: British Museum Press.

Fuller, T. (1869). *A Pigsah Sight of Palestine and the Confines Thereof; with the History of the Old and New Testament Acted Thereon*. London: William Tegg.

Gébelin, A. C. de (1781). *Monde primitif : analysé et comparé avec le monde moderne*. Vol. 8. Paris.

Hirschvogel, A. (1538). *Aureolus Theophrastus Bombastus von Hohenheim [Paracelsus]*. Woodcut. Wellcome Library no. 2200305i. Wellcome collection.

Hornung, E. (1999). *The Ancient Egyptian Books of the Afterlife*. Ithaca and London: Cornell University Press.

Hornung, E. and T. Abt (2007). *The Egyptian Amduat: The Book of the Hidden Chamber*. 2nd ed. Tr. David Warburton. Zurich, Switzerland: Living Human Heritage.

Keats, J. (1820). "Robin Hood: To a Friend". In: *Lamia, Isabella, The Eve of St. Agnes, and Other Poems*. London: Taylor and Hessey, pp. 133–136.

Kretschmer, M. (1927). "Atrox Fortuna". In: *The Classical Journal* 22.4, pp. 267–275.

La Fontaine, J. d. (1868). *Fables de La Fontaine avec les Dessins de Gustave Doré*. Paris: Hachette.

Levi, E. (2011 [1855]). *The Dogma and Ritual of High Magic*. San Diego: St. Albans Press.

Lichtheim, M. (1976). *Ancient Egyptian Literature Volume II: The New Kingdom*. Berkeley and Los Angeles, California: University of California Press.

Newton, I. (n.d.). *Keynes MS. 28*. Cambridge: King's College Library.

O'Brien, E. (1964). *The Essential Plotinus*. Indianapolis: Hackett Publishing Co.

Olmstead, A. T. (1948). *History of the Persian Empire*. Chicago: The University of Chicago Press.

Osiander, A. and H. Sachs (1527). *Eyn wunderliche Weyssagung von dem Babstumb*. Nuremberg: Hans Guldenmundt.

Phillimore, J. S. (1912). *In Honor of Apollonius of Tyana*. Vol. 1. Oxford: Clarendon Press.

Pratchett, T. (1993). *Lords and Ladies*. Discworld 14. London: Transworld Publishers.

Quirke, S. (2013). *Going out in Daylight – prt m hrw: the Ancient Egyptian Book of the Dead: translation, sources, meanings*. GHP Egyptology 20. London: Golden House Publications.

Rolfe, J. C. (1927). *The Attic Nights of Aulus Gellius*. Vol. 1. The Loeb Classical Library. Cambridge, Massachusetts: Harvard University Press.

Rouse, W. H. D. (1942). *Nonnos: Dionysiaca*. Vol. 3. The Loeb Classical Library. Cambridge, Massachusetts: Harvard University Press.

Russell, B. (2004 [1946]). *A History of Western Philosophy*. London: Routledge.

Sheppard, M. and J. McCarthy (2017). *The Book of Gates: A Magical Translation*. With illustrations by Stuart Littlejohn. Quareia Publishing UK.

Simpson, W. K. (1980). *Mastabas of the Western Cemetery: Part I*. Giza Mastabas 4. Boston: Museum of Fine Arts.

Tesla, N. (2001). *My Inventions and Other Writings*. New York: Penguin Books.

Tolkien, J. R. R. (2005). *The Fellowship of the Ring*. The Lord of the Rings. London: Harper Collins.

Waite, A. E. (1894). *The Hermetic and Alchemical Writings of Aureolus Philippus Theophrastus Bombast, of Hohenheim, Called Paracelsus the Great*. Vol. 2. London: James Elliott and Co.
— (1906). *Strange Houses of Sleep*. London: Philip Sinclair Wellby.
— (1933). *The Holy Grail: History, Legend and Symbolism*. London: Rider and Co.
— (1971 [1910]). *The Pictorial Key to the Tarot: Being Fragments of a Secret Tradition under the Veil of Divination*. 2nd ed. London: Rider & Company.
— (1992 [1938]). *Shadows of life and thought: A retrospective review in the form of memoirs*. Whitefish: Kessinger Publishing.
Walker, C. Z., ed. (2001). *The Art of Seeing Things: Essays by John Burroughs*. Syracuse: Syracuse University Press.
Zajda, J., S. Majhanovich, and V. Rust (2006). "Introduction: Education and Social Justice". In: *International Review of Education / Internationale Zeitschrift für Erziehungswissenschaft / Revue Internationale de l'Education* 52.1/2, pp. 9–22.
Zerin, R. (n.d.). *Angels, Humans, and Prayer in the Kedushah d'Yotzeir RZ*. https://www.sefaria.org/sheets/99258.6?lang=biwith=alllang2=en [Accessed 7th June, 2020]: Sefaria.

Quareia

a New, Free School of Magic
for the 21st Century

*Advancing education in Mystical Magic
and the Western Esoteric Mysteries.*

www.quareia.com

schooldirector@quareia.com

Quareia is a practical magical training course founded by Josephine McCarthy and Frater Acher. It is a complete and freely available course designed to develop a student from a complete beginner into an adept. There are no barriers to entry: the course is accessible regardless of income, race, gender, religion, or spiritual beliefs.

Quareia is aligned to no particular school or specific religious, mystical, or magical system; rather it looks at and works with various magical, religious, and mystical practices that have influenced magical thinking in the Near Eastern and Western world from the early Bronze Age to the present day.

The entire course is free and openly available on the Quareia website.